ISLAMIC EDUCATION

The Academic Circles at al-Azhar, *c.* 1800

(A Water-Colour by P. W. Hunt in the Author's possession)

ISLAMIC EDUCATION

Its Traditions and Modernization into the Arab
National Systems

A. L. TIBAWI

Distributed in the United States by
CRANE, RUSSAK & COMPANY, INC.
347 Madison Avenue
New York, New York 10017

1972

By the same author

Arab Education in Mandatory Palestine, 1918–1948
British Interests in Palestine, 1800–1901
American Interests in Syria, 1800–1901
A Modern History of Syria including Lebanon and Palestine

English-Speaking Orientalists
Al-Ghazali's Tract on Dogmatic Theology
Jerusalem: Its Place in Islam and Arab History
Russian Cultural Penetration of Syria-Palestine in the Nineteenth
    Century

Muhadarat fi Tarikh al-Arab wal Islam
    (Lectures on the History of the Arabs and Islam)
    2 volumes in Arabic

SBN 7189 0161 4

© A. L. Tibawi 1972

PRINTED IN GREAT BRITAIN BY HEADLEY BROTHERS LTD
109 KINGSWAY LONDON WC2B 6PX AND ASHFORD KENT

And hasten not with the Koran ere its
revelation is accomplished unto thee;
and say, "O my Lord, increase me in knowledge."

The Koran, xx, 114

To the Memory of Shaikh Khalil,
my first teacher

INTRODUCTION

The plan, material and ideas of this book have been formed, tested and corrected in the course of a career in educational administration and university teaching, and have been improved through historical and educational research and writing. The result of this labour is now offered, as the first comprehensive study of the subject in English and Arabic, not only to the specialists but also to students as a textbook and a work of reference.

In writing this book care has been taken to avoid the occupational hazard of modern scholarship in education which is sometimes accused of producing accounts obscured by excessive jargon and vitiated by verbosity and vague ideas. Every effort has been made to achieve clarity of expression and exposition without relaxing the scientific rigour in marshalling the facts, weighing the evidence and drawing conclusions.

But it may not be out of place, in a book where footnotes have been dispensed with, to emphasize that, allowing for human error, every fact or figure has its warrant in the sources, and every conclusion is preceded by factual evidence. In addition the author may be allowed to state that a great many of the questions here discussed have been more exhaustively studied, and fully documented, in his previous works cited in the Bibliography.

Part One is a history of Islamic education, its theory and practice, from the rise of Islam to the dawn of the nineteenth century when the impact of Western ideas and methods began to be felt. The ideas of modernization and their application are then studied up to the fragmentation of the religious system into regional or national systems.

Part Two takes the fragments, country by country, and traces the development of the educational system in each generally down to 1967. With a few exceptions no attempt has been made to record developments since that date. Part Three is an interpretive review of purely educational and general cultural problems of common interest to the fourteen systems studied in Part Two.

Limits had to be set for the space allotted to Part Two, the longest of the three. Within these limits each system receives approximately the same space unless particular circumstances dictated otherwise. Except for the Arabian Peninsula and the Levant, states are listed, and their educational systems discussed, in the order of achieving independence from foreign control. In this way all the fourteen member states of the Arab League are covered. Appendix 2 deals very briefly with four of the emirates of the Gulf.

Within each national system the treatment is primarily concerned with the main activities and institutions controlled by the ministry of education. Limited educational work of, for example, the ministry of agriculture, health, defence, and other official or unofficial bodies is only incidentally mentioned, if at all. Private schools, native and foreign, are covered, but not in the same detail as state schools. In a book on Islamic and Arabic education, the schools of native non-Muslim and non-Arab minorities, such as the Armenians and Jews are mentioned only if relevant.

The passage of time between writing and publication would naturally affect the figures in Part Two but not the history in Part One or the ideas in Part Three. While every national system would have expanded at different levels the problems attending educational development would still be substantially the same as here portrayed.

A great difficulty was encountered in the writing of the second part of this book, and much time was wasted waiting for information sought from the Arab ministries of education. A circular issued from the University of London, signed by the author and two British professors as a committee of the "Arab Education Project", requested the supply of reports, statistics, syllabuses and the like. (Appendix 5). Only five of the fourteen ministries replied and sent the required sources. Reference to the diplomatic representatives of the others in London produced no results. We had to depend on what colleagues in these countries could send, but more particularly on the cultural department of the Arab League which supplied most of the material. But through no fault of the department the facts and figures were at least three years out of date.

The paucity or absence of information in official reports on the transition from religious to secular systems, or from colonial to national controls, involved the author in considerable research in non-educational works and in colonial records. Care has been taken to fill in the gaps and to establish links between one era and another. This is naturally essential for an understanding of the historical development of each national system.

It is recognized that our interpretation of little known facts, assembled here for the first time in a consistent whole, produces a picture of education under the British, French and Italian colonial control which is not flattering. This is inevitable. Few educationists who study at least the official colonial reports could fail to observe that political rather than educational considerations often dictated the amount of expenditure on education, the type of schools and even the content of the curricula. Fewer still could read such reports consecutively for a period of years without concluding that none of the colonial systems was designed with the definitive objective of uplifting society as a whole.

The historical background is that before the First World War the colonial powers concerned established their rule over a number of Arab countries by conquest and maintained it by force. They did so primarily to serve their own ends not to promote the education, conventional or otherwise, of the indigenous population. The end of the First World War witnessed Britain and France extending their rule over more Arab countries, but this time their position was legitimized behind a facade of mandates from the League of Nations. According to the League's covenant, these powers were trustees and agents of civilization. It was incumbent upon them to uplift society, socially, economically and politically. Their neglect to do so through education is described in this book.

The evidence of this educational neglect is almost entirely derived from official colonial sources, particularly regarding Palestine, Trans-Jordan, Iraq, Syria and Lebanon. A great deal of the evidence concerning these countries is also derived from the minutes of the League of Nations' Permanent Mandates Commission. More evidence was derived from other British and French sources. The accumulated material was studied critically, but care has been taken to do so in the social, economic and political setting at the time. Thus our present notions about "foreign aid" were not allowed to influence any of the conclusions. No colonial power was blamed for not making grants towards educational development in the territory under its control, but simply for failure to make adequate provision from local resources. No colonial administration was blamed for not creating a demand for schooling, but simply for failure to meet actual and spontaneous demand.

A British colleague criticized sections in Part Two as rather too harsh when dealing with colonial systems and rather too indulgent with the national systems. On the other hand, an Arab colleague criticized Parts Two and Three as dwelling too much on the inadequacies of the national systems without making due allowance for the retardation of colonial rule and its crippling legacy.

These two points of view command respect, and I did my best to profit from them. But taken together they seem to suggest that apart from verbal changes there is little I can do without altering my own point of view, based as it is on solid facts. I am not aware that the

educational or other shortcomings of the national systems are concealed or minimized anywhere in this book. The severity or mildness
of stricture noted by my British colleague must be largely unconscious depending on my expectation of performance by a
European administration on one hand and a native one on the other.
In my view most of the shortcomings of the national systems are due
to inexperience or inefficiency, but not lack of concern. Those of the
colonial systems had more complex causes—political, financial,
cultural and on the whole lack of imagination. As the Arabic
proverb has it—the mistake of the great is indeed great.

Three technical points require mention. First, despite efforts to
unify educational usage and nomenclature, there are still some confusing differences. In Egypt before the revolution there was a primary
(*ibtidai*) as well as elementary (*awwali*) school. They were two different schools of different standards. At present in Tunisia the ministry
of education is termed secretariat of state. Care has been taken to
make the meaning clear in such cases.

Secondly, as a rule no living Arab educationist is mentioned by
name. This is deliberate, so also is the omission of the names of
living heads of states and ministers of education.

Thirdly, the second part of this book contains the essential amount
of statistical material incorporated in the discussion and in the
proper context. It was therefore deemed unnecessary to burden the
text with fourteen tables and the same number of charts and
diagrams. There is another consideration. Apart from lack of uniformity in reporting statistics, occasional and limited checks of certain
returns weakened my confidence in their accuracy.

A.L.T.

ACKNOWLEDGEMENTS

Much of the material of Part Two and the headlines of the other two parts formed subjects for discussion at my postgraduate seminar at the University of London Institute of Education from 1966 almost to the time of going to press. I wish to record my appreciation of the stimulating contributions by my students. To mention them all by name would produce too long a list. But three deserve mention for special services. Mr. M. Hibshi (King Abdul Aziz University, Jiddah), Dr. M. Morsi (Ain Shams University, Cairo) and Mr. J. Whelen (British Council.)

For the supply of information or documents I am grateful to my friends Professor N. Hatoum (University of Damascus), Professor H. Kurani (American University of Beirut) and Mr. M. Akhal (British Embassy, Beirut).

Unique among Arab educational authorities in promptness is the cultural department of the Arab League, without whose supply of reports, documents and statistics the writing of the second part of this book would have been very difficult. It is a pleasant duty to record here my gratitude to the director, Dr. M. T. al-Nimr and his colleague, Dr. N. al-Asad (the tiger and lion indeed!)

I am grateful to my colleagues, Professor J. A. Lauwerys and Professor L. J. Lewis, who agreed to sign with me the circular now published as Appendix 5 and were helpful in other ways. And once more I thank my wife and our daughter Raya, ever my most vigilant critics, for reading the manuscript and making numerous suggestions for its improvement.

Sincere thanks are due to Mr. H. L. Elvin, Director of the University of London Institute of Education, for reading the final typescript and making a number of remarks. But neither he nor any of my other kindly critics is responsible for any inaccuracies or heresies that may still be found in these pages.

It is a pleasant duty to acknowledge the generosity of a number of Arab governments, ministries of education, universities and other institutions in ordering copies of the book in advance of its publication.

A.L.T.

CONTENTS

Appendices

PART I

The Tradition and Its Modernization

1

ISLAM AND ISLAMIC CIVILIZATION

[1]

The national states in the Arab world today are essentially fragments formed and re-formed, through the vicissitudes of history, from the universal Muslim community first forged from discordant tribes by the Prophet Muhammad some fourteen hundred years ago. Arab education in modern times is likewise a direct development of the Muslim education which Muhammad's mission had initiated. Because they are so deeply rooted in Islam as a religion and as a civilization, modern Arab society and modern Arab education cannot be truly appreciated without some accurate understanding of the Islamic faith and Islamic civilization. This is the more essential because Islam is still very widely misunderstood or distorted in western literature.

"Islam" means submission, the submission of man's will to God's commandments. These were revealed through a succession of prophets, including Moses and Jesus. The last and seal of prophets was Muhammad through whom the final divine message to mankind was revealed. This final message, which supersedes all previous messages, is enshrined in the Koran. The holy book contains the principles which regulate man's life and govern his conduct towards his creator, his fellowmen and the rulers of his community.

In the Koran ethics is very closely connected with theology, and morality is enunciated as commands from God: Right conduct receives equal emphasis as right belief. Charity, patience, fulfilment of promise, kindness and gratitude to parents, forgiveness of offenders are among the virtues that constitute right conduct.

As to beliefs in general the Koran insists on the absolute unity and majesty of God, and repudiates the Christian trinity as contrary to that unity. Jesus, like Muhammad, was God's prophet but not His son. Man has direct access to his creator without an intermediary, be he a prophet or saint. Hence no prophet is to be worshipped; he is only to be revered and emulated as God's chosen messenger.

On the basis of the Koran and the practice and pronouncements of Muhammad, scholars have constructed and elaborated a whole system of conduct for the individual, the community and the state and their inter-relations. Approved conduct, in accord with divine command, is rewarded by God's blessing in this world and paradise

19

2

in the next. Disapproved conduct may lead to social penalties in this world or torment in hell in the next, depending on its gravity and divine mercy. All of man's actions are reviewed on the Day of Judgement.

The duties of the true Muslim, "the five pillars" of the faith, signify both its devotional and social aspects. The Muslim must testify that "there is no god but Allah and Muhammad is His Messenger". He must pray, according to a prescribed form, five times daily. He must fast from dawn to sunset a whole specified month every lunar year. He must give alms to the poor if his wealth or his income is within the prescribed limits. He must visit Mecca at least once in his lifetime if his circumstances and wealth permit.

Just as the relationship of man with his creator is stressed in the formula of the profession of faith in God and communion with Him through prayer, so the role of man as a member of a social order is inherent in the duties of alms-giving and making the pilgrimage to Mecca. The one shows concern for the less fortunate members of the community, the other affords opportunity for the faithful to commune with other members of the universal brotherhood in the birth-place of the faith.

Concern for the social order is more emphasized in the theory of the Islamic state. Because of the all-embracing nature of Islam there is no separation between religious and political affairs, between church and state so to speak. The law governing both is the divine law, one and indivisible. As elaborated by jurists, Islamic law is very inclusive indeed. It details the rules of statecraft in peace and war, and regulates the political, social and economic life, as well as the religious. It defines the rights and duties of the individual in this world, and provides guidance for earning eternal bliss in the next.

Under the state, as within the faith, the community lives ideally in obedience to divine command. The ruler, be he the first ruler Muhammad himself or any of his caliphs or later sultans, is the guardian, not the maker, of the law. His duty is to see it applied among believers and, so far as it is within his power, to extend its sway to non-believers. Members of the community owe him obedience as a religious duty.

As conceived in the Koran and expounded by those learned in the law, the Islamic community was a large brotherhood which transcended all barriers of race and colour. No member is distinguished from another except by piety and good deeds.

On the individual level, Islam is at once a faith and a moral code, a constant reminder of God's creative activity and predestination in each and every human deed and thought. To those outside the fold of believers, God's predestination is grossly misunderstood as fatalism. God had indeed predestined man's actions, but He had also created in him the power of responsibility to decide which course to follow. There is no fatalism in this, for fatalism implies acceptance of physical determinism in a fortuitous universe, and this is the opposite of the Islamic view of an ordered universe, subject, not to physical accident, but to pervasive divine government and wisdom. Its working may sometimes be beyond the comprehension of mortals, but its validity must be believed.

[2]

This is not the place to give a survey of Arab, still less Islamic history. Suffice it for our purpose to say that before his death in A.D. 632 Muhammad left the Arabs as a community and as a state bound together by the bond of religion. Within a century after his death the Arabs had extended their political sway outside Arabia eastward to India and westward to Spain. All the territory of the Persian Empire in Asia and most of the territories of the Byzantine Empire in Asia and Africa, in addition to those of the Visigoths in Spain, were conquered.

But contrary to popular belief, Islam was not imposed on any of the various peoples within this large empire, nor was the Arabic language forced upon the conquered races. By a slow process, however, both Islam and Arabic were adopted freely by the majority so that gradually the empire became a multiracial cultural unit in which Islam was the dominant faith and Arabic the sole vehicle of literary expression.

As a civilization Islam proved very receptive and adaptable. It absorbed and assimilated into its system much of the Greek, Persian and other heritages and succeeded in retaining its essential character. The result of the cultural ferment, in which all nations shared, was an Arabic-Islamic civilization truly cosmopolitan. It reached its zenith about the fourth century after the rise of Islam. That was the golden age of the caliphate.

At this point if not earlier, however, the political power of the caliphate began to decline. Internal as well as external factors combined to bring about its eventual fall. Before and after this event new states had risen in Persia and the countries to the east, in Syria and Egypt, and in North Africa and Spain. The greatest of all these new states was to be the Ottoman Empire. Except for Persia and central

Asia in the east, and Morocco and Spain in the west practically all the lands of the caliphate fell under Ottoman control.

The political disruption in Islam did not always produce cultural retrogression. Indeed, cultural unity and progress survived political anarchy and disunity. Even amidst the darkest political misfortunes considerable cultural advance was scored. But ultimately a relative cultural stagnation began to set in, just about the time Europe was emerging from the dark ages to the Renaissance and all that followed. Stagnation in Arabic-Islamic culture was masked for a time by the might of the Ottoman Empire whose armies in the name of Islam penetrated into Europe as far as Vienna. But soon the tide began to turn.

For once Europe had passed through the Renaissance and begun to apply its scientific discoveries to the art of war it became possible not only to check but also to defeat the hitherto invincible Ottoman Turk. When the rulers of the Ottoman Empire considered the changed situation their confidence in the superiority of their faith, political system and way of life was unshaken. Hence they merely searched for ways of adopting as much or as little of Europe's technological knowledge as would redress the military balance in their favour. Little did they suspect that technology could not be isolated from the civilization that produced it so as to be borrowed on its own.

The consequences of the borrowing which continued to increase in extent and intensity throughout the nineteenth century is now writ large in the modern educational systems of the national states in the Arab world, successors of the Ottoman Empire. No clear understanding of this important historical fact is possible without some acquaintance with the origin and development of Arab-Muslim education upon which the modern systems were grafted.

2

HISTORICAL VIEW OF EDUCATION IN ISLAM

[1]

Every classical Arabic work that deals with Muslim education begins with some discussion, detailed or short, of a single theme: the tracing of the roots to the Koran and the traditions which represent the sayings and the practice of Muhammad. It is therefore essential to take a brief notice of this deep-rooted conception of the origin and character of education in Arabic and Islamic tradition. Education, like everything in the social order, was divinely ordained, and like the society it served education had the definite purpose of conducing to approved conduct and happiness in this world and eternal bliss in the next.

It is singular that Muslim education was launched by a man who was, according to tradition, an illiterate. The orthodox count this circumstance as a miracle. It began with Muhammad's first experience of the divine revelation. He was commanded by the angel-messenger: "Read!" To the plea that he was no reader the command was repeated in the name of God "who taught Man that he knew not".

Muhammad belonged to a noble if poor family in Mecca. Such families counted a few literate persons among their members. But illiteracy was almost universal in Arabia before Islam. The literate exceptions lived in the cities and smaller settlements. The merchants of Mecca could scarcely conduct their domestic and foreign trade without the rudiments of reading, writing and reckoning. Some of such men were among the first converts to Islam, and served as scribes to the Prophet or later as high officials in the Islamic state.

But on the whole pre-Islamic Arabian tradition was oral, and its rich heritage in poetry was transmitted orally. There is little or no evidence that literacy was a necessary qualification in a poet or in the transmitter of his poems. Indeed, the Koran itself, revealed piecemeal in the lifetime of the Prophet, was first proclaimed orally and transmitted by word of mouth. Not before the end of a generation was it written down in an authorized version.

To an illiterate environment, and in the face of an oral tradition, the Koran's message was revolutionary. Apart from its purely religious content proclaiming the unity and majesty of God, the

23

message insists on the high value of learning and associates it with
wisdom. Men of learning are placed in a position second only to
prophets. But this learning was, of course, concerned with the divine
revelation, its understanding and its propagation by preaching and
teaching. The Koran represents Muhammad as a teacher of this
divine message, but a teacher who, unlike others, expected no reward
for his labour except from God.

In the discharge of his mission Muhammad provided both commentaries on the revelation and set precedents for the future action
of his community. Thus preaching the new faith was accompanied
by two practical measures of special educational significance:
literate believers were required to teach illiterates, and only literate
preachers were sent out to new communities that embraced Islam.
Such men were the first teachers just as places of worship, the
mosques, became the first schools in Islam. It would be equally
true to say that the Koran was the first textbook.

The association of the mosque with education remained one of its
characteristics throughout history. In the early days it was the focus
of all communal activities. From its pulpit religious edification and
state policy were proclaimed; within its walls justice was dispensed;
on its floor sat preachers and teachers surrounded by adults and
children seeking learning or instruction.

The very first teachers acted by commission from the Prophet, and
like him they taught gratuitously. Next to him they were the architects of an educative society whose leaders were truly its teachers.
Members of this society, the leaders and the led, the teachers and the
taught, were collectively and individually responsible for upholding
its moral standards and correcting lapses: "bidding to honour, and
forbidding dishonour."

When they were finally recorded the canonical traditions, the
repositary of Muhammad's dicta, were simply amplifications of the
Koran. Take for example the verse which proclaims that there is no
limit to learning and that man's share of it remains necessarily small.
Muhammad developed the theme in a number of ways, but two
traditions must suffice: "Quest for learning is a duty incumbent upon
every Muslim, male and female"; "Wisdom is the goal of the believer
and he must seek it irrespective of its source." Other traditions speak
of learning and wisdom as equal if not superior to worship, and of
men of learning and wisdom as the successors of prophets. Here
again are two notable examples: "God eases the way to paradise for
him who seeks learning"; "Angels spread their wings for the seeker
of learning as a mark of God's approval of his purpose."

Thus were the foundations laid, solid in the theoretical and rudimentary in the practical sphere. Little change was effected in the lifetime of the Prophet. Nor was there a radical change after his death and the eruption of the Arabs from the Peninsula and the expansion of the political power of Islam. There was, however, a significant development. Hitherto the Islamic community was relatively small and its prominent members, the companions of Muhammad and the authorities on Koran readings and authentic traditions, were concentrated in a few centres in Arabia. Now they were dispersed. Many were settled in Iraq, Syria, Egypt and elsewhere combining administrative with religious and educative functions.

To verify the correct reading of a Koranic verse or to establish the veracity of a tradition it became necessary to travel to distant lands in order to question and learn from authorities. The zeal with which this movement of seeking the authorities was inspired by the fervour with which the faith was held. But the practice soon acquired all the characteristics of a permanent institution, and remained one of the prominent features of Muslim education in the classical age.

But as may have been inferred from the above discussion all the enthusiasm for acquisition of learning was by its nature confined to adults. No formal and universal provision appears to have been made for the prerequisite of teaching the elements to children. Thus the second caliph, who established a working system of administration in which the religious education was as hitherto entrusted to the administrators or leaders of the community, neglected to make specific provision for elementary education. To him, however, is ascribed the injunction to the Arabs outside the Peninsula: "Teach your boys swimming, archery, horse-riding and appreciation of poetry." The second, third and fourth injunctions accord well with Arab tradition, but the first is a reflection of the caliph's well-known awe of water, whether it was in the sea or in large rivers like the Euphrates, Tigris and Nile, so much so that he was reluctant to approve a contingency whereby water would separate him from his armies.

But if poetry was to be taught who was to teach it? Was it possible to do always without teaching the art of writing? Could the Muslims in the new environment do without teaching their children arithmetic? In the words of a jurist of a later age, the early Islamic community established no institutions and the Islamic state assigned no funds for direct expenditure on teachers of reading and writing to the young. "They regarded this," he wrote, "as the private concern of parents." This very circumstance contributed to the rise of a class of private teachers, ever present before Islam in small numbers, who taught the elements and charged fees.

At first private teachers taught in their homes, where individual pupils or small groups sought their services. But both the demand and the teacher's need to earn his living formalized the service. Enterprising teachers soon began to receive pupils in special places possibly a room in a house. A place thus assigned for instruction became ultimately known as *Maktab* or *Kuttab*, both derived from the Arabic root "to write". The first term was more used in the classical period and the second in more modern times, but throughout Islamic history the two terms are really interchangeable.

According to the sources, what was taught in such places—and I deliberately avoid the use of the technical terms of "schools", "teachers" and "subjects"—included indeed poetry, in addition to reading and writing and some reckoning. Boys much more than girls were taught to recite short chapters of the Koran and to commit to memory some short poems. Given the oral tradition in which they were brought up the process could have presented no insurmountable difficulty to the teacher or the taught. What must have been difficult was the teaching of writing, for two reasons. Firstly, out of religious motives, as well as on account of lack of other written material, the Koran with its majestic and highly poetic language was the sole textbook. Secondly, the Arabic script was at this early stage, and before it was standardized, such a chaos of symbols that a single word could be read in several different ways with only the sense as guide.

[2]

With the establishment of the Arabs and the spread of Islam in territories inhabited by civilized peoples such as had lived under the sway of the Byzantine and Persian empires, cultural fertilization was inevitable. It was preceded, or at least accompanied, by an internal movement for the verification and recording of the Arabic and Islamic heritages. The first step was taken when the text of the Koran was established in an authorized version. This was somewhat tardily followed by the writing down of the traditions of Muhammad. Both necessitated the extension of the process to the Arabic language itself and its rich poetry, folklore and history.

The written word had thus become an aid, if not a rival, to oral authority. Apart from increased use in the service of religion, the written word acquired a new and practical significance in the service of the state. An essential element in early Muslim administration was the toleration of "the People of the Book", the Christians and Jews, who enjoyed internal autonomy under their spiritual leaders. So unconcerned with details were the early Muslim military commanders and administrators that they suffered official records, including even those of taxes, to remain in the hands of natives and in their own languages, not in Arabic, the language of the rulers.

This peculiar anomaly remained in force for nearly half a century. When government business was at last "Arabicized" there was a sudden demand for large numbers of literate Arabs who could act at least as clerks and accountants. But the state still failed to take the logical step of establishing the institutions that would train them. Hence the new importance of the *Maktab* and the emphasis now laid in the sources on its teaching of arithmetic. The rudimentary education hitherto provided at this private "school" was auxiliary to religious purposes. It had now to serve also another material and secular purpose.

There were other signs of the changed atmosphere. One was the rise of a class of special teachers, very highly qualified and entrusted with the education of princes and sons of the wealthy. Such tutors naturally served the needs of a small minority. Another small minority was the exceptional scholars who journeyed in the land in quest of the widening range of Arabic and Islamic learning. Still another minority of seekers of enlightenment frequented the "circles" of learned men, usually held in mosques, where discourse and question and answer were the received method. These and other advanced scholars availed themselves of an increasing number of private or public collections of books made available through princely or wealthy patrons. But all had to acquire first a facility in reading and writing. The *Maktab* remained for the first four centuries of Islam the only universal institution where these skills could be acquired.

Such, in brief, were the main lines of development stimulated from within. External stimuli became operational when Islam came into contact with Greek and Persian civilizations and absorbed considerable numbers of Christians and Jews. These contacts opened new horizons for material and intellectual adaptation and development. The fraternity of Islam, which began with the Arab tribes, had now been greatly enlarged by an admixture of races with various religious and cultural backgrounds. Any such development was bound to create tensions and to present challenges. There were

two possible courses to follow: Islam's attitude to the foreign
civilizations and cultures might have been one of hostility and
rejection, as was the attitude of the Jews to Greek culture, and the
results would have been an exclusive and one-sided civilization; or
it might have been an attitude of reception and assimilation, as was
the attitude of medieval Christendom to the heritage of the ancient
world.

On the whole Islam adopted the second alternative. The greatest
assimilation was from the Greek heritage. Translation of Greek
philosophy and science was gradually followed by assimilation and
comment. The introduction, reputably from China, of the art of
manufacturing paper greatly aided the process of duplication by
copyists who had hitherto depended upon papyri and parchment.

The cultivation of "the sciences of the ancients", often with the
active support of caliphs, produced after the end of the third century
of Islam a philosophical stream in what we must now term as
Islamic-Arabic thought, a complex organism that developed from
religious studies, grew to maturity under the patronage of the
Islamic state and was expressed in the Arabic language.

The main stream remained religious in content and direction. But
while its guardians, the theologians, rejected philosophy as putting
Reason in opposition to Revelation, they adopted the dialectic
methods of the philosophers. A subsidiary stream of religious
thought was sufism, the mystical philosophy in Islam. It began, as
in the other great traditions, with the yearning of the spirit for a
personal communion with God. The early ascetics who practised
piety and meditation were the forerunners of the sufi mystics who
preached gnosticism and pantheism and shocked the orthodox just
as much if not more than the philosophers.

But on the whole the orthodox theologians succeeded in silencing
or at least isolating the philosophers, and more by infiltrating the
ranks of the mystics than by direct assault reduced the influence of
the extremists. The outcome of these struggles, discernable from the
end of the fourth century of Islam, was the establishment of the
supremacy of a theology that was essentially orthodox but containing important concessions to mysticism or even philosophy.

Despite all its capacity for compromise, however, orthodoxy
failed to establish a universal unity among the faithful. The Sunni
majority remained opposed to the Shi'i minority's doctrine of an
infallable imam, which the Koran does not concede even to Muhammad. This doctrinal division led ultimately to political divisions and
consequently to rivalry in the realm of education.

Within the orthodox field, however, remarkable adjustments had in the course of time been made. The Koran and the prophetic traditions remained the main sources of inspiration and guidance, but the learned in the community permitted the resort to analogy, consensus and opinion. Thus where a given case was not explicitly covered by the divine revelation or prophetic tradition the learned permitted themselves the resort to analogy, and where this was inapplicable they deemed their own consensus as valid and binding. This means the validity of the collective opinion of the learned. Individual and independent opinion was permitted, but it was not as binding as the consensus.

In the preceding paragraphs three main streams in the Arabic-Islamic thought were identified. These were, in the order of their impact on society and influence on education, theological, mystical and philosophical. To generalize, with little risk of simplification, it is correct to say that the education of the majority remained firmly in the hands of theologians. This is not to say that the mystics and philosophers did not resort to teaching in order to propagate their ideas. The mystics in particular were very active in this field, employing an elaborate system of initiation and promotion from one stage to another through study, meditation and precept. They achieved a considerable measure of success and their following was numerically great. The philosophers, on the other hand, could influence only very small sections of the community.

An early attempt at a comprehensive synthesis deserves to be noted. In the fourth century of Islam [or the tenth A.D.], a secret society of "lovers of philosophy" named the Brethren of Purity published in Basra and elsewhere in the lands of Islam some fifty tracts in which they sought to integrate Greek philosophy with the Islamic tradition. Distributed anonymously, the tracts represented a popular encyclopaedia of the entire knowledge of the time. Their underlying assumption that religion needed philosophy, or that in other words Revelation depends upon Reason, was unacceptable to the orthodox, and the attempt ended in failure.

A century was to elapse, and radical political changes were to take place, before another and more successful attempt was made. Such semblance of political unity as the Sunni caliphate in Baghdad had maintained was shattered when a Shi'i caliphate was established in Cairo before the end of the fourth century of Islam. To the doctrinal differences between the two camps there was now added political rivalry for supremacy. Education was one of the weapons used in the contest.

[3]

The rival caliphs in Cairo claimed descent from the Prophet, and fortified their claim through a well-planned state education, designed principally for adults and disseminated from a central institution known as *Dar al-Ilm* (literally house of learning). A mosque established on the morrow of the capture of Cairo was soon used as another repository of learning according to the doctrine of the new rulers. This mosque is now well known as al-Azhar, supposed to be the oldest university in the world.

It is difficult to exaggerate the significance of this first active and direct intervention in education, despite the fact that it was limited to the post-elementary level and the elements had still to be learned privately or more formally at the *Maktab*. For the lesson of this Cairo initiative was not lost on Baghdad, which in response to the challenge took a tardy but identical step. The fifth century of Islam witnessed the rise of a new institution for adult education known as *al-Madrasah*. Like its parallel in the rival camp it was established by the state for the dissemination of the dogma of the rulers. Here again elementary education was left to private initiative; in the east as in the west the state was in need of preachers, judges and other officials, but cared very little how or where they prepared themselves for admission into higher institutions.

For the first time in the history of Muslim education teachers in the new institutions became practically civil servants paid by the state. Students received free tuition, and under certain foundations also free lodging and food. Allowing for doctrinal differences, the new institutions had similar curricula. The central core was religious studies: exegesis, theology and jurisprudence with their handmaid Arabic studies. Philosophy as such had no place in either the eastern or the western institutions, though the latter tended to be more tolerant of it.

It was the principal teacher of al-Madrasah an-Nizamiyyah in Baghdad whose attempt at a synthesis proved permanently successful. Al-Ghazali [well known to medieval Europe as Algazel] received his elementary education from a mystic and then sat at the feet of famous men of learning until he himself became renowned for his learning. In his thirties he reached the top of his profession as the principal teacher in the foremost institution in the eastern caliphate. But like many saintly characters in history, his lofty spirit recoiled from worldly vanities. He gave up his post, donned the garb of a mystic and proceeded to Mecca on pilgrimage, stopping to preach and meditate in Damascus and Jerusalem.

In an autobiography of convincing candour, al-Ghazali recorded his search for "the hidden meanings and ultimate goals" of the various branches of learning, and for "the secret base" of the different doctrines. He wrote that his search had led him to the conclusion that "the essential truth" and spiritual satisfaction could be found in the tenets of the sufi mystics. He was led to this conclusion not by the evidence of the senses nor by logical argument nor even by pure reason, but by divine guidance.

Of the three strands we identified in the Islamic tradition al-Ghazali thus ruled out the philosophical, but rehabilitated the mystic with the theological. In what amounted to a *summa*, he recast the whole Islamic tradition in a synthesis of dogma, ritual, and ethics at once authoritative and rational. In his method of treatment he frequently employed syllogism and invoked the authority of Reason, but he decidedly reserved the final authority for the divine Revelation.

A compromise more enduring has never been achieved. But it contributed to the isolation of the philosophers who, despite repeated attempts at reconciling Reason with Revelation, could never make a permanent impression. After al-Ghazali they remained a race apart, ignored, admired or declared heretics according to the occasion. The theologians and the mystics emerged as the guardians of Islamic learning, and the transmitters of the Islamic tradition through teaching and preaching. The character of Muslim education, in aims, content, methods and institutions was determined for centuries. It hardly changed till the last hundred and fifty years.

There were indeed doctrinal and regional variations, but innovations were very few. Special mention may, however, be made of certain developments that varied the traditional conventions of Muslim education. At the lower level the custom of charging fees for teaching the elements and even the Koran became so universal that jurists were compelled to lay down rules governing it, particularly when the teaching of reading and writing involved, as it often did, the use of the Koran. There are even isolated instances when, if not the state at least some individual rulers, patronized or established institutions for teaching the elements and the Koran where the teachers were paid and the pupils provided with free material.

The reference is, of course, to al-Hakam II who is reputed to have opened in Cordova a number of primary schools of *Kuttab* type and paid their teachers from his private purse. But it is not clear whether these schools were preparatory to the more renowned higher institution which operated as a form of *Madrasah* in the mosque of Cordova.

Another related innovation was the sale of copies of the Koran which at first was frowned upon. It was not beyond the ingenuity of jurist teachers here again to legalize the practice "in the public interest." The price, they said, was not for the priceless word of God but for the labour of the copyist who had to earn a living while satisfying a communal and religious need.

The break with tradition was, however, more universal at the higher level. Here both teachers and taught were generously rewarded. The spread of this practice was challenged by vigorous protests. "Hitherto," one protest proclaimed, "learning had been sought by the highly intelligent and diligent class who wanted it for its own sake and for the attainment of personal perfection. Hence they came out truly learned and they and their learning were useful to the community. If now material reward is to be had for the pursuit of learning the lazy and the mean will come in great numbers pretending love of learning—a circumstance that will lead to its disappearance."

There is no doubt that the trend was towards accepting the innovation. But despite this trend a class of pious and less necessitous teachers continued to uphold tradition by teaching gratuitously. No class of teachers was more assiduous in this than the sufis. It was a natural consequence of their system, the essence of which was the striving for personal favour and communion with God. It taught that while for this purpose much depended on the exertion of the individual, a great deal was to be gained from the guidance of a spiritual teacher. Almost all great sufis were also great teachers. The followers of great teachers eventually organized themselves into orders.Their members were drawn from all classes of society, and in later history claimed powerful following in the craft guilds. Spiritual and moral education was the central core of the system in all these orders. Teaching and devotion were practised anywhere, but formally in the *Zawiyah*. This was a parallel to the *Maktab* in that it taught the elements, but superior to it in that it provided education at a higher level.

Even a self-restricting curriculum admitted some innovations. It is true that their admission was not universal, but the innovations themselves were significant. Thus we infer from what al-Ghazali wrote that in his days enterprising teachers in the *Maktab* resorted to dramatization and games in order to hold the attention of young pupils. There is no specific mention by him or by other writers of comparable activities in the *Madrasah*, but there is a general mention of, *inter alia*, horsemanship, chess and music, although it must be assumed that these activities were cultivated privately.

As to teaching methods the oral tradition had never been superseded, and at all levels teachers continued to rely on recitation and oral exposition, and pupils on learning by rote. Even after the whole of the Arabic-Islamic tradition was recorded, distinguished teachers in the classical age were more comfortable, and indeed more profound, without than with the aid of the written word. However, as the classical age was followed by one of less vitality and originality teachers became increasingly the slaves of texts. They conceived their task to consist of merely expounding and "dictating" commentaries. Dictation was the more formal stage in the development of teaching methods of which we have already distinguished two others: oral transmission and exposition followed by question and answer.

[4]

After the disruption of the historic caliphate, and amidst the chaos that followed, the theologians and jurists as a class lost their point of anchor in a central political power. They lost also some of the vitality that characterized men like al-Ghazali, but they continued to monopolize teaching in the endowed institutions that survived the holocaust of the Mongol invasion. On the other hand the sufi orders lost little or nothing of their internal cohesion and external activity. They survived, perhaps more than the theologians, as the guardians and transmitters of culture much as the monastic orders were in medieval Europe.

It is a singular fact, with no exact parallel elsewhere, that political upheavals, and even the eclipse of the central political power in Islam, did not result in a decrease in educational institutions. On the contrary there was a remarkable increase. An explanation may be sought in the disturbed religious conscience of society. The calamities that befell it were interpreted by many as God's wrath for its iniquities and its neglect to live, as the early Islamic community lived, in obedience to His commands. Hence, in addition to pure acts of genuine piety and prayer, there was a profusion of expiatory acts by petty or illegitimate rulers, wealthy notables and others. These acts included the building and endowment of educational institutions, including the *Maktab*, *Zawiyah* and *Madrasah*. The process continued, henceforth the successor simply emulating predecessors, to comparatively modern times, and covered major cities and smaller towns and some villages.

But all the increase in quantity was not matched by improvement in quality. Rather on the contrary: the academic and teaching standards of al-Ghazali's era could not be maintained, and began to deteriorate in the following centuries. With very few notable exceptions, the literary product as a whole betrayed authors who were no more than imitators and commentators. The curriculum of higher institutions became confined to religious and Arabic subjects. Arab philosophy beat a gradual retreat until it was adopted by Europe. Of the sciences cultivated by the Arabs medicine managed to survive largely in hospitals, and alchemy with a few individuals who pursued its study privately.

Such was the educational and general cultural set-up when roughly by the beginning of the sixteenth century the Ottoman Turks succeeded to the greater part of the heritage of the Sunni caliphate and re-established a central Islamic power. Practically all the Arab lands formed part of this mighty empire and remained so for the next four hundred years. As a restoration of a central Islamic power, the rise of the Ottoman Turks was not all-embracing: their expansion in Europe was indeed great, but the expansion in Africa did not embrace Morocco, nor did the expansion in Asia embrace Persia. In this country a rival Shi'i state was established.

In this distribution of power the Arab loss was double. That they themselves did not regain political power was perhaps mitigated by the fact that those who gained most of it were brother Muslims, but there was no mitigation of the cultural loss. The Arabic language, the *lingua franca* of Islam, ceased to be official in Persia, and in the Arab lands suffered degeneration both as a classical model and as a spoken language. Not before the beginning of the nineteenth century did its revival begin in earnest, preceding by nearly a century the restoration of Arab political independence.

3

EDUCATIONAL THEORY IN ISLAM

[1]

The essence of Muslim education is stated in the divine revelation in the Koran, and is restated in greater detail in the traditions of the Prophet Muhammad. It took more than two centuries of practice for still more detailed exposition of theory to be formulated. Most of the formulations were necessarily close to the first principles laid down in the divine revelation, but some of them were designed partly to accommodate lapses from the ideal and partly to rationalize innovations.

During this long period of practice that preceded the detailed formulation of theory there developed in the public mind an unfavourable image of the teacher who taught for material reward. In anecdotes, proverbs and poetry he is depicted as a person of little intelligence and less judgement, an object of caustic and pitiless ridicule, very much like the pedagogue in Greek history. Two examples must suffice. A famous general and administrator, who lived half a century after Muhammad, had risen from such humble beginnings, and his enemies spared no effort to remind him of his antecedents, as the following lines show:

Has he forgotten the lean years when he taught the Sura of
    Abundance
For loaves, some scarcely visible and others as round as a full
    moon?

The second example comes from the famous poet Abu Nuwas, known to European readers of the *Arabian Nights* as the boon-companion of "the good Haroun alraschid". In lines of singular charm the poet depicts a *Maktab* run by one Hafs where corporeal punishment was inflicted on a lazy inmate:

Lo behold Hafs in his Maktab!
Stern, sitting on a mat surrounded by slaves.
"Whip him!" he cried, "Whip the lazy boy!"
He was bared of silk and streaky garments
And with a leather strap they chastized him.
"O dear master!" he cried. "I will reform."
I begged Hafs to pardon the boy—
"He will do well anon" was my plea.

It was in this atmosphere that the first notable contribution on the theory of education was written outside purely religious circles. Its author was the famous belletrist al-Jahiz whose accomplishments included a mastery of Islamic theology and Arabic philology as well as Greek philosophy and science. He flourished in Basra in the third century of Islam, and wrote on a variety of subjects in a prose style that was to be a model for centuries. A short chapter on teachers is to be found in one of his books. Since its author had acted as a tutor to the sons of the caliph, the chapter may be regarded as an apology for this class of teachers. Otherwise it is a balanced account, valuable alike from an educational and historical point of view.

The historian will find, within the compass of a short chapter, a classified list of teachers particularly of tutors and men whose circles attracted numerous students. And the educationist will find a judicious assessment of the professional and social status of teachers. The account opens with a survey of the popular and unfavourable view of the teacher whose foolishness and small-mindedness was proverbial. Thus it was said "more foolish than a *Kuttab* teacher" and "how could intelligence and wisdom be found in one who rotates between an infant and a woman!" Al-Jahiz discounts this view in a striking passage: "There are, in my view, two classes of teachers: men who raised themselves above teaching the children of the common people to specialize in teaching those of the nobility, and men who raised themselves above teaching the children of the nobility to devote themselves to teaching princes who would succeed to the caliphate. ... The unfavourable views of teachers cannot apply to either class. It cannot even apply to all teachers in village *Kuttabs*, for they are like any other class of men; they include the superior and the inferior."

Neither poetry nor polite literature was, however, the main channel through which the spirit of Muslim education was preserved for posterity. It remained for theologians, jurists and mystics, those who formed the bulk of teachers, to expound that spirit in a more serious vein and on traditional lines. The earliest concise treatise on the subject of teachers was written in Tunisia by a contemporary of al-Jahiz. Its author was the jurist Ibn Sahnun who had travelled to the east both to perform the pilgrimage and in quest of learning. His short treatise, only twelve pages in manuscript, was written from a purely religious point of view, and naturally begins with citation of traditions on the virtue of learning and teaching the Koran.

It is evident that by Ibn Sahnun's time the practice of charging fees, among other innovations, had become well-established. A gloss over a prophetic tradition provided a sanction for the practice so that material reward became legitimate even on teaching the Koran:

"The community cannot do without a ruler for upholding justice lest transgression prevails, without sale and purchase of copies of the Koran lest its diffusion diminishes, or without teachers to instruct the children against payment lest the people remain illiterate."

For the rest the treatise lays down such rules for the conduct of teachers as betray the author's legal training. Thus he insists that once he accepted a fee for his services the teacher must treat his pupils on a basis of absolute equality without any distinction between the rich and the poor. He must not inflict corporeal punishment while in a temper, for punishment is corrective for the sole benefit of the pupil and not to assuage the teacher's anger. At any rate he must not inflict more than three strokes without the consent of the parents, and on no account must he hit the face or the head or withhold food or water. The teacher may employ a monitor, but he must have mastered the Koran and require no further instruction in the elements. Then Ibn Sahnun expresses his personal preference for boys and girls to be taught separately.

[2]

The preceding translated excerpts and summaries are fairly representative of Arabic-Islamic thought on important aspects of elementary education down to the end of the fourth century of Islam. Rooted in a distinctly religious tradition the theory was expanded and interpreted on the basis of long practice. Although the practice in post-elementary education, comprising the Koranic and Prophetic with allied Arabic studies, had also been greatly expanded, there were as yet no comparable interpretive accounts of this development by theologians, jurists or linguists. The earliest account is to be found not in the works of any of these but in the philosophic tracts of the Brethren of Purity whose publication symbolized the beginning of state intervention in education.

With skilful if unorthodox interpretation of the Koran and prophetic traditions, the Brethren sought to integrate Greek philosophy with the Islamic heritage. Through the diffusion of this integrated learning they hoped to establish "the kingdom of the Righteous", a utopia ruled by philosophers. In their tracts the Brethren mention Plato quite frequently, and their utopia bears close resemblance to his *Republic*. It also resembles closely the *Virtuous City* by the Muslim philosopher al-Farabi (well-known in medieval Europe as Alpharabius), a student of Aristotle and called after him "the second teacher".

Nevertheless the substance of the tracts includes much of neo-platonism and Islamic mysticism, and both of these elements are reflected in the theory of education scattered in the odd fifty tracts. The supreme and ultimate aim of education remains strictly ortho-dox: happiness in this world and eternal bliss in the next. However, the nature of the process of learning is in the tracts based on the Platonic doctrine of reminiscence which may be simplified as follows: The soul of man came to be attached to his body through emanation by stages from God. Hence it is potentially learned and needs instruction only by reminding in order to become actually so.

It is not easy to establish why the Brethren failed to apply this principle to elementary education. Not only did they adopt the traditional attitude to elementary education but inexplicably failed to pay enough attention to those whose opinion had been formed. They deliberately directed most of their attention to youths after the age of fifteen. "Concentrate on youth", they instructed their members, "and do not tire yourself in the vain hope of reforming the old."

One reason for this attitude seems to have been a desire to achieve quick results; the Brethren were certainly not ignorant of the educa-tional process. Their tracts clearly state that the mind of the child before receiving instruction or embracing beliefs is like a *tabula rasa*: "It is like a white clean paper; once anything is written on it, right or wrong, it will be difficult to erase it or to superimpose new writing upon it."

There is indeed frequent if incidental reference in the tracts to the *Maktab*, its teacher, the subjects he taught and the articles used by pupils. But the main concern is with the next stage which led, under the Brethren's system, to further stages in a continuous education unto death. There is in addition more than lip-service to the venera-tion of learning in the Islamic tradition, although it is frequently invoked in support of philosophical aims. Appeal to Reason and the injunction "Know thyself" figure prominently on the pages of the tracts.

In the purely educational sphere I would single out two new contributions to theory. The first is concerning the relationship between teacher and pupil, and is closely related to the ideas of the mystics. The relationship, is a spiritual one and is superior to physical relationships:

"Know, o brother, that your teacher is the begetter of your soul just as your father is the begetter of your body. Your father gave you a physical form, but your teacher gives you a spiritual one. Your teacher nourishes your soul with learning and wisdom and guides it to attain everlasting bliss. Your father brought you up and trained you to make a living in this transient world."

The second contribution to educational theory envisages teaching as one of the crafts, the more perfection the craftsman acquires the nearer he comes to God: "Excellence in every craft is imitation of the Wise Creator, and He loves the skilful craftsman. . . . Hence philosophy has been defined as imitation of God in knowledge, wisdom and goodness. He who acquires an increase of these comes correspondingly nearer to God."

Let these quotations suffice as a justification for regarding the Brethren as representatives of the philosophic strand in Muslim educational theory. For there is surprisingly little philosophy of education in the writings of Muslim philosophers, and the Brethren's treatment of the subject is more sustained if necessarily sporadic. It has the added merit that it combines theology not only with science and philosophy, but also with mysticism in its Islamic and Neoplatonic forms. In admitting the mystic element the Brethren were the forerunners of al-Ghazali by nearly a century.

In the meantime the institution of *al-Madrasah*, under this or other names, became universal and more formality had been introduced in the relationship between teacher and pupil. If translated in modern parlance the words of the Brethren on this relationship mean that it was personal, not institutional. Until their time, a seeker after learning generally went to study a given subject, or even a given book, with a famous teacher, not necessarily to a particular place of learning. The pupil could either join the public circle of the teacher in a mosque or elsewhere, or seek more intimate relations with him by personal attendance. The latter method was peculiar to the mystics. Nowhere was such relationship closer than between a novice and his guide in any of the mystic orders. It was the truly spiritual relationship that transcended even blood ties.

[3]

Classical Arabic literature contains no theory of education more authoritative, systematic and comprehensive than had been bequeathed by al-Ghazali. His giant mind roves over the entire field and nothing is too small for his eagle eye. His insight is that of one who himself was a great teacher in addition to being a great thinker. He naturally wrote as a theologian and mystic, but within a religious framework he is humane and liberal; his writings sparkle with piety, common sense and compassion.

He begins with the infant child before the age of conventional education. "The child", he wrote "is a trust [placed by God] in the hands of his parents, and his innocent heart is a precious element capable of taking impressions". If the parents, and later on the teachers, brought him up in righteousness he would live happily in this world and the next and they would be rewarded by God for their good deed. If they neglected the child's upbringing and education he would lead a life of unhappiness in both worlds and they would bear the burden of the sin of neglect.

Al-Ghazali's view of the *Maktab* and of what should be taught in it corresponds to that of his predecessors and current practice in his time. But he surpasses them in the high moral standards he expects from the teacher. He who undertakes the instruction of the young, insists al-Ghazali, "undertakes a great responsibility". He must therefore be as tender to his pupils as if they were his own children. He must correct moral lapses through hinting rather than direct prohibition, gentle advice rather than reproof. Above all he himself must set an example so that his actions accord with his precepts.

Higher education is dealt with under the curriculum and the qualities of teachers and pupils. The question of remuneration is theoretically resolved by a classification of the branches of knowledge into purely religious and auxiliary studies. Pursuit of the former is a personal duty of the believer, while the study of such subjects as arithmetic and medicine in the latter is merely desirable. While it was legitimate to accept material reward for teaching auxiliary subjects, it was still the duty of the ideal teacher to teach religious subjects gratuitously. He may, however, accept such remuneration as would free him from material worries and make him devote himself entirely to the diffusion of religious learning. This is an oblique excuse for al-Ghazali's own employment as a paid teacher in Baghdad. There is similarly a trace of an autobiographical note in the qualities he expected in the teacher and student at this higher level. Both must approach learning with humility and must free their minds from wordly concerns.

In discussing the process of learning al-Ghazali re-echoes the doctrine of reminiscence: "Knowledge exists potentially in the human soul like a seed in the soil; by learning the potential becomes actual." And yet there are two distinct channels in his system through which learning is acquired: actual application and divine inspiration, the efforts of mind and body on the one hand and a "light from God" on the other. Here the mystic in al-Ghazali asserts the firm belief in a divine illumination more efficacious than human reason.

This is not a denial of the operation of reason; it merely places it in a hierarchical order second to divine grace. Al-Ghazali's system is so balanced that its preoccupation with things divine and mystical experience leave room also for rational thinking, logical deduction and empirical observation. Nor does it neglect the needs of the body. While al-Ghazali warns against luxuries that lead to laziness he recommends that the primary school pupil should be allowed physical exercise including walking. "After school", he writes, "the pupil must be allowed to play for recreation but not to the degree of exhaustion. To prevent play and to insist on continuous study leads to dullness in the heart, diminution in intelligence and unhappiness." There is no specific provision for students in higher institutions, but there is an incidental mention of chess. It was, however, part of the life of adolescent and older students to ride horses, to go hunting and to attend musical and poetry recitals.

Al-Ghazali's ideas dominated Islamic educational thought for centuries after his death. With one notable exception, practically all educational literature down to the beginning of modernization in the nineteenth century is either inspired by his writings or directly derived from them. Nothing of special value was added to theory; authors were content to reproduce their predecessors often in rather condensed form. An author who lived about a century after al-Ghazali may be noted here. Zarnuji's short book contains, in addition to a summary of the traditional ideas, some curious remarks which indicate that superstition had penetrated the educational citadel.

He warns students against the use of red ink on the double ground that it had not been used by their predecessors and that its use was peculiar to philosophers. He shows a capacity for combining the ridiculous with the absurd when he asserts that among the causes of forgetfulness was "the eating of the seeds of coriander and sour apples or the passing through a file of camels."

And yet Zarnuji had been translated into Latin and quite recently also into English. In Arabic his book has run into several printings. The reason for this popularity may be the brevity of the book, its simple language and a style enlivened with anecdotes, proverbs, and lines of poetry, in addition to curious assertions such as given above.

[4]

Two centuries after Zarnuji the reputation of Muslim scholarship was more than redeemed by the historian Ibn Khaldun. He was born in Tunis and received his early education from his father and then pursued the traditional Arabic and Islamic studies under various teachers till the age of twenty. He then held political, diplomatic and judicial posts in North Africa, Spain and Egypt. Only in Cairo did he experience teaching when he combined the post of judge with lecturing at al-Azhar.

His reputation rests on his history and particularly on its *Prolegomena* in which he expounded his philosophy of history and sociology. The distinguished English historian Arnold Toynbee wrote of Ibn Khaldun that he had "conceived and formulated a philosophy of history which is undoubtedly the greatest work of its kind that has been created in any time or place." As part of his philosophy Ibn Khaldun devoted important sections to education and these are our sole concern here.

Ibn Khaldun starts from first principles: education is a social phenomenon and teaching is one of the social crafts; man is a social animal and his prosecution of learning is conditioned by the nature of the material, intellectual and spiritual forces of the civilization in which he lives. But like his illustrious predecessor al-Ghazali, Ibn Khaldun manages to be original within the Islamic tradition. Thus under the proposition that learning and education thrive only in a civilized society he writes: "Man is distinguished from animals by a capacity to reason. His reason guides him to make a living, to co-operate with other members of his society and to accept what God has revealed through His prophets for man's welfare in this world and the next. Man is therefore a reasoning animal, and reasoning is the foundation of all learning."

And yet Ibn Khaldun is very close to al-Ghazali in setting limits to the capacity of human reason in the process of learning which ultimately must depend on divine guidance. He advocates gradual imparting of knowledge according to the capacity of the learner, asserts that proficiency in one branch of knowledge prepares the learner for acquiring another, and approves of the custom of travel in order to learn from different teachers as conducive to a deeper understanding and wider vision.

Then he explains that in the whole process of learning reason enables the learner to grasp the meaning through the spoken and written word and to deduce laws establishing order and relation between different meanings. Not every learner is capable of reaching this final stage. To him who is in difficulty, Ibn Khaldun's advice is this: "Abandon all artificial means of learning and appeal to your natural reason innate in you . . . and seek God's guidance which had illuminated the way of learners before you and taught them that which they knew not."

This is clearly addressed to the advanced student who is Ibn Khaldun's main concern. His mention of elementary education until the age of adolescence is less direct or detailed. Like his predecessors he recommends the treatment of young children with compassion, not only because harshness dulls the child's capacity to learn but also because it "depraves his humanity." There is a valuable review of elementary education in Ibn Khaldun's time concerned mainly with the curriculum. In Andalusia teachers tackled, in addition to the Koran, Arabic grammar and poetry, letter-writing and penmanship. In Morocco nothing more was taught than the Koran and writing through learning it. In Tunisia the Koran and prophetic traditions were taught with penmanship as an auxiliary subject. As to the people of the east, who to Ibn Khaldun included the inhabitants of Egypt and the rest of the Islamic countries, his knowledge is clearly not first hand. He is therefore cautious when he says that, according to report, the curriculum was "mixed" which means that it was similar to that of Andalusia.

Commenting on these methods Ibn Khaldun quotes the view of an Andalusian pupil of al-Ghazali that the best order of approach was not to begin with the Koran which is too difficult for children, but with Arabic language and poetry, then arithmetic and finally the Koran. Ibn Khaldun agrees that this was a better method of approach but he says custom was against it. Furthermore, it carries with it a danger that adolescents may be tempted to neglect the study of the Koran once they had learned the elements and left school.

There was no substantial divergence either in curricula or methods in higher education. There was, however, a difference in educational advance between the eastern and the western parts of the Muslim world. Ibn Khaldun's critical mind ascribes it to a different level of civilization: "The people of the east are on the whole more steeped in the craft of teaching as well as in other crafts, so much so that those who travel from the west to the east in quest of learning presume that the people of the east are naturally endowed with better minds . . . and that the difference between them is one of a difference between two species of human beings, ... whereas it is simply the result of an increased intelligence through civilization . . ."

Different levels of civilization in the Arab countries no doubt existed in Ibn Khaldun's time, but they all shared in the misfortune of a general decline of Islamic learning. This is reflected in his criticism of its methods. He deplored, for example, the greater dependence upon memory in learning texts with commentaries and super-commentaries thereon, "repetitive in words while the meaning is one and the same." He equally deplored as confusing and discouraging to students the custom of condensing whole disciplines in short treatises to facilitate memorizing. But this decline was still accompanied by increased endowment of educational institutions of the *Madrasah* and *Zawiyah* type. This was particularly true of Egypt and to a lesser degree of Syria. Hence, according to Ibn Khaldun, students flocked to these institutions from the east and from the west attracted both by the educational facilities and the generous living allowances.

[5]

"We learn by report that in the lands of the Franks on the north shores of the sea philosophical sciences are much in demand, their principles are being revived, the circles for teaching them are numerous, and the number of students seeking to learn them is increasing."

Thus was the beginning of the Renaissance viewed from North Africa, brought to Ibn Khaldun's notice. He had just written a chapter on the refutation of philosophy in which he argued against the study of physical science unless the student had first been saturated with religious science. This rejection of philosophy and science by Ibn Khaldun was no more than a confirmation of an attitude begun nearly a century before al-Ghazali and was finally formalized by him. It contrasts very sharply with the early enthusiasm for translating Greek philosophy and science under the patronage of caliphs.

Greek philosophy and science were, however, cultivated by a line of distinguished Muslim philosophers who passed the heritage enhanced to medieval Europe. The value of this contribution to the Renaissance is a debatable question, but it is a fact that Aristotle continued to be studied for a long time at the University of Paris and elsewhere through the works of Averroes.

From the Renaissance down to the Industrial Revolution the general trends in Islamic and European education and learning in general are discernible in formalism and stagnation on the one side and re-birth and development on the other. A reversal of roles more radical can hardly be imagined: At a time when Europe was semi-barbarous and Charlemagne could scarcely write his name, the Islamic world enjoyed a high degree of civilization and its educational institutions were unrivalled. The forces that shaped European development were on the whole internal springing, to start with, from the Greco-Roman tradition and Christianity. By comparison Islamic development or stagnation was greatly influenced not merely by the conservatism of theologians but also by formidable external factors.

Successive waves of foreign invasions, beginning with the Crusades, followed by the Mongol sack of Baghdad and other cities, and culminating in the gradual end of Muslim life in Spain, resulted in large scale destruction of seats of learning and general devastation of the land. Each of these events contributed its share to a hardening of attitude to external influences. It was a protective reaction springing more from weakness than from strength. At the height of its power and glory Islam accepted and adapted much of the culture of the peoples it came in contact with. In the ages of its decline confidence was lost and the guardians of its tradition feared and resisted all foreign intrusion.

After the eclipse of the historic caliphate in Baghdad chaos reigned supreme. It was left to the Arabicised Mamluk rulers of Egypt to pick up the pieces and establish a kingdom that embraced the central Arab home lands including Syria and Hijaz. The Mamluk sultans were great patrons of learning and endowed a great many institutions some of which survive to this day. They were supplanted by the Ottoman Turks whose dominions included virtually all the Arab lands in Asia and Africa except Morocco. The Ottoman Empire was strictly Islamic in policy and organization, and its educational system was a replica, in theory and in practice, of its Arab predecessors.

But the Empire was also, at least in the territorial sense, a European power, for its dominions embraced the whole of the Balkan Peninsula almost to the gates of Vienna. And yet for centuries relations with Europe were confined to war. No interest was evinced in the political, religious, intellectual or social developments in Europe. A small change of attitude began to take place in the eighteenth century and gathered momentum after the French Revolution. It was prompted by a desire to examine the source of a new European strength displayed in weapons and techniques in the battlefield.

At the time when this change began the educational system in the

Arab (and Turkish) provinces of the Empire was still based on the *Maktab* and the *Madrasah* with their curricula and methods hardly changed. There is, however, an occasional mention of women taking charge of girls whose education together with boys was discouraged. These women acted independently or as paid employees of parents. There is little evidence that they benefited from special endowments. Nor is there any evidence that, apart from private tuition received at home by daughters of noble or wealthy families, there was any provision for higher female education. In addition to learning to recite the Koran daughters of well-to-do families learned privately some needlework, embroidery and domestic science.

Of the Arab provinces Iraq in the east never recovered the primacy in learning after the Mongol invasion. In the west the splendour of Arab civilization in Spain was no more, and in North Africa the surviving educational institutions were relatively small in number and poor substitutes for those of Cordova and Granada. In the heart of the Arab world, Hijaz, Egypt and Syria, the mosques and other seats of learning either escaped unscathed or were less affected by the cataclysm. To these centres in Mecca, Medina, Jerusalem, Damascus and Cairo, scholars from both ends of the Arab world resorted for further study and meditation.

Turkish rule had little influence on the educational institutions in these centres except perhaps in the form of endowments and donations. Except for the private *Maktab* all educational institutions were managed by trustees belonging to the powerful corporations of theologians, jurists and mystics. The stability and security which Turkish rule brought about had the double effect of increasing both the number of institutions and their conservatism. To the governing bodies of these institutions their function was to maintain tradition and preserve the accepted norms of society, not to mould it or transform it.

This attitude had, of course, been formed by the operation, over centuries of social and religious factors. An essential part of the child's upbringing, before as during and after the age of attending school, was respect for elders. It began with respect for parents and members of the family, but was automatically transferred to teachers. At a higher level it became a respect for authority, a conspicuous element in all branches of Islamic learning and indeed the political system.

Such was the general attitude to education in the closing decades of the eighteenth century, on the eve of the reception of European methods.

4

EARLY MODERNIZATION

[1]

On the eve of the introduction of European methods the educational institutions in the central Arab lands of Hijaz, Syria and Egypt were superior to their counterparts elsewhere. For centuries they enjoyed the protection of a single political power and munificence of successive Mamluk and Ottoman sultans. So successful were these institutions in establishing their supremacy that they served not only indigenous students but also those from other Arab and Muslim lands in the east and west. The sketch portrait in the following pages may therefore be regarded as typical and representative.

The mosques in the holy cities of Mecca and Medina, which had since the early days of Islam been seats of learning, remained the goal of pious and aspiring students. Throughout the ages they attracted scholars from all parts of the Muslim world who, after performing the pilgrimage, took residence in the precincts and for longer or shorter periods engaged in learning, teaching and writing. The facilities for these activities were ample thanks to endowments, donations and the annual bounty from the reigning monarchs. But while the term *Madrasah* was not formally applied to the mosque circles in the holy cities, their range of studies and methods were not widely different from those of such institutions elsewhere.

In Egypt as elsewhere the *Kuttab* was maintained in towns and villages, but the *Madrasah* existed only in the cities. The largest of this type of institution was al-Azhar in Cairo. Its long history, rich endowments and central position in the heart of the Muslim world gave it unrivalled primacy. While it was by no means rare for a *Madrasah* to exist with its own endowment and to be run by a single teacher, al-Azhar had at the time of the French invasion in 1798 some fifty senior teachers apart from junior assistants. Its students then numbered about three thousand, about a third of whom came from other Muslim lands. The sultan of Morocco sent an annual gift as an act of piety, but probably also because al-Azhar received students from his distant land.

Syria appears to have had more educational facilities but no single institution of the size and importance of al-Azhar. Syrian students, as students from other lands, did in fact seek higher education in Cairo at al-Azhar and had special quarters assigned for their lodging and received free rations. The only educational centre in Syria that rivalled Cairo was Damascus. It had at this time some fifty *Madrasahs*, and some of them attracted students from other lands, probably because the city was an important assembly station on the pilgrim route to Mecca. Other seats of learning in Syria were Jerusalem, Nabulus, Acre, Sidon, Tripoli and Aleppo. Ambitious Syrian students who did not go to Cairo for further training went to Istanbul, the capital of the Ottoman Empire. Its institutions were the recruiting ground for high posts in the central and provincial government.

The courses followed at traditional institutions were very similar. With no recognized standard students had to adjust themselves to the lectures given by different teachers. A student moved freely from one circle to another till he found his level or despaired. There was no time limit. The process could have taken a few years or might have lasted for the greater part of a lifetime. It was of course harder for students who joined with imperfect knowledge of classical Arabic. They had first to master it before they could make any progress in other branches of learning. Progress was marked not by a diploma of an institution but by a licence of one of its teachers. (Institutional diplomas are comparatively recent innovations).

Methods of teaching followed well-defined lines. An established teacher taught, from a given text by commentary or dictation, those who chose to join his circle. He sat supporting his back to a pillar in the mosque or school and the students sat round him in rows of a semi-circle. Once he concluded the lesson with the formula "and God knows best", it was customary for students of all ages to come forward spontaneously in order to kiss his right hand.

Later on an assistant would repeat the master's lesson for the benefit of those who did not follow all its intricacies. A repeater was usually one of the bright students chosen by the master. It was a recognized practice for students to raise questions and to argue with the teacher in the course of a lesson. Many a student made a name for himself and became an assistant in this manner. Such assistants eventually became leaders of circles themselves.

The picture of the educational system at the beginning of the nineteenth century must suffice. Viewed within its own limits the system afforded a good deal of freedom and was by its own standards tolerably efficient. It adequately served the needs of society as they then were. But this is not to say that it was perfect. For it allowed certain debilitating features to develop in its fringe and failed to detect their harmful influence. One of these was the cultivation of pseudo-science.

There is contemporary and reliable evidence that apart from a formal religious and linguistic curriculum, Azhar shaikhs and others cultivated informally the study of arithmetic, algebra, geometry, astronomy, geography, medicine, logic and even philosophy. While we do not know exactly what was studied of philosophy it is probably correct to infer that mathematics and logic were studied as auxiliary to religious science. It is, on the other hand, certain that much of astronomy was astrology and that even medicine became infested with occultism. That the learned profession tolerated such lapses was a serious blow to the rational element in the Islamic tradition, and tended in the long run to undermine the general intellectual atmosphere.

And yet if an educational system may be judged by its best products then that of the era now under review can boast of at least three men of outstanding intellectual power and creative originality: the Syrian biographer Muradi, the Palestinian mystic Nabulusi, and the Egyptian historian Jabarti. Their different interests indicate mere facets of the essential unity of Islamic learning, each of them representing in his own sphere the best of its traditions at the time.

To such men was due the maintenance of the unity of Islamic learning and the upholding of its conventions. Each was the typical scholar who according to tradition remained a learner all his life: "seek learning from the cradle to the grave". He moved in quest of learning from one country to another but found himself always at home among brethren who lodged him and entertained him in public or private houses, and facilitated his task of attending lessons or giving such lessons himself. This solidarity of the learned was not simply professional. The best minds among the learned formed themselves into semi-formal corporations which served to maintain moral and academic standards in the public services, in the educational institutions and in such professions as medicine and such crafts as calligraphy. Similarly members of the mystic orders among the learned maintained spiritual and moral standards in their own institutions and in the craft guilds.

The above discussion reveals that the Islamic oral tradition had greatly been transformed. Teachers were now tied to fixed written texts, and their oral exposition of texts was valid only if it had some textual authority. The totality of "knowledge" was recorded on paper. Although paper was introduced into Europe by the Arabs they shunned the European invention of printing books on it for nearly three centuries. Religious scruples regarded the mechanical reproduction of the word of God or material connected therewith as irreverent.

Printing of non-religious matter was authorized to Muslims in the eighteenth century in Istanbul. Non-Muslim, Ottoman subjects and foreign residents were permitted to print religious and other literature in their own languages. Until the beginning of the nineteenth century printed books in Arabic consisted mostly of Bibles and Christian literature emanating from the press of the *Propaganda Fide* in Rome and some lithographic hand-presses in convents on Mount Lebanon. The Arabic section of the Propaganda was confiscated by Napoleon who used it, with its Maronite translators, for the issue of proclamations in Egypt and Syria. It was removed with the French expedition after three years of occupation.

The claim that the brief French presence in Egypt and Syria initiated a revival in learning is one of the myths of modern history propagated by the French and their admirers. There is ample evidence to show that on the contrary the French occupation caused, in addition to physical destruction, disclocation in educational institutions and left them the poorer by the execution of notable teachers of al-Azhar and frigthening away others. The French were far too busy in military campaigns and suppression of risings to pay serious attention to native education. Their ventures in the cultural field were designed for their own benefit, and the efforts of the team of savants who accompanied Napoleon were directed towards the advancement of European knowledge of Egypt rather than towards the education of the Egyptians.

[2]

The first essays in modernizing education had native not foreign stimuli. They began at the top in Istanbul, but the aim was military, not educational. The method of approach was not through the modification of the traditional system, but by the gradual and almost unconscious creation of a new and parallel system. It was of a very limited scope to start with. In the last quarter of the eighteenth century a school for army engineers and another for naval officers were established in the capital. French and Swedish instructors were employed to train Turkish cadets in gunnery, fortifications and navigation, through the medium of French. But even this limited innovation was unpopular in the army and among some religious leaders, and a powerful reaction resulted in the deposition of the sultan and the shelving of his modernization plans, only to be taken up more vigorously by his successor.

Not before the first quarter of the nineteenth century did educational modernization, still military in intention, restart on a considerable scale. This time it was started almost simultaneously in the capital Istanbul and in the important Arab province of Egypt. From the turmoil following the end of the French occupation there emerged Muhammad Ali Pasha as a semi-independent governor in Cairo. Like his master in Istanbul he was bent on creating an army on European lines. Both used education as an instrument. But henceforth we must keep the purely Turkish activity in the background and concentrate on the more relevant Egyptian.

Muhammad Ali's enterprise and daring surpassed those of his master. The sultan was always careful not only to seek the formal sanction of any new measure from the highest religious authority but also to have it announced as in strict conformity with Islamic law. The pasha freed himself from all such controls. He came to power through the help of the ulema but once in power he disregarded them. He watched astutely for precedents in his master's action, and while professedly following these precedents exceeded by far any limits the sovereign himself dared to reach.

Soon after his confirmation in office, Muhammad Ali realized the need for experts. He met this need largely by the employment of Italian and French personnel and partly by luring one or two Turks with first-hand experience of the modernizing measures adopted by the sultan in Istanbul. At the same time he began to send an increasing number of selected students for training in Europe. At first he sent a few individuals, but in 1826 he sent the first large mission consisting of forty-four students to France.

Already in 1816 the pasha opened a new school near his residence in the Cairo citadel. In addition to the Koran, reading and writing Arabic, the pupils were taught Turkish, Persian and Italian as well as horse-riding, use of arms and military tactics. Turkish and Persian were with Arabic the languages highly educated Muslims learned at the time. Italian had, since the ascendency of Venice and other Italian cities, become the language of foreign commerce in the eastern Mediterranean lands. The first students from Egypt were in fact sent to Italy partly because of this commercial ascendency and partly because at the time that country presented no political dangers.

A second school was opened also near the pasha's residence and specialized in teaching geometry and mathematics. Pupils at these

first schools were given free clothing and food and monthly allowances. Teachers of technical subjects were mostly Italians, some of
whom were in the service of the pasha in other capacities, notably
translators and land-surveyors. Thus the first schools were virtually
staffed by European Christians, Italians and Frenchmen.

There is no evidence that the pasha sought the approval of the
ulema for his action. Indeed, there is evidence that he acted contrary
to their interests when, on various pretexts, he confiscated considerable property belonging to religious foundations. Then by a
ruthless system of monopolies he made himself the chief farmer and
merchant in the land, Egypt's wealth became virtually his personal
wealth, and he employed much of it to build a modern military
machine.

His first fully-fledged military school was established under a
French army officer assisted by other French instructors. An arsenal
and a medical unit also started under French direction. The medical
unit was established in 1827 as a medical school. Other similar
establishments followed in quick succession. To serve their needs a
printing press was established near Cairo in 1820. Most of the books
it printed in Arabic and Turkish were translated texts on military and
allied subjects, with some books on medicine and a few on literary
and religious subjects. At first Syrian Christians but later Azhar
shaikhs were employed together with specialists in the translated
matter. As finally established the system was as follows: Once an
Arabic version was produced by a specialist it had to pass two checks
by shaikhs, the first to correct its grammar and the second to polish
its style.

The success of the new institutions in producing the officers who
trained an efficient army was proved in Arabia and Greece, where at
the command of the sultan it was sent to quell revolts. So successful
was his army that Muhammad Ali decided to introduce further im-
provements in the institutions. Thus returning students from Europe
were absorbed in the system and Italian instructors were gradually
reinforced or replaced by French instructors, with the result that
French replaced Italian as the European language taught as such
and used as a medium of instruction. Arabic, Turkish and Persian
continued to be taught together with such subjects as arithmetic,
geometry, trigonometry, geodesy, physics, gunnery, military tactics,
fortifications and reconnaissance.

The teaching of such highly technical subjects by foreign instructors presented great difficulties. Let us take the methods adopted at
the medical school as an example. Its students were drawn from

native Egyptian elements, and hence those coming from al-Azhar and similar institutions predominated. Such students were by their former training ill-prepared for learning medicine, specially through a foreign language. To overcome the language difficulty translators, mostly Egyptian and Syrian Christians were employed, so that a lecturer faced his students with a translator by his side. But it was soon discovered that no matter how patient a lecturer was, and no matter how often he repeated his lecture and checked the accuracy of its translation before and during the lecture, there were limits to the comprehension of ill-prepared students. Hence the establishment of a preparatory department which gave instruction in such subjects as mathematics and French. Hence also the importance of a special bureau for translation which later served the pasha's wider purposes as the school of languages.

Except for the medical school none of the new institutions had a preparatory department. Nor did the pasha care before the middle thirties to establish elementary schools as recruiting ground for his new system. The Turkish element of the population was a very small minority, and the pasha had to depend on the traditional schools for more recruits. He used both material inducements and compulsion in recruiting students. The inducements included free clothing, food and monetary allowances, but when these failed the pasha recruited by force. The reluctance of parents and students was due largely to fear of conscription, for it was obvious that all the new schools, whether purely military, ancillary or even civil, were geared to serve a military machine. None of them was for the purely intellectual or professional training of young Egyptians.

At least one of the by-products, however, had a profound intellectual influence. The large educational mission sent to France in 1826 had Rifa'a Tahtawi as its imam. He had passed from the *Kuttab* to al-Azhar where he became a junior teacher. He was twenty-four when he went to Paris. During his stay of five years he learned enough French to read Voltaire, Rousseau, Montesquieu and Racine. He was encouraged to train as a translator, and on his return he was employed in that capacity. Eventually he became head of the school of languages. He, his assistants and pupils produced a great many of the translated texts for the schools and other purposes.

[3]

From the beginning the administration of the new schools was a department of the war office. Its first head was a French army officer who established himself permanently in the service of the pasha by embracing Islam. In 1837 the department of education was re-organized and re-established as an independent office, but its military character remained.

Indeed, urgent military necessity seems to have dictated the insti-tution of new primary and preparatory schools within the new system and as far as possible independent of the traditional system. As a result of his rebellion against his suzerain the sultan, Muham-mad Ali found himself in occupation of the whole of Syria. Both for garrisoning that country and for another expected encounter with the sultan's forces a large standing army was necessary. Apart from money an expanded army was in great need of *literate* officers. A crash programme to produce them was adopted by the re-organized department of education.

Fifty elementary schools, each still called *Maktab*, with an Azhar shaikh for headmaster were established. The total number of pupils in these schools was 5,500. The curriculum was similar to that of the traditional type consisting of the Koran, reading, writing and arithmetic. The course was fixed for three or four years, beginning from the age of seven. All pupils received free clothing, food and were lodged in the school under semi-military discipline.

The next stage consisted of two preparatory schools with a total number of 2,000 pupils selected from the fifty elementary schools. Here the curriculum, spread over four years, included the three languages (Arabic, Turkish and Persian), algebra, geometry, history, geography, calligraphy and drawing. Discipline was strictly military and pupils were treated as drafted soldiers. From among them some were selected for further training in the specialized schools which at this time included a polytechnic, a school for infantry, another for cavalry, a third for artillery, in addition to the schools of medicine, veterinary and languages and one or two others.

It is noteworthy that the teaching of French (or any other European language) had disappeared from the curriculum. The necessity for its use during the early years of improvization was no longer opera-tive. We are told that students returning from Europe were each given a book on the subject of his speciality and all were kept con-fined to quarters in the citadel for three months until translations into Arabic or Turkish of the assigned books were produced. Further-more, the staff of the school of languages did, in addition to teach-ing, a great deal of translation. Students trained in Europe and employed as teachers had thus no need to teach through the medium of a foreign language.

The shortcomings of this system are very serious. It neglected female education and omitted to make provision for training teachers at least for the elementary and preparatory schools. It was not co-ordinated with the traditional system and appeared to operate as a rival or even substitute. Its administrative and executive élite consisted of non-Egyptians elements of which the Muslims were principally Turks and the Christians were Armenians. The native Muslim majority provided cannon fodder and the native Copt minority small clerks and accountants.

Above all the system had little or no direct intellectual purpose. At any rate its general cultural value remained restricted by its limited aim of educating army officers. There was no attempt at establishing even a nucleus of a *public* system. The use of foreign Christian instructors and technicians was a purely utilitarian measure conceived on a "business" basis: To increase Egypt's productivity and the pasha's income and thereby his military and political strength. Foreign instructors and teachers were in fact employed in capacities well expressed by the Arabic-Turkish term applied to them "those who receive orders". The orders came from one man, Muhammad Ali, who was just as eager to take advice as ready to dispense with it, and had no hesitation to change or even scrap any scheme at any time if its utility was not according to his expectations or its cost too high according to his own estimate.

Both utility and cost were the tests which some four years after re-organization dictated the virtual dismantlement of the system. Following another Egyptian victory over the sultan's armies, the five major European powers jointly intervened to curb Muhammad Ali's power. The settlement they imposed gave him the hereditary rule of Egypt but deprived him of Syria and forced him to reduce his armies from about a quarter of a million to some twenty-thousand.

Suddenly the schools lost their *raison d'être*. Disillusioned with Europe, and his finances greatly strained, the pasha began to scrap the new schools. Before his death in 1849 little was left of the system more than a bare skeleton: three elementary schools and nine specialized schools. According to their whims his two successors did not always spare even this skeleton. The system was thus virtually liquidated within a decade after the death of its founder. The sending of students for training in Europe was, however, continued, although now they went not exclusively to France, but also to England, Italy, Austria and Bavaria. Students returning from training in Europe served in the surviving schools and government departments. They and their predecessors represented the real net gain of the system initiated by Muhammad Ali.

Meanwhile the traditional system, neglected, undermined or exploited by Muhammad Ali, began to recover. Its role as the only public system, in the true meaning of the term, had never changed. But weakened throughout the first half of the nineteenth century as indicated above it faced a new challenge, more direct and immediate, in the second half. It was a double challenge presented on the one hand by its old products who had been exposed to European influences, and on the other by the growth of European interests in Egypt. By the beginning of the second half of the nineteenth century there were large French, Italian and Greek colonies in Alexandria, Cairo and elsewhere. The foreigners enjoyed extra-territorial rights in the Ottoman Empire of which Egypt was a part, and exploited these rights in commerce, industry and education. It is true that such schools as were established by foreign agencies attracted mainly Christian minorities dissatisfied with their native parish schools, but the number of Muslims who for various reasons patronized foreign schools was increasing.

Furtive Catholic missionary activity among native Christians in Egypt began as early as the seventeenth century, through the efforts of the Franciscans. But it never struck the deep roots it did in Syria where there were indigenous communities that accepted the supremacy of the Pope and formed a point of anchor for all Catholic religious and cultural activity. In the nineteenth century, with the growth of European political influence, missionary activity, Catholic and Protestant, became more widespread in the Near East. Muhammad Ali, tolerated this activity both in Egypt and in Syria so long as it remained confined to non-Muslims, but as regards Christians he appears to have disapproved of its proselytizing side.

[4]

The decade or so that preceded the introduction in Egypt of new legal and administrative measures with a view to creating a nucleus of a public school system on new lines witnessed the depression of the system initiated by Muhammad Ali, the revival of the traditional system and the flourishing of foreign schools. The Egyptian measures coincided with similar ones taken by the imperial government in Istanbul. Both left the foreign schools virtually untouched. But while the Egyptian practice of sending students for training in Europe was maintained, the authorities conceived a new scheme whereby some relationship between their new schools and the traditional system was established.

The credit for the move goes to Ali Mubarak Pasha, himself a product of both the old and the new systems. After the usual *Kuttab* education he enrolled in one of Muhammad Ali's new schools, and in 1844 was selected for training as artillery officer in France. He was thus more prepared for the experience than Tahtawi was. Both had profound influence on modern Egyptian thought and educational practice. But Mubarak was better placed to use the machinery of government. He was in charge of education, religious foundations and public works when he used the opportunity to apply the first education decree issued late in 1867.

There was a simultaneous attempt at reforming the curriculum of al-Azhar. In 1865 a new rector submitted detailed proposals for this purpose. He deplored both the narrowness and low standards of the studies then pursued. Few graduates, he said, were masters of grammar and able to write tolerable Arabic composition. Fewer still were those who were steeped in linguistic, literary, historical, physical and astronomical studies. It was indispensible "to renew the pursuit of these esteemed studies."

But the attempt proved abortive and the rector was dismissed. Mubarak's scheme, however, had a better reception. Its application resulted in the constitution in a few centres of two grades of "civil" schools, elementary and central. The former category included official schools and some *Kuttabs* taken over, with their endowment if any, and placed under official control. This first attempt to integrate part of the traditional schools with the new was necessarily on a very small scale and encountered immense difficulties, chief among which was the inevitable conservatism of old institutions and their refusal to change their character by the simple magic of an official decree. The majority of the *Kuttabs* remained, however, outside the new measure and entirely unaffected by it.

Only in the official elementary schools in a few towns, and more particularly in the central schools in a few cities, was it possible to introduce more than the traditional curriculum. For one thing they had more qualified teachers; for another they were under direct government control and inspection. Their curriculum included, in addition to religious instruction and Arabic, arithmetic, the elements of history, geography and science, penmanship and Turkish (or another foreign language).

Admission to the central schools was by selection from the two types of primary schools. Unless their homes were within easy reach of the school, pupils were lodged and boarded in the premises, and all had to wear uniform. The theoretical age of admission was ten, and of completion of the course was fifteen. A significant move towards a "national" system was the provision in these schools for the admission of Copt pupils and the teaching of Christian religious instruction for their benefit.

The new "civil" schools were about thirty with one or two schools for girls in a special category. There is no exact estimate of the number of pupils. The teachers were a mixed lot: they included those who had been educated entirely under the traditional system, those who had been educated under both the traditional and the new systems, and a good proportion of Europeans mainly for teaching languages.

Foreign teachers were employed on a large scale in the specialized schools, remnants of Muhammad Ali's system. These schools were now very few in number and included the military school, the naval school, the school of medicine and other schools for administration, accountancy and surveying. The majority of their staff were men who had completed their education in Europe or in the schools themselves. Most, if not all of them lacked professional training. This great handicap was even more serious in the new primary and central schools. It was, however, remedied after a period of experimentation, by the opening of Dar al-Ulum in 1872.

Although the recruits to this first training college came mainly from al-Azhar, they were intended as teachers not in the old, but in the new schools. They were admitted by selection, and like students at similar institutions, they were given free board and tuition in addition to small allowances. Members of the staff of the new institution were partly Azhar shaikhs and partly "modern" teachers educated in the new schools or in Europe. The former taught religious and Arabic subjects and the latter taught mathematics, physics, chemistry, history and geography. There was no provision, and indeed there was no staff, for the teaching of the theory and practice of pedagogy.

Despite its imperfection the scheme represents another effort to transform the old system, by the 'indoctrination" of its own products. Like the symbolic effort to integrate the old system with the new at the elementary school level the teacher training scheme was on a small scale—the number of students being fixed at fifty. But small or symbolic both moves sowed the seeds of tension between the old and the new systems at close quarters. They were to produce mixed fruit in the next generation or two under the British occupation.

Of Muhammad Ali's successors Ismail was perhaps the most enlightened and progressive, though he was ostentatious and a spend-thrift. During his reign the opening of the Suez Canal was inaugurated amidst greater growth of European penetration of the country. His personal extravagance and ambitious schemes of public works led him to raise huge loans in Europe at ruinous rates of inter-est. European business and banking houses exploited the situation under capitulatory rights and European nationals became, after the formation of the mixed courts, virtually beyond Egyptian law. When the public debt exceeded ninety million pounds sterling Disraeli bought Ismail's shares in the Suez Canal Company for the British Government. Soon afterwards Egypt was declared bankrupt and Britain and France forced the acceptance of their dual control of the public services through the *Caisse de la Dette Publique,* ostensibly to safeguard repayment to the creditors, mostly of French and British business interests.

The institution of dual foreign control was the signal for the beginning of widespread resistance to foreign influence. It was a complex movement, religious, political and cultural. The agitation in religious circles was initiated by the fulmination of Jamalud-Din al-Afghani and gained adherents among Azhar shaikhs, notably Muhammad Abduh of whom more will be said later. More serious was the discontent in the army and among the intelligentsia, products of the new schools. Ismail was suspected of having encouraged the agitation, and under Anglo-French pressure the sultan agreed to depose him and appoint his son in his place.

But a drift towards violent eruptions was only temporarily arrested. First the chamber of notables ignored the dual control and prepared the budget without reference to the foreign body. Serious and bloody riots took place in Alexandria against foreigners. A national government with 'Arabi Pasha, a native Egyptian, as minister of war proved even more of a challenge to the Anglo-French control. It is an irony of fate that it was the Liberal Government of Gladstone that, after the defection of France, went to war with Egypt. By the middle of September 1882 the country was in British occupation.

This is a turning point not only in Egypt's political history but also in the history of education in that country. Under the circumstances of severe financial stringency, political upheavals and foreign control and ultimately foreign occupation, the new schools suffered severe cuts in budget with their inevitable consequences. Under British control education had a different history which will be taken up in due course.

[5]

The discussion of the course and effects of modernization in state education in Egypt had been intended as an illustration of the earliest and greatest impact of European ideas and techniques. There is therefore no need to treat in detail smaller educational developments on similar lines elsewhere in Arab lands. It is, however, essential for an understanding of the new currents of thought and experience to allude to some contrasting historical situations in other parts of the Arab world.

It has already been pointed out that successive waves of foreign invasions, among other factors, created in the long run an attitude of rejection, or at least suspicion, of external cultural influence. We may add that it also contributed to the development, among leaders of religious thought, of a reaction against internal innovations. We have suggested that this hardening attitude to both external and internal stimuli was a sign of weakness that stands in sharp contrast to the earlier attitude when Muslim political power was supreme.

One of the earliest and strongest notes of protest against innovation was struck by a Syrian theologian in the fourteenth century. His battle cry was "Back to the Koran and Tradition!" He waged a relentless war against the speculative individualism of philosophers and mystics as well as against the compromises of the theologians in a supreme effort to re-establish formalism. His cause was ultimately taken up in the eighteenth century by the preacher Muhammad Ibn Abdil Wahhab who hailed from Najd. He was afforded protection and support by the Saud princes, and from this alliance the Wahhabi movement was born with a distinct militant character.

The Wahhabi political power was crushed by Muhammad Ali's modernized army, but the religious movement lived on and was destined in the fullness of time to rally under Saudi leadership and to become the dominant power in the Arabian Peninsula. In the Saudi dominions education was throughout the nineteenth century and down to the Second World War distinctly and exclusively religious in character. Such changes as were introduced in it are of very recent date and their treatment will therefore be reserved for the right place later in this study.

Iraq likewise remained for a long time unaffected by any modernization in education, not only because it was relatively inaccessible to European enterprise, but also because official Ottoman modernization was applied in it rather late. Iraq had, however, preserved some of the cultural heritage of the classical age in a few institutions. An important survival was a famous *Madrasah* in Baghdad bearing the name of the distinguished Sunni jurist Abu Hanifah. Then the powerful shi'i section of the population had also maintained some continuity in the pursuit of traditional learning in its institutions at Karbala and Najaf. But on the whole it is correct to say that up to the closing decades of the nineteenth century there was little substantial change.

In the meantime far in the western end of the Arab world momentous developments had been taking place. Algeria which had acknowledged the suzerainty of the Ottoman sultan was the first object of European territorial expansion. In 1830 France pounced on Algiers the capital and began a protracted and savage war of conquest. Almost immediately French settlers began to arrive and take possession of tribal land or establish privileged commercial enterprise. Various methods were attempted in order to impose what France conceived to be her *mission civilisatrice* and what the Arab Muslims regarded as a deliberate plan to change their national and cultural character. Nowhere were the French measures more pernicious and in the end self-defeating than in the field of education. Even according to French official reports Algeria was at the time of the conquest thickly covered with the traditional Muslim schools at the primary and higher level, and Arabic and Islamic studies were flourishing.

What was the fate of this legacy under French control? After placing the religious foundations and the schools that benefited from them under strict control, the French began systematically to introduce the French language and promote its teaching, almost always at the expense of Arabic. The curriculum may otherwise be regarded as "modernized", but the purpose of the operation was not the protection or development of native culture. The object was rather to force French civilization upon the rising Algerian generations, both its welcome and unwelcome elements.

France had been in Algeria for half a century when in 1881 she forced a protectorate on the neighbouring Arab state of Tunisia which like Algeria had acknowledged the suzerainty of the Ottoman sultan. As in Egypt financial difficulties coupled with the growth of foreign interests in the country led to the institution of an international commission to administer the revenue. The climax of competition among foreign powers for a dominant position was reached in the French intervention.

The educational set-up was then not much different from that

obtaining in Algeria when it fell under French control. The traditional educational system had at its apex the Zaitunah mosque school
which occupied in the city of Tunis a position analogous to that of
al-Azhar in Cairo. But following precedents set by the Ottoman
sultan in Istanbul and by Muhammad Ali in Cairo, the Tunisian
rulers established at least two schools on modern lines independent
of this traditional system. One was military and the other civil. In
both institutions a new curriculum was introduced and foreign
instructors employed for teaching technical subjects and French,
Italian and Turkish. In the "civil" school the new subjects and foreign
languages were taught together with Arabic and Islamic subjects.

A milder version of their educational policy in Algeria was
followed by the French in Tunisia, if only because here they preserved the façade of native sovereignty, whereas in the Algerian
territory they recognized no sovereignty other than the one they
acquired by conquest. There was, however, little difference in the
practical application of the educational policy between the one
territory and the other. The subject will be taken up in due course
when we discuss developments after the 1880's. It now remains to
tackle, with a little more detail, peculiar educational developments
in Syria up to this date.

[6]

Syria's cultural contact with Europe may be regarded to have
begun during the Crusades, but as is well known Europe had then
very little to teach and much to learn from Arab civilization. However, during the Crusades the seeds of future cultural connections
were sown when the Maronites on Mount Lebanon allied themselves
with the Franks. The alliance ceased to have any practical value
after the failure of the Crusades, but the connection was re-
established from the seventeenth century. Early in the eighteenth the
Pope concluded a concordat with the Maronites by which they
accepted his supremacy and set a precedent for certain other
Christian minorities to do likewise.

The way was thus opened for Catholic missionary activity in
Syria, both in the purely religious field directed from the *Propaganda
Fide* in Rome, and in the religio-educational field sponsored increasingly by French religious orders and other organizations. The
activity which began in the seventeenth century assumed special
significance only in the nineteenth when Syria became the object of
rivalry between European and American missions, Catholic and

Protestant. From the beginning all foreign missions had to build with native material or on native foundations.

Every church in the land had already its own educational facilities in community schools. The legal basis of these schools was the *millet* system in the Ottoman Empire, a confirmation of earlier Muslim practice. According to this system every community enjoyed internal autonomy under its spiritual head and managed communal affairs including education with little or no interference by the state. This was substantially the system obtaining in Syria when foreign missionary competition began in the early decades of the nineteenth century.

To conduct their educational work was relatively an easy matter for Catholic missions, since they had a point of anchor in native communities. It was a very hard struggle for Protestant missions, since they had first to create native Protestant communities from members of existing churches. The largest Christian community was the Greek Orthodox, and Protestant converts were made in greater numbers from its members.

Catholic missions enjoyed more or less official French protection; Protestant missions, British "countenance" which in the days of empire amounted to the same thing. While engaged in fierce competition, Catholic and Protestant missions had a free run during the first half of the nineteenth century. The second half witnessed the active intervention of Russian Orthodox missions. They were intended positively to further the education of the Orthodox community and negatively to protect it against Protestant and other encroachment.

Ultimately the Catholic schools had their apex in the Jesuit College in Beirut (now the Université St. Joseph), and the Anglo-American schools in the Syrian Protestant College (now the American University of Beirut). The Russians schools, a late development, did not go beyond teacher training, but promising students were sent for further study in Russia. It must not be supposed that the educational scene was monopolized by American, British, French and Russian agencies. There were indeed others, notably German, not so conspicuous but nonetheless significant among the Protestant agencies.

It is important to bear in mind that the educational work of all foreign agencies among Christians in Syria was privileged. If the activity was welcome to the community concerned it was a mere extension of its right to provide for its children the kind of education it chose. But even when disapproved by the community, foreign religious and educational work was in a sense covered by the extra-territorial rights of foreign powers under the capitulation, unless it was contrary to public morality and likely to lead to a disturbance of the peace.

Christian missions of all affiliations were, however, restricted by law and practice to the Christian Arab minorities. The Muslim Arab majority remained unaffected. But its traditional school system described above began in the second half of the nineteenth century to be transformed, partly by the modernizing measures introduced by the Ottoman government and partly by local initiative: a new national system on European lines by the government, and private schools on the same lines by individuals and voluntary societies.

Syria's first experience of a modern state school system was during the Egyptian occupation when a few quasi-military schools were opened in the 1830's, but disappeared at the end of the occupation. Not before 1869 was there another determined effort in this direction. The Ottoman education law promulgated in that year instituted a new school system modelled on the French. Although it took some time before the law was applied in Syria, its application involved not only the establishment of new elementary and secondary schools with new curricula, but also the placing of the traditional schools under some official supervision through local committees, and the extension of some control over foreign missionary schools.

The new state schools were legally open to all children of all communities irrespective of religion. In practice, however, the majority of Christian children either continued to attend the various mission schools or preferred their own church schools. The attempt to create a national system was thus defeated. The law did not make attendance compulsory. But it would be sheer simplification to say that the national system was frustrated only by the presence of foreign schools. It would nevertheless be correct to say that these schools, despite the benefits they conferred, played havoc with the religious, linguistic and national orientation of their products, and created conflict of loyalties and a cultural chaos.

By their very nature foreign schools were sectarian. The Protestant schools in particular contributed to the creation of new sects in an already sectarian environment. The French schools were most assiduous in cultivating the French language and culture often at the expense of Arabic and native culture. Their products tended to be more French Catholic than anything Syrian or Arab, still less Muslim. By contrast the Americans encouraged the teaching of

Arabic and through it; so did the Russians. In this matter British practice was more according to American and Russian than French practice.

[7]

Of all the Arab countries only Syria and Iraq were around 1880 under the most direct Ottoman control. Tenuous control was exercised over Hijaz in the Arabian Peninsula largely because of the holy cities, over Yemen and over the vast desert land of Libya. Egypt, Tunis and Algeria were in foreign occupation. The Kingdom of Morocco in the far west was then struggling to maintain its existence as an independent state in the face of competition among the European powers for influence or control.

The Moroccan educational system was still the traditional, with the Qarawiyyin mosque school at its apex. This famous school was established at Fez, like Zaitunah at Tunis, long before al-Azhar was founded in Cairo. But neither of them was equal to it in wealth or scholarship or reputation in the Arab and Muslim worlds. In the last quarter of the nineteenth century Sultan Hasan tried to modernize the Moroccan educational system by sending a few students for training in Europe, but his efforts proved fruitless.

The Ottoman sultans were more successful. The modern system they introduced in the Empire was both on a larger scale and more directly educational in its intention than the earlier and utilitarian system inaugurated in Egypt by Muhammad Ali. The operation of this new Ottoman system in Syria and Iraq deserves more than a passing notice.

Its basis was, of course, the law of 1869 and the regulations made under it. This law provided for a minimum compulsory schooling of four years from the age of seven. But under the social, economic and educational conditions then prevailing, the provision was not more than a pious hope. So was another provision of the law seeking to extend state control to private schools, native and foreign. While it was easy enough to place the traditional Muslim schools under the supervision of local education committees on which officials and local notables served, it was not easy to do so with private Christian schools of the different denominations, still less with foreign mission schools.

Regarding mission schools, special mention is necessary of a clause in the education law, no doubt specially designed for these schools without specifically saying so. According to this clause all schools were prohibited from any teaching which was calculated to assail the religious beliefs of any recognized community. For this purpose all foreign schools were required to register their teachers with the local education authority and to submit to it copies of its curricula and textbooks. This clause was not applied rigorously, but occasional recourse to it was made.

Nor was it easy to implement the law regarding the establishment of a modern school system independent of and parallel to the traditional system. It was first applied in Istanbul and its vicinity, but later on was extended to the provinces until it embraced those in Syria and Iraq. Different levels of social development were reflected in the actual application of the law. Thus Syria's share was at first relatively greater than that of Iraq, and in general urban areas benefited more than rural districts. The opening of schools for girls presented special difficulties, and indirect pressure had to be applied to secure enough pupils for the new schools. Improvization was perhaps inevitable. Hired buildings and makeshift equipment were not great handicaps. But shortage of teachers was a serious problem especially for girls' schools where teachers had to be often the wives or daughters of Turkish officials stationed in the district.

The new schools were basically elementary and secondary, each stage divided into two cycles. The very first cycle was the four-year "compulsory" school, the lower elementary, followed by the school for the adolescent (*Rushdiyya*). Thereafter a preparatory school led to the higher secondary (*Sultaniyya*), and this in turn led to higher schools, technical and teacher training. The system had a military element, but was on the whole a public and "academic" one, the military element consisting of a parallel section at the secondary level which led ultimately to the military academy in Istanbul.

From the upper secondary classes students were selected for higher education in the capital where, apart from the military academy, there were schools of medicine, civil administration, law and letters. These schools formed later on *Dar al-Funum*, the University of Istanbul. Most of the future Arab leaders were educated in this way and only a few of them in foreign institutions in Beirut or in Europe. The graduates of the traditional schools were not superseded; they had to share the responsibility of leadership with the product of the modern schools.

But even when finally established the modern state schools fell far below the level of a compulsory or universal system. Lower elementary schools were established in cities and large towns, but villages had still to depend upon the *Kuttab*. Higher elementary and secondary schools were restricted to the capitals of districts or provinces. So were the few technical and preparatory military schools as well as the training colleges.

The importance of the new schools was, however, in their curricula more than in their numerical strength. The four-year cycle was theoretically an improvement on the *Kuttab*. It taught in addition to the traditional Arabic subjects some arithmetic, history, geography and hygiene. From the lower elementary cycle upwards additional subjects were attempted including mathematics, physics, chemistry, biology, civics, Turkish, French and Persian. The programme of girls schools was less loaded and stressed such subjects as domestic science, sewing and embroidery.

At all levels and in all schools the teaching of any subject naturally depended on the availability of qualified teachers. As already stated these were from the beginning in very short supply. A greater obstacle for Arab pupils was the use of Turkish as the medium of instruction from the *Rushdiyya* upwards. It seems that the measure was at first due to the fact that there were more Turks than Arabs trained as teachers. But this expediency was soon converted into a state policy that placed Arab education under complete Turkish control. This policy caused a great resentment, particularly when Turkish officials were not men of high education, as seen in these lines by the poet Rusafi:

> A director for education came to Baghdad,
> Long pastured in the meadows of levity.
> An ass, yet he speaks!
> A child, yet with a beard!
> O Learning—depart from the city!
> O Ignorance—roam free!

5

PHILOSOPHY OF MODERNIZATION

[1]

It has been demonstrated in the preceding pages that about the time of the British occupation of Egypt the greater part of the Arab world had been exposed for longer or shorter periods to various forms of European influence, whether introduced deliberately by the Egyptian and Ottoman governments, or imposed by European powers following military occupation, or insinuated gradually through educational missionary work.

Each of the three forms of exposure presented a challenge to the established order, more immediate and serious than that seen clearly or dimly by the first students sent to Europe. It was one of these students, the Egyptian Tahtawi, whose reflections set the pace for rationalizing modernism. For he was the first to put forward the comforting notion that what was good in the European system was already enshrined in the Islamic tradition. Those who followed him went one step further when they declared that what was good in the European civilization had, to a great extent, been borrowed from the classical Arab civilization. Hence it was not beneath the dignity of the modern Arabs to resume part of what was their heritage.

Educationalists and men of letters even more eagerly than rulers and administrators readily adopted this rationalization of modernism. The process itself had of course begun and continued for a long time without active rationalization. But henceforth the protagonists were at pains to represent the process as valid and legitimate, on the double plea that it agreed with the Islamic tradition and represented in fact a mere resumption of a heritage.

Beside the conservative majority there was a powerful minority which was for a measured, selective and controlled westernization, in education and science as well as in other aspects of life. But this modernist minority was baffled by details: what precisely was good and what was not; what was to be adopted and what was to be avoided? The choice was no longer entirely in Muslim hands in those territories occupied by France. Nor was it entirely in Arab hands in those lands still forming part of the Ottoman Empire.

The British occupation of Egypt in 1882 proved a beginning of a new era in the educational no less than in the political field, with far-reaching consequences that gradually touched other Arab countries to the east and west. The era that may conveniently be reckoned to have begun then had distinct characteristics, manifested in the cumulative effects of the Ottoman, Egyptian and other measures of modernization. The most significant of the educational effects was a duality in the school systems that created a cleavage in society by the institution of two types of education and two ways of thought. It was a perplexing dilemma. The most authoritative voice that provided intellectual guidance on facing it was raised in that citadel of conservatism al-Azhar in Cairo. But it was a voice for modernism, not conservatism. It was the voice of Shaikh Muhammad Abduh.

Abduh was educated in the traditional way, and was a student at al-Azhar when he fell under the influence of Afghani who was then preaching in Egypt and elsewhere the necessity for self-revival in Muslim education, unity of purpose among the Islamic peoples and the emancipation of those of them who were under foreign rule. We are concerned here only with the call for educational revival which captured the imagination of Abduh.

Underlying the call was a conviction that as a universal faith and a way of life, Islam was not only suitable for all peoples at all times, but also reconcilable with modern European science. The political and cultural conditions of the Islamic peoples at the time were not due to any deficiency in their faith but to the neglect of its adherents to live up to its ideals and apply them to changing conditions. In the words of the Koran "God changes not what is in a people, until they change what is in themselves".

Education was regarded as the most efficacious of the means of change. The first of Abduh's contributions on this subject were published in the form of articles while he was still a student. He called for the study of all branches of science, including those that had been taught in the traditional institutions such as mathematics and logic, and "the new sciences, useful for our life in the new age". The secret of European advance and wealth, of European excellence in the arts of peace and war, was education and science. These were precisely the means of attaining similar results in Egypt and other Muslim lands. Accordingly Abduh advocated more translations into Arabic of books on physics, chemistry, medicine and other sciences. He also advocated the translation of books on politics and history of civilization.

But neither Abduh nor his master Afghani was popular except among a minority of teachers and students at al-Azhar. Their modernism and radicalism were more popular among a minority of men who had been educated in the new schools or in Europe. So hostile was al-Azhar to the new approach that when Abduh's candidature for a licence or diploma was considered there was a critical moment when approval was in serious doubt. But once he passed that hurdle he was free to show his originality and to indulge his intellectual adventure.

He was a born teacher and had a commanding presence with a firm grasp of the Arabic and Islamic sciences. On that foundation he built, and used his imagination and intellectual power to enrich it with the fruits of modern knowledge. He learned French well enough to read books on history, philosophy and education. On the last subject he read and was influenced by the French translation of Herbert Spencer's *Education, Intellectual, Moral and Physical*. But how much Abduh was influenced is not easy to determine, because he was a highly intelligent assimilator who adapted foreign ideas to suit Islamic situations. Thus Spencer's main point that science not the humanities should be made the principal instrument of education was disregarded by Abduh who merely pointed out that science had had its place in early Muslim education and its restoration was an imperative necessity in modern times. (While in England in 1903 Abduh called upon Spencer, then very old and retired, at Brighton.)

Abduh taught simultaneously at three key institutions: at his *alma mater* he offered a course of lectures based upon a classical work by Ibn Miskawaih on character training, and used for another course of lectures on political science a recently translated work from French. At Dar al-Ulum he used Ibn Khaldun's *Prolegomena* as a basis for a course on Islamic history and civilization. At the School of Languages he taught the Arabic language and literature. In all his teachings he introduced an element of rationalism and encouraged personal judgement. He often appealed to common sense and reason as aids not rivals to authority. He demonstrated in practice how to write Arabic in a clear and simple style, yet conforming to classical standards.

His ideas and methods earned him the appellation of *failasuf* (philosopher), a mark of admiration by his followers and condemnation by opponents. The two different attitudes to his intellectual adventure and liberal interpretation of religious questions soon crystallized into two opposing schools of thought. His orthodoxy was called into question and he was even accused of infidelity. The tenor of the argument against him was on these lines: "What kind of a shaikh is this who speaks French, travels in European countries, reads European books and teaches the ideas of European philosophers?"

With Abduh's involvement in politics and its influence over his career we are not concerned here. Unlike his master Afghani he did not advocate revolutionary action, and remained convinced of the need for evolutionary change through education. But he was far from satisfied with the traditional system, and had important reservations concerning the modern systems in Egypt and the Ottoman Empire as a whole. He viewed even with less favour the schools under direct foreign control. He was indeed for the adoption of suitable foreign curricula and methods, but only as a free choice by the native population.

To reform the old system and to improve the modern system was Abduh's first concern, and he advanced toward this goal with caution and skill. It was paradoxically while acting as editor of the official gazette that he conducted a campaign for the reform of the education service. He used the strategy of representing himself as the mouthpiece of anonymous critics and was careful, while publishing the criticism, to defend or extol the education authorities. Thus he introduced one of their circulars in 1880, reminding teachers of their duty to pay special attention to religious instruction, with a contribution of his own, nearly double the length of the circular. In this introduction, reminiscent in tone and content of the Brethren of Purity, Abduh wrote that the real aim of education was the cultivation of the mind and the training of character through which man attains happiness.

The subject of foreign schools he treated with characteristic tact and tolerance. It was natural, Abduh wrote, that such schools should seek to propagate the religious faith and national culture of their founders. If a native Christian or Muslim child is enrolled in a foreign school at an early age it was likely to become acquainted with a faith other than that of its parents, and to become prepared to forsake their faith and become Catholic or Protestant. Should this happen the parents had only themselves to blame. Accordingly he cautioned parents in terms which forecast a remote possibility of complete secularism in education: "Let parents refrain from sending their children to foreign schools that tend to change their habits and religious faith, until God ordains that religious instruction be excluded from all schools throughout the world, that it be given in special institutions only, and that the schools be restricted to teaching subjects other than religion—an impossible development in our lands."

But Abduh's objection to the influence of foreign schools was not purely religious. For while he welcomed their teaching of languages, he deprecated in the products of such schools the use of foreign speech in conversation and the blind imitation of European manners. To him the primary function of all schools, native and foreign, was the cultivation of the mind and the uplifting of character. Such exhibitions, as foreign expression in conversation and foreign dress, were poor evidence of either.

Abduh's first campaign for the reform of all schools was not fruitless. It was in fact a contributory factor in the creation of a new advisory council on education with himself as one of the members. It was probably under his influence that one of the council's first proposals was to place foreign schools under official supervision through the issue of grants-in-aid. The proposal was overtaken by revolutionary events. The internal political upheaval and the British occupation resulted in Abduh's exile to Beirut where he began new efforts for the reform of education in Syria and in the rest of the Ottoman dominions.

[2]

Abduh was the true author of the "philosophy" of modernism in education as in theology and other fields. He, and after him his disciples, led the modernist movement in Egypt and Syria, and their influence reverberated throughout the Arab and Muslim worlds well into the twentieth century.

Immediately he settled in Beirut he formed a circle in the great mosque for Koranic exegesis on lines so appealing in their originality and liberalism that some non-Muslims were attracted to it. He also held a smaller circle in his house for reading and commenting on the biography of the Prophet. Then he was invited to teach at the Sultani School, the highest boarding establishment of the modern state system. Here he exercised a great influence on the curriculum by introducing and teaching theology, jurisprudence, Islamic history, logic, rhetoric and Arabic composition.

None of these subjects was taught in the school before. It was largely due to Abduh's personality and method of teaching that they became attractive to students. His teaching notes on theology, couched in modern rationalist terms, had since become a classic and run into several editions and been translated into foreign languages. In teaching the Arabic language he relied on the Koran and the standard classics. His greatest influence in this direction was the demonstration of the futility of imitating the rigid style of the age of decadence and the insistence on flexibility and clarity in diction. To aid his teaching he edited from manuscripts two famous classics with copious notes. "Although his methods were entirely novel" wrote one of his pupils, "they rendered learning difficult subjects comparatively easy".

Abduh's zeal for modernizing the curricula and teaching methods went beyond his own model teaching at different levels in Beirut. He wrote two memoranda on the subject, one concerned with schools in the Ottoman Empire as a whole and the other with those in Syria. The broad principles of the two documents are essentially the same, springing from a dissatisfaction with the conditions in the traditional as well as in the modern schools. The first memorandum was addressed to the highest religious authority in Istanbul and made recommendation in respect of three types of schools. First, that elementary state schools should teach, in addition to reading, writing and reckoning, Islamic history, and should give sound religious and moral education. Secondly, that the curriculum of the specialized state schools, for training the future officials and army officers, should also include thorough religious and moral instruction. Thirdly, that the curriculum of the other specialized schools for the education of the ulema should be widened to include, among other subjects, Islamic and general history.

In the curricula of two specialized categories of schools, there must be room, according to the needs of the future occupation, for foreign languages, mathematics and physical and natural science. Each of the three categories of schools should be geared to serve the different needs of society not to create exclusive social classes. Indeed, Abduh's egalitarian and liberal mind clearly stipulates for free movement from one class to another, solely on grounds of merit.

A special place is reserved in this memorandum for a strong complaint that religious education in the modern state schools at the lower and higher level was inadequate. Abduh regarded such instruction as had then been given as little more than memorizing formulae and mechanical performance of the ritual without in either case understanding the meaning or symbolism. He singled out for particular notice the product of the military schools, many of whom were in his judgement, devoid of religion and ignorant of the fundamentals of the faith.

The same spirit breathes through the second memorandum submitted to the local Ottoman governor, who under the education law of 1869 was the *ex officio* chairman of the provincial education board and had powers to implement reforms. The memorandum pointed out the sectarian composition of the Syrian people, whether Christian or Muslim, and how foreign schools had catered for some of the needs of the different sects with results inimical to the interests of the state and religion. Nothing could avert these dangers except state schools in sufficient numbers. Shortage of funds was no excuse for neglect, since the voluntary opening of new schools by the Muslim Benevolent Society had demonstrated that the people were willing to share the burden with the state.

Abduh's recommendation meant in effect the application of universal, though not compulsory, elementary education, with selective boarding secondary schools in large centres. No doubt this was the ultimate goal of the state system as provided for in the law, but Abduh's concern was more with quality than quantity, with the content of education more than with apparatus. In particular, he wanted to re-establish the moral basis of education for Muslim children and to restore loyalty to the Ottoman state, shaken by foreign influence, in non-Muslims.

He therefore assailed foreign schools as fostering other loyalties and using textbooks with offensive reference to the Ottoman government and the state religion. He pointed out that the French schools in particular tended to alienate pupils from their national culture and to instil in them love of France rather than of their native land. Pupils in Protestant schools, whether American or British, tended in a similar though less obvious way to look up to Britain. (The memorandum does not dwell on German or Russian schools whose influence was to become equally potent later on.) Even some of the private Christian schools followed foreign models, chiefly French, and did not shrink from using textbooks written by Europeans with hostile statements against the government and the religion of the majority of the people.

This second memorandum contained a recommendation of special significance. It was an echo of one of the grievances of the Syrian Arabs against the new Ottoman educational policy—the use of Turkish as a medium of instruction in the modern schools. This grievance was one of the causes of early national stirrings, with the limited aim of restoring Arabic to its rightful place in the schools. It is an historical fact that under the banner of language Christian Arab and Muslim Arab in Syria forged the beginning of a national unity that ultimately led to liberation from Turkish rule.

Abduh was a consummate master and teacher of the Arabic language. He was dedicated to its renewal and revival of its classics.

Like all highly educated Arabs he regarded it, next to the Koran, as the most precious national heritage. In this sentiment he was one with the Syrians. Accordingly he recommended, with complete disregard of the Ottoman practice, that Arabic should be the sole medium of instruction for Arab children. He conceded to Turkish only the place he conceded to a foreign language like French, which he thought must be taught, but only after Arabic had been mastered.

He continued the struggle for educational reform in Egypt after his return from exile. He was appointed judge but he preferred the classroom to the bench and succeeded in lecturing at al-Azhar part of the time while engaged in other tasks. By then Egypt was effectively under a British control exercised behind a façade of native government. To the subject of education during the British occupation we shall return, but first we must complete the account of Abduh's efforts for educational reform.

Once more he embodied reform proposals in a lengthy memorandum, in which he enunciated a few fundamental principles beginning with the need to base all education on morality and religion. He reiterated that neither the traditional system nor the modern system was satisfactory. It was wrong to gear the state system to the single aim of producing government servants. At the lower level, where the majority of pupils did not proceed to higher schools, the curriculum should be so designed as to prepare such pupils to act as useful members of society. Thus what was to be taught of arithmetic and Arabic was to be of practical use to the community in ordinary bookkeeping and correspondence. In addition to religious education and national history the curriculum should include an element of training in agriculture and crafts.

At the preparatory and higher school level Abduh was aware that the specialized schools served specific government needs. He refrained from criticizing their curricula in detail, but he insisted that there was little true learning and education in these schools since they all neglected "the cultivation of the mind and the refinement of character." To parents and pupils the aim was nothing more than securing government employment. Teachers did not venture beyond mechanical repetition of set textbooks to students who were expected to reproduce the material in order to pass examinations. The curricula of these schools required enrichment by intelligent teaching of the creed and training in free and correct expression. All students must be taught that government service was not the only purpose of education. Education and learning was by itself necessary for "good living".

Turning to the traditional school system Abduh recommended the reform of the *Kuttab* where the children of the majority received their primary education and from where state and other schools recruited students. He was aware that reform required time and money. He proposed to begin with the improvement of the educational standards of the teachers through the preparation for their use of simplified textbooks that they can understand and teach, under such supervision as the state can exercise. But that was no substitute for the professional training of teachers. On this subject Abduh made detailed suggestions, mainly concerned with the expression and improvement of Dar al-Ulum, the only institution for this purpose.

The greatest problem was, however, the reform of al-Azhar which Abduh knew so well as a student and lecturer. He regarded most of its teachers as too conservative and the range of studies pursued too narrow. He particularly deplored the absence of any academic or moral guidance to students. He realized that only gradual reform could succeed, but it must embrace, to begin with, the curriculum, institution of a system of supervision, introduction of examinations, and a change of emphasis in teaching from memorizing to comprehension. Then Abduh added a remark which concealed a revolutionary suggestion (and in fact took over seventy years to implement.) "It may be useful", he wrote, "to place al-Azhar under the control of the Ministry of Education or the Ministry of Religious Foundations, with a special statute."

It is clear from the preceding discussion that his educational thought embraced every aspect of public and private education of his time. He was consumed by a desire to reform the traditional system, but not at the expense of depriving it of its essential character. He never disguised his disappointment with the modern schools, principally because of the inadequacy of the ideal and moral content of its curricula. He assailed the different foreign school systems, largely because they created social and religious cleavage. For similar reasons he deplored the multi-sectarian character of private schools. Nowhere did he discern in this bewildering diversity any forces working for unity. Instead of welding society he saw education promoting its fragmentation.

There were ranged against his proposals for reform formidable, though not concerted, forces. In the traditional field he had to contend with the strong conservative elements in the government and in the educational system itself. His proposed reforms of the state schools were thwarted by unimaginative authorities pleading inadequacy of resources. His fight against the influence of foreign schools failed because of their privileged position under the capitulations. Even against native sectarian schools he could make no impression, for these were, especially in Syria, protected by their established right to autonomy.

Abduh's influence was to appear through his disciples and works. His educational thought, except on al-Azhar, had hitherto received little of the attention it deserves. His three papers discussed above constitute the first systematic approach to modern Arab and Muslim education; they sum up the vital problems for the half century after their date.

[3]

It comes as a surprise to the uninitiated that the educational reforms proposed by Abduh were rejected by Sir Evelyn Baring (better known as Lord Cromer), the British Agent and Consul-General and the real ruler of Egypt for some twenty-five years. Britain was professedly in Egypt temporarily for the purpose of restoring order and safeguarding an administrative and financial efficiency that would make the country solvent and regulate payment to foreign creditors.

Any detailed discussion of the political, strategic and other considerations which prolonged the British occupation are outside the scope of an educational study. But such a study would be incomplete without an understanding of British influence directly bearing on education. A report on Egypt completed by Lord Dufferin a few months after the occupation contains a section on education of which two matters deserve special notice here. The first is the number of schools in 1883. There were twenty-seven elementary state schools with 4,664 pupils, a preparatory school with 292 pupils, specialized schools with a total of 384 students, plus 60 at the training college of Dar al-Ulum and some 300 at the only girls' school. Outside the state system there were 5,370 Kuttabs with 137, 553 pupils. Al-Azhar had 8,000 students and 300 professors. The second important matter in the Dufferin report was the recommendation of the employment of colloquial not classical Arabic as the medium of instruction.

At the end of his long stewardship, Cromer published in 1908 two volumes running into some twelve hundred pages. Yet "consideration of space" made him allow less than twenty pages for a chapter on education, consisting mainly of an apology and a rebuttal of a charge of deliberate neglect of education.

Citing very few facts and figures, Cromer sets out to answer questions he himself formulated: "What has been done in the direction of moral and intellectual progress? Have the English made any endeavour to educate the Egyptians?... Have they discouraged the acquisition of knowledge, with a view to keeping the Egyptians in a position of servitude?... Have the English ... endeavoured to educate the Egyptians and to lead them ... [to] self-government?"

Cromer quotes with approval Lord Macaulay, who in 1833 replied in the negative to his own question in a speech in the House of Commons: "Are we to keep the people of India ignorant in order that we may keep them submissive?" Having stated that his policy was to educate, Cromer proceeded to answer his critics why he did so little. First, he pleaded that a quarter of a century was too short a time; secondly, "the unpromising nature of the [human] material on which the English had to work; thirdly, want of money; fourthly, "the undisciplined minds of pashas"; and lastly, British control was not direct or complete from the start.

Considered in the light of the educational thought and practice in the last half century these arguments recall to mind the second Caliph's rebuke to a provincial governor who was called upon to answer certain charges: "Your explanation betrays a man whose conscience is troubled by the justice of the accusation". Few educationists would accept the validity of the first and second of Cromer's explanations. The third is, of course, the standard excuse usually offered by deficient administrators, foreign and native alike, and is never convincing. The fourth is unjust at least to two men whose actions and ideas were discussed above, namely Ali Mubarak Pasha and Shaikh Muhammad Abduh. As to the last of Cromer's explanations, it is sufficient to state the fact that he had absolute control of finance, and hence education like other services was at his mercy.

There is no need to go into further discussion of Cromer's apology. For educationalists and historians will no doubt draw their own conclusions from specific aspects singled out for brief mention below. Most of them were directly or indirectly influenced by the British presence in Egypt. First, the medium of instruction in state schools. Dufferin's suggestion for the adoption of colloquial Arabic was too revolutionary for any British administration to sanction. But the place of classical Arabic in the curriculum was undermined by another not less radical measure. It was replaced as the medium of instruction by English or French, the former ultimately displacing the latter, not only in secondary schools but also from the third year in the elementary schools, and not only in teaching science but also such literary subjects as history. To execute this measure English teachers had to be employed, then inspectors and finally an English adviser to the ministry of education whose advice had to be accepted. Apart from any purely pedagogic and administrative objections to the measure the reduction of Arabic, the mother tongue of all pupils, to a mere school subject carried with it incalculable cultural dangers against which the nationalists voiced loud protests.

Secondly, the charging of fees at state schools. Before the British occupation the system was almost completely gratuitous, with stipulation for payment only under certain circumstances. After the occupation it became completely fee-paying, and this made it the preserve of the rich and put it beyond the reach of the poor. An annual fee of twelve to fifteen pounds was in a poverty-stricken society prohibitive indeed. Only a few months before his death Mohammad Abduh wrote of the rigid application of this system and the discontent of parents in towns and villages: "It is pitiful to see fathers and mothers bringing their little boys to the ministry of education, pleading poverty or some service rendered to the state by a member of the family, and requesting admission to school without payment, only to be disappointed."

Thirdly, the restrictive and selective character of state schools. Because they had only one aim, the production of a fixed annual number of junior government officials, it was necessary to restrict admission by the demand of payment of fees, and to select from among those admitted against payment by a rigorous examination system. As a result there were at the turn of the century only three state secondary schools in all Egypt, two in Cairo and one in Alexandria, with a total number of pupils of 515. The school curriculum had to be purely utilitarian, with little or no intellectual or moral content. Given their social background and the kind of education they received the product formed a class that tended to have little sympathy with the common people, thus widening the gap between the rich and the poor.

Fourthly, female education. The single school for girls inherited by the British administration and noted in the Dufferin report remained the only one till 1895 when another was opened. Parents' ignorance of the true religious injunction on the education of women, their partial dependence on the earnings of their children and general social prejudice, no doubt militated against more schools for girls. However, daughters of the rich were educated privately or even at foreign schools, and their parents were indifferent to promoting female education at state expense. For their part the British administration regarded the matter as a sleeping dog, and took no initiative at least in voting the necessary money. A year or two before the turn of the century a significant step was taken by the ministry of education, probably with British approval. In offering grants-in-aid to *Kuttabs* that submitted to official inspection they encouraged the admission of girls by assigning a *per capita* rate twice as much for the girl as for the boy.

Fifthly, the traditional system. According to Cromer, "the British reformer" left this system alone for some fifteen years. As we noted above Abduh's proposals for its reform and the reform of the state system were rejected. Tardily two small steps towards reform were taken: the issue of grants-in-aid to *Kuttabs* with a view to improving their standard through official supervision, and the appointment of a committee to supervise the introduction of reforms in al-Azhar. The first measure began to show results as more and more of the traditional schools were affiliated to the state system. The second, with Abduh's active participation, had some initial success, but the committee's work was thwarted by the Khedive Abbas Hilmi Pasha who became suspicious of the growing influence of Abduh, by now holding the highest religious office in the land, the Mufti of Egypt. In despair, the veteran reformer resigned his membership of the committee, and with his death a few months later reform of al-Azhar was indefinitely postponed.

Lastly, the specialized schools and higher education. The specialized schools and educational missions to Europe represented the only facilities for modern higher education down to the end of the First World War. Such military aspects of these schools that survived till the British occupation were changed or suppressed. But the introduction of civil courts of justice under Ismail, in consonance with their introduction in the rest of the Ottoman Empire, directly influenced the opening of a new school of law in 1868. Similar consideration led later on to the opening of an independent French school of law which attracted sons of wealthy families. However, all the specialized state schools, including a new one for agriculture and another for commerce and two new schools for the training of teachers, were intended to keep the state services supplied with teachers and other officials. None of them had the deliberate aim of promoting the intellectual education of the citizen.

Nor was an enlightened policy of sending students for training in Europe adopted. Cromer had genuine distrust of higher education for political reasons. He saw little in such education more than a machine "manufacturing demagogues". At any rate he was determined to divert Egyptian students from French to British institutions, and succeeded in doing so. The majority of students were sent to Britain and only a minority to France. But French educational influence had been so well-established among the educated and wealthy classes that they continued to send their sons to France at their own expense.

Cromer had no power to stop them, and remained long enough in Egypt to experience the outcome of such education. Although he subscribed to the principle enunciated by Macaulay he pointed to India as a warning against leaving the ignorant masses defenceless against the "half-educated charlatan". The logic of this argument might have led its author to recognize the need for a co-ordinated educational plan at lower and higher levels. He failed to do either, even according to his own statements.

In 1889 the state budget showed a surplus of over two hundred thousand pounds, but not a penny of it was invested in education. In that year only £69,479 was allowed, of which £12,745 was recovered in school fees. Cromer's policy was frequently criticized in the House of Commons, and had since been censured by several English writers. Even his aim of preventing political opposition was defeated. A nationalist party led, by a French educated "demagogue", Mustafa Kamil Pasha, and composed of men educated on modern lines, called for the end of the British occupation, and accused the British, *inter alia*, of a woeful neglect of education.

At the end of Cromer's term of office, a committee of Egyptian leaders opened with voluntary contributions a private institution under the ambitious name of "the Egyptian University." When it began to function in 1907–1908 the institution was in fact a school of arts, the nucleus of the university. Lectures were given in history and philosophical subjects by Egyptian scholars and by invited European savants. Several of the future educationalists and men of letters had their initiation in these lectures which moreover attracted a number of Azhar students. The intellectual stimulation and fermentation that this first modern Egyptian venture in liberal arts promoted was to prove a major factor in Egyptian education.

The idea of a university was a symptom of the dissatisfaction among the Egyptian intelligentsia with the educational service under Cromer. It was Sa'd Zaghlul Pasha, for sometime minister of education in the last days of Cromer, and later the foremost leader of the Egyptian national movement, who presided over the committee that sponsored the university. It was moreover he who began while minister of education to reverse British policy in one important matter. In the same year that the university was launched a new elementary school syllabus was adopted, and the occasion was taken to begin gradually the restoration of Arabic as the language of instruction and the reduction of English to the status of a foreign language only.

[4]

Education was equally if not more prominent in the programme of the Syrian nationalists. In Egypt educational grievances against the British were submerged in the political struggle against the occupation. In Syria there was, to start with, little or no political element in the reaction of the Arab leaders to the Ottoman educational policy. The new State schools were established and expanded without serious difficulties. The incorporation of the traditional schools, particularly those in villages and smaller towns, into the new state system was accomplished in Syria on a greater scale than in Egypt. Local education committees composed of officials and local dignitaries ensured a smooth transition. The protests of conservative elements were little more than murmurs. They were effectively silenced when it was proclaimed that the change was by the will of the sultan-caliph.

Indeed, so widely was educational modernization accepted that native private schools began to adopt curricula accommodating the traditional with the modern elements, religious and linguistic subjects with science and foreign languages. Because they enjoyed an autonomous status in education, or because their religious faith provided a bridge to Europe, the Christian Arabs were pioneers in this direction. The Muslim Arabs took a longer time, largely because of a built-in suspicion of foreign influence. However, by the turn of the century there were native schools in Syria, both Christian and Muslim, that compared not unfavourably with the longer established foreign schools. But there was no native institution to rival either the Jesuit College or the Syrian Protestant College.

The spread of modern schools, state and private, was bound to limit the attraction of foreign schools. Indeed, there is reliable evidence from American and British consular and missionary sources to show that at least Anglo-Saxon institutions began to feel the pinch. One illustration must suffice. In 1884 the agent of the Church Missionary Society in Nazareth wrote that "Orders have been issued forbidding Mohammedan children from attending [foreign] Christian schools, and what is more efforts have been made to establish schools for boys and girls, not in towns only, but also in villages."

One of the negative aims of the new state schools was to render foreign schools unnecessary for the children of the Muslim majority. There is little doubt that this expectation was fulfilled. At the turn of the century Syria was in fact served by a growing system of elementary and secondary schools. It was augmented at the elementary level by the absorption of numerous *Kuttabs*. At the secondary level it was sufficiently diversified to embrace literary, technical (including crafts for boys and domestic science for girls) and teacher training.

During the first decade of this century there was established in Damascus institutions for higher education in quick succession: a school of medicine, a military school, a school of law and finally a school for arts and sciences. For still higher training Syrian students went to the University of Istanbul. Many joined the military academy with a view to becoming officers, and the rest trained as doctors, lawyers, engineers and teachers.

It has been suggested above that educational modernization was protected by the prestige it derived from the sultan-caliph. But he scarcely realized that these modern schools were to be the hotbeds of sedition. Whether in Syria or in Istanbul they inevitably produced generations that looked through a widening window to nationalist, secularist Europe. Slowly but surely nationalist ideas began to develop in the minds of Turkish and Arab students, who later on assumed positions of responsibility in the army, government and professions. While hitherto Turks and Arabs were united in an Islamic state, now a nationalist *mystique* began to divide them on racial and national grounds, irrespective of their common religion.

In Syria the immediate cause of rupture was educational first and political or rather administrative next. The Arabs had two basic demands: that Arabic, not Turkish, should be the medium of instruction in state schools in the Arab provinces, and that the Arabs should have greater share in the administration of their homeland, if not also in the central government. The Young Turks who were then in power entertained certain Turkish and Ottoman nationalist notions which hindered an amicable settlement. The First World War broke out with the issues still unresolved. It proved a turning point in Turco-Arab relations. An Arab revolt, inspired in Syria and proclaimed in Hijaz, in alliance with Great Britain, had the declared aim of securing independence from the Turks.

6

Since this was the end of an era, a statistical picture of at least the state schools would be useful. There are, however, no reliable records, and in the heat of political antagonism Arab authors tended to minimize the Turkish contributions. The figures here given must therefore be viewed with caution. They represent a composite picture for the whole of Syria (which then included the present republics of Syria and Lebanon and Palestine east and west of the River Jordan.) In this whole area there were roughly 400 schools of all grades, with some 21,000 pupils in the elementary and some 900 in the secondary and higher schools.

The broad outlines of this educational set-up in Syria, and its problems, applied, *mutatis mutandis*, to Iraq, the other Arab country that was under direct Ottoman rule. But here the schools were comparatively fewer in number, and apart from three schools for teacher training there was a school of law in Baghdad. Iraq had fewer and less developed foreign schools. Even its native private schools were less advanced than their counterparts in Syria. Here again only of state schools can a statistical picture be drawn, but with the same reservations made concerning Syria. At the outbreak of the First World War there was a total of about 170 schools of all grades with some 7,400 elementary and 1,200 secondary and high school pupils.

In the Arabian Peninsula only Hijaz and Yemen were affected by this educational modernization as provinces of the Ottoman Empire. More radical changes were effected in two Arab countries in North Africa through violent European intervention. In 1911 Italy landed troops on the coast of what is now Libya, then part of the Ottoman Empire, and began a long war of conquest. In the following year France imposed a protectorate on the independent Kingdom of Morocco, in the face of an armed revolt. Spain took the opportunity to claim a portion of the Kingdom as a sphere of influence which France had to recognize.

On the eve of the First World War therefore the Arab countries in Africa were divided between France in Morocco, Algeria and Tunisia, Italy in Libya, and Britain in Egypt (and the Sudan). In Asia most of the Arab countries formed part of the Ottoman Empire which though Muslim was increasingly regarded by Arab nationalists as foreign. The principal cause of alienation was cultural deriving its force from love of the Arabic language and its literature. In a word it was resistance to a process of "turcification" and fear of loss of cultural identity through education as conducted under Turkish control.

More fearful was the educational prospect in North Africa where active "frenchification" had long been in progress, particularly in Algeria. Not only were young Algerians taught French and through its medium but those who successfully passed through French schools were also offered French citizenship, since Algeria was regarded by the French as part of metropolitan France. There is no doubt that French education was successful in so far as young Algerians found it profitable to learn the language of their rulers and to acquire French professional qualifications. But the process of "frenchification" failed where it touched Islam. That very few accepted the offer of French citizenship was a proof that even French education could not weaken its hold on its adherents. Algerian Muslims as a whole refused French citizenship because it involved surrender of personal status under Islamic law.

The educational policy of the British in Egypt had no "anglicizing" aims. It was, however, criticized on the lines discussed above, particularly because it advanced English at the expense of Arabic. No criticism could be levelled against the British administration on religious grounds. Not only did they not interfere directly in religious affairs, but refused to allow Christian missionaries a free hand to publicly assail Islam.

France's educational policy in Morocco followed on the whole Algerian and Tunisian precedents. Discussion of Italy's policy in Libya must be reserved for a later occasion, since the Italians had first to fight a prolonged war in order to establish an effective control. They met the most stubborn resistance from the Sanusi order, a religio-political fraternity, based on religious education, founded by Muhammad Ibn Ali in the first half of the nineteenth century. Unlike similar orders, the Sanusi was militant, and used the sword as effectively as the Koran.

Thus in 1914, Arab prospects on the national and cultural levels were very dark indeed. No Arab country had any effective control over shaping its future as a national or cultural entity. The modest attempt by the Syrian Arabs to redress a cultural grievance against the Muslim Turks ended in failure. If it was impossible to come to terms with brother Muslims it was harder still to do so with alien Christians.

While the Turks laid no claim to a superiority over the Arabs in civilization, the Europeans did so with undisguised arrogance. For in their different ways the British, the French and even the Italians and Spaniards took it for granted that they had special insight into what was in the best interests of their Arab subjects, and accordingly rejected or side-tracked Arab attempts at improving their political or at least educational lot. In these circumstances of frustration and unrelieved tension it was inevitable that alienation and rupture would be the outcome. Once more the Syrian Arabs made the first move. They conceived an Arab revolt against the Turks which was, for a variety of reasons launched from Hijaz. The revolt was a result of a secret agreement with Britain, and through this British connection the revolt served the cause of the allies in the war against Germany by weakening her ally Turkey.

It is impossible to deal here with the war-time tangle of agreements between the Arabs and Britain, between Britain and the Zionists, and between Britain, France and Russia, concerning the various Arab countries in Asia. Impartial historians have since found them contradictary, irreconcilable and inspired more by imperial ambitions than by promoting the well-being of the indigenous population. Small wonder that the Arabs found the peace settlement most disappointing. The pre-war position of Britain, France, Italy and Spain remained unchanged in North Africa. Syria and Iraq, now detached from Turkey, were divided into British and French spheres of influence, later legalized by the League of Nations as mandates.

Out of the Turkish provinces in Iraq an Arab monarchical state under British mandate was established. Out of those in Syria the two republics of Lebanon and Syria were carved as French mandated territories, and Palestine east and west of the River Jordan fell under British mandate. It cannot escape notice that in the semi-nomadic east an Arab state was recognized, but the more settled and civilized west was denied any form of national government. All the political divisions in Syria and Iraq were potentially independent states. To make an exception of Palestine west of the River Jordan was solely due to the British promise to facilitate the establishment of a Jewish national home which the overwhelming Arab majority refused to recognize.

From the end of the war an Arab national movement was conducted on a regional basis with the declared purpose of shaking off foreign domination. Since this domination was established by force, the resistance assumed diplomatic as well as armed resistance. Within seven years of the end of the war there was a revolt against British rule in Egypt and another in Iraq; a third was declared against the French in Syria, and the Palestine Arabs staged a series of revolts. In Libya the Italians had a continuous war for nearly two decades. In the far west a revolt against French and Spanish rule assumed the dimension of a full-scale war.

The whole Arab world was up in arms against its European masters. The greatest scores to be settled were with Britain and France. The first had after the war extended her sway from Egypt to Palestine, Trans-Jordan and Iraq, and the second extended it from North Africa to Lebanon and Syria. The Arab struggle against the two powers was in its manifest aspect political, seeking the achievement of self-government. In a deeper sense, however, it was cultural and educational: the Arabs were nowhere satisfied with the conduct of the education service by foreign masters. The reaction of their leaders, many of whom were educated in Europe or on European lines, was a mark of disillusionment with European liberalism and disappointment at the failure of two great powers to conduct their policy according to the best principles in their own tradition.

It took nearly half a century for the Arab lands to be freed from foreign rule, one after the other, with the sole exception of Palestine. But political liberation revealed colossal problems of cultural orientation and educational adjustment. To the study of these problems of modern Arab education in a national setting we now turn.

PART II

The Modern National Systems

After the First World War the Arab lands outside the Peninsula formed two large areas of British and French dependencies. Sandwiched between the two areas there was an Italian dependency in Libya, and in the extreme west, a Spanish one in Morocco. In the Peninsula there were the three independent states of Hijaz, Najd and Yemen as well as a string of British dependencies along the coast from Aden to Kuwait.

The following account of the educational systems in these countries, beginning with modernization down to roughly 1967, shows how a great tradition had been fragmented and transformed. The countries outside the Peninsula are taken first, generally in the order of their attainment of national independence.

IRAQ

A few days after Turkey's entry into the war, a British expeditionary force was despatched from India to Iraq. It captured Basra almost at once, but the occupation of the rest of the country had to be accomplished piecemeal over four years. The British army found in Basra a school for boys run by an American missionary of the Dutch Reformed Church, and they made use of the school and its headmaster to meet their immediate need for native interpreters and clerks. Every youth who had acquired a smattering of English at this school was immediately engaged, and the missionary was given money to open five other schools and to concentrate on producing the native personnel the army then needed.

There was as yet no plan to pay any attention to education as such, and no attempt was made even to re-open the Ottoman schools. After the capture of Baghdad, however, the military administration paid more attention to the civil services including, of course, education. The entire senior staff of the education department consisted of two British army officers and a civilian Arab, specially seconded from the Egyptian ministry of education. The three men began with re-opening some of the Ottoman elementary schools in the cities and large towns, adopting, on the whole, the system and methods of the Egyptian schools.

Even within these modest limits the authorities were, according to a British eye-witness, unable to satisfy the demand for elementary schools. None of the four or five secondary schools that functioned under the Turks was re-opened, and of the three schools for training teachers only the one in Baghdad was re-opened with the Egyptian expert as the principal teacher. A crash programme was adopted which within three months' time was supposed to produce teachers suitable to put in charge of classes.

Nor was the position much changed when after the armistice, another British army officer, educated at Eton and Oxford and with educational experience in Egypt, became director of education. He had three British assistants, each in charge of a province with an Arab assistant. The new team continued the process of re-opening elementary schools, but still no secondary schools were re-opened, nor was the training of teachers extended. Of the twelve girls' schools inherited from the Turks, only the one in Baghdad was re-opened, under an English, instead of a Turkish, headmistress.

92

Under these circumstances, it is inexplicable why only the re-opening of the school of law and the school for crafts, both in Baghdad, was given priority. In the school year 1919–1920, the total number of schools under the British director was only seventy-five, or roughly half the number in the last year of peace under the Turks. Again in the words of the same British eye-witness, educational reconstruction was "at a pace always disappointing". He gives the usual explanations that apologetic authorities everywhere give: insufficient funds, trained staff and apparatus.

There is no doubt that these inadequacies hindered advance, but their operation was itself the result of an uncertainty concerning British policy. For without clear guidance from London, the military authorities on the spot assumed that occupied Iraq formed a de-pendency of the Indian Empire or an extension of the British sphere of influence in the Persian Gulf. If so education was no urgent matter, and must not at any rate outpace whatever then existed in India or the Gulf.

This uncertainty was publicly removed by an Anglo-French declaration issued in November 1918, some five weeks after the armistice with Turkey. It proclaimed, *inter alia*, the determination of Britain and France to establish in the Turkish provinces of Iraq and Syria native governments deriving their initiative from the wishes of the native population. Unfortunately, Britain took too long to implement this promise in Iraq, and the long delay contributed to the national armed rising in the summer of 1920. One of its conse-quences was that "two years' educational work went by the board". The writer of these words, the director of education, had himself also to go.

That was the end of an interregnum, as much in education as in form of government. It is, therefore, important to note a few prece-dents set during this brief period of direct British control. First, the medium of instruction in the training school became Arabic instead of Turkish. The change was dictated more by practical considerations than by a desire to satisfy Arab aspirations, for the Turkish teachers had gone and the British officers had no teaching experience through the medium of Arabic or even English at training school level.

Secondly, the British officers found themselves powerless for lack of qualified teachers to secure for English in Iraqi schools a place similar to that it had gained in Egyptian schools. But they com-pensated for that by introducing the teaching of English wherever possible.

Thirdly, they made concessions to racial and linguistic minorities on the question of the language of instruction in state elementary schools. Arabic was of course the medium of instruction in most schools, but Kurdish and Turkish were sanctioned, instead of Arabic in areas where these were the languages of the majority of the population.

Fourthly, official patronage and material assistance was at once given to foreign schools before the native demand for schools was satisfied. Most of the foreign schools thus aided were missionary in character. The Archbishop of Canterbury had long maintained in north Iraq an educational mission whose main task was to improve the educational standards of the Nestorians. Not unnaturally the British officers were favourably disposed towards this mission.

When a national government was formed, it did not approve of all these precedents. It retained the teaching of English but only from the fifth year; it ended the issue of grants-in-aid to foreign schools, but found it impossible to abolish the concessions concerning the language of instruction.

The revolt and its cost in British lives and treasure hastened the formulation of a new British policy favouring the conversion of direct rule to one through a native agency. Accordingly, a provisional Arab government was set up, and soon afterwards the election of Faisal, son of the Sharif of Mecca, as King of Iraq was arranged. (He had already been elected King of Syria, but the French ousted him by force of arms.) The new Anglo-Iraqi relation was to be expressed in a treaty and the British mandate from the League of Nations would then operate behind the façade of a native government. Thus for a decade under the monarchy every Iraqi minister had a British adviser whose influence went beyond the mere tendering of advice.

The ministry of education was the first to be placed under native executive authority, but its British adviser still wielded considerable authority. Hence many Arab nationalists blamed this arrangement for what they regarded as a slow progress in educational development. But Britain honoured her promise to end the mandatory regime and to recommend the admission of Iraq to the membership of the League of Nations. When this was arranged in 1933, it marked the legal if not the practical end of British influence on internal Iraqi affairs.

During the decade of Arab control with British advice there was, despite all difficulties, a remarkable advance in education. The two sides differed over priorities, but the number of elementary schools rose from 88 to 336, of secondary schools from 3 to 22, and the education budget more than doubled. From the beginning such "Egyptian" imprint, as British army officers had left on elementary schools was removed. Furthermore, the educational system as a whole was, in the words of its director general, harnessed to the ideas of Arab nationalism.

The relatively rapid expansion in elementary education was matched by the development of secondary schools and teacher training. While it is certain that the British military administration was responsible for the revival of the Ottoman training school in Baghdad, the evidence is conflicting as to who, and when, opened other post-elementary state institutions. The British director of education up to the summer of 1920 specifically states in his memoirs, that he "purposely" did not revive or open any secondary schools. It must, therefore, be assumed that the three secondary schools that existed under the provisional government in 1920–1921 were partly if not entirely a resurrection of the Ottoman schools.

From the beginning the ministry of education realized that the new secondary schools needed time to yield results and that the training of teachers itself required the services of trained teachers. Therefore, teachers were recruited from other Arab countries, and an increasing number of Iraqi students were sent for further education, mostly at this stage to the American University of Beirut. As noted above, the training of teachers in Iraq itself had a humble beginning in the crash programme conducted by the Egyptian expert. This venture was to develop as the first training college, which was ultimately followed by others for men and women, and for urban as well as for rural teachers.

Educational administration was from the beginning centralized in the ministry in Baghdad, no doubt in accordance with the inherited Ottoman tradition and the precedents set by the British-Egyptian officials. The schools followed a uniform curriculum, varied only in respect of the language of instruction. Such a curriculum may be criticized on intellectual grounds, but it cannot be denied that for a nation in the making it was fully justified.

Education laws under successive regimes, monarchical and republican, provide for a primary school of six years from the age of six, free for all children of all races and creeds and compulsory in areas to be specified from time to time by the minister. Post-primary education is now six years, the first three are termed intermediate, and the second three secondary. The first secondary year is general, but the second and third are of two trends, literary and scientific.

Vocational education is provided for at different levels from the end of the primary school.

Neither the content nor the standard of education can be gauged merely from a written syllabus designed for any level of schooling. The reference here to the primary school syllabus is only to show the triumph of modernization, begun by the Turks, continued by the British and now completed by the Arabs. The traditional syllabus had, with very few exceptions, been either edged out or revised beyond recognition. The very first subject in the state school syllabus is not the Koran but simply "religious education", obviously for Muslims and non-Muslims in a national school. Arabic comes next, followed by the foreign language which is English in Iraq and is taught in the fifth and sixth years. The rest of the subjects are arithmetic, history, geography, elementary biology and science, civics, health education, art and crafts, singing and athletics (with domestic science for girls in the fifth and sixth years).

The Iraqi educational system had from the beginning to overcome immense difficulties: it had to cope with the linguistic requirements of minorities, to meet the religious scruples of the Shī'a, and to soften the social and other prejudices of the beduins, and to a lesser degree, the rural population. Above all it had, as a modern system, to reconcile itself to what survived of the traditional system, to tackle the problem of female education, to integrate or control private schools, native and foreign, and finally to plan for higher education.

All these problems were tackled with varying degrees of success. It is not intended to go into details. However, the two questions of foreign schools and development of higher education each deserve some special mention.

It has been observed above that the national government put an end to the practice begun by the British military authorities of paying grant-in-aid from public funds to foreign schools. This negative move was ultimately followed by positive action when by law foreign (and all private) schools were brought under official control. Parents were explicitly forbidden from admitting their children to foreign elementary schools. Pursuing no doubt, the policy of a uniform curriculum, such schools were required to submit their syllabus for official approval, and had moreover, to teach Arabic, history, geography and civics according to the national curriculum, to use the prescribed textbooks in these subjects, and to accept and pay the teachers selected by the ministry of education for teaching the subjects.

Native private schools, Muslim and non-Muslim, were also covered by similar stringent regulations. They were, however, eligible for grants-in-aid, provided they adopted the official curriculum and their efficiency was certified after inspection. By these measures, Iraqi children attending foreign schools or sectarian native schools were reasonably guaranteed instruction in the most "sensitive" subjects similar, if not identical, to that received by those attending state schools. Uniformity in the early and formative education of the future citizen was thus ensured in all schools. But as the state system became firmly established the authorities became more tolerant of private schools, native and foreign.

The question of higher education was not so neatly solved. The idea of a university was mooted as early as 1921 under most discouraging circumstances. First, the training school and the school of law inherited from the Turkish regime were quite elementary in standard. The new secondary classes, in the cities and larger towns, had just started, and at least three to four years must be allowed for pupils to complete the course. Equipment, apparatus and above all trained teachers left much to be desired. Therefore, academic and practical considerations rendered the idea of a university rather unrealistic.

And yet a beginning was made there and then. It was decided to begin with a college of religious sciences. This was not as fantastic a step as it seems. There were traditional schools that could immediately feed the college with students to pursue higher studies. These schools belonged to the two major sections of the Muslim population, the Sunni and the Shiʿa. To enrol students from both communities in an institution with a common curriculum was regarded by King Faisal and his ministers as a useful step towards national unity, through a broad but uniform education of the future religious functionaries and leaders. With these high hopes construction of the building was authorzied, and the college was inaugurated in 1924.

The development of the schools of teacher training and of law into colleges, and the rise and development of other schools and colleges took place long before they were in the end joined to form the University of Baghdad. In the early days, the practical needs of government departments, rather than a concerted effort to develop higher education, inspired the establishment of these institutions. Thus the first institution not connected with teacher training, the school of law, was connected with the ministry of justice, and its teachers and the majority of the students were government officials.

Similar were the circumstances of the school of engineering, established in 1921, in connection with the public works department, and of the school of medicine, established in 1927, in connection with the public health department. Even the college for religious science was connected, not directly with the ministry of education but with the department of religious foundations. In 1923, however, a higher training college for men was established under the ministry of education, and in addition to the men's elementary training school with which the system began, another for women was added in the same year.

Thus were the foundations laid. Upon these foundations an imposing edifice has since been erected. It is the structure as it stands at present rather than the stages of its evolution that will be discussed below.

As stated above the educational ladder begins with six years of primary school, followed by six years of post-primary school. Vocational education of four trends (agricultural, technical, commercial and domestic science) is provided for at different levels after the primary school.

Higher education for those who successfully pass three examinations at the end of the primary, intermediate and secondary (including vocational) is for a minimum of three years at teacher training colleges or of four years at the various institutions and colleges affiliated or constituting the University of Baghdad.

The emergence of this university has a long history beginning as we have seen with the establishment of the college for religious sciences. Its closure some six years after inauguration was a setback to the idea of a university. Another set-back was the discouraging opinion of a commission of experts under Professor Paul Monroe of Columbia University which visited Iraq in 1931 at the invitation of the government. The commission regarded the establishment of a university as inopportune and recommended instead the continuation of the scheme then in operation of sending students to foreign universities.

In 1940 the idea of a university was again revived, under changed conditions. For in the meantime, high schools and colleges had been improved and new institutions of similar standard came into being, though each as hitherto in connection with a government department. Perhaps more significant was the expansion and improvement of the secondary schools from which the higher institutions could recruit students. But the deterrents were still great. The number of secondary schools especially for girls was small, and the academic standard was not high enough. Each of the existing colleges was run under its own rules and regulations, independent of the other. There was no common body, such as an examination board, to equalize standards which even to Iraqi educationists were not of a university level.

The establishment of a university was therefore not as simple as uniting by legislation the existing and largely professional colleges of various academic standards. Apart from the considerations just mentioned, there was as yet no college or colleges for arts and sciences, the central core of any university. Successive ministers of education sought advice from several British and Egyptian experts, and considered arguments for and against the project submitted by Iraqi experts.

A practical step was taken in 1949 when a college for arts and science was established, but later split into two colleges. So great was the unpreparedness of Iraq that a number of professors had still to be invited to these and other colleges from foreign (largely British) and Arab (largely Egyptian) universities. Parallel development in other fields was also undertaken. A higher training college for women was established, the improvement of existing colleges was continued, and new colleges were founded.

At last the University of Baghdad, uniting the colleges, was incorporated by a royal decree in 1956, revised by a republican decree in 1958. The University then comprised twelve colleges, including arts, science, law, medicine, education, engineering, agriculture, commerce, and one college for women. An important provision in the two decrees is that Arabic was to be the language of instruction, but that the senate may approve in special circumstances the use of another language. This was, of course, an indication of how far the university had to depend on foreign teachers.

The number of the colleges and institutions of various descriptions has since been increased. A branch opened in Mosul, was in 1965–66 raised to the status of an independent university. A third was inaugurated in Basra in the following academic year, and a fourth is projected at Kufa.

Mention may be made here of an American Jesuit college in Baghdad, known since 1956 as al-Hikmah University. Run on American college lines and charging fees, it has powers to grant first degrees in science. The number of students is around 300. (This has since been absorbed by the University of Baghdad.)

TRANS-JORDAN

Following Turkey's entry into the war in 1914, military preparations were undertaken in southern Syria to free Egypt from British occupation. The attempt was not successful, but before the British army took the offensive across Palestine an agreement had been reached with the Arabs to fight on the British side in return for certain promises of independence. Accordingly, the sector of the front east of the River Jordan was assigned to the Arab forces commanded by Faisal, son of the Sharif of Mecca. The British army faced the Turks on the main front to the west of the river. In 1918 the Turks were finally defeated and the Arab army entered Damascus in triumph where a national government was proclaimed under Faisal with jurisdiction over the Syrian interior from Aqaba to Aleppo.

But Britain had also a secret agreement with France by virtue of which a special French position in the northern Syria littoral was recognized and priority of French interest in the interior. The same agreement defined British and French spheres of influence in the Syrian interior, French in the north and British in the south. The British sphere was extended by another agreement with France to embrace Palestine west of the River Jordan. However, unable to establish its claim to the interior by peaceful means, France invaded it and ousted Faisal.

In its sphere Britain was pledged to facilitate the establishment in Palestine, west of the River Jordan, of a national home for the Jews, and to uphold a native Arab government to the east. This eastern part was conveniently labelled Trans-Jordan, and was administered by the Amir Abdullah, second son of the Sharif of Mecca, with British advisers. The British position in both parts of Palestine was legalized by a mandate from the League of Nations, and Abdullah's position in Trans-Jordan in relation to Britain became similar to that of his brother Faisal in Iraq.

The country now named Trans-Jordan had been a mere district in and at the southern end of the province of Damascus. After the war, it formed part of Faisal's national government. The territory, large in area, small in population, poor in resources, contiguous with the desert on the east and south, had a large proportion of nomads. The settled population was either peasants or small merchants. For centuries the major pilgrim caravan to Mecca passed through the country, and early this century the caravan route was replaced by a railway which brought a measure of prosperity and civilization to the countryside.

On the eve of the war there were in the whole area 21 Ottoman state elementary schools with 1,039 pupils (including two schools for girls with 59 pupils). The Muslim majority was of course served also by some schools of the *Kuttab* type, and the small Christian minority by comparable church and missionary schools. Since the middle of the nineteenth century agents and associates of the Anglican Bishop in Jerusalem, notably the Church Missionary Society, maintained a handful of schools for Christian children. There were other similar agencies.

The short-lived Faisal Government had scarcely more than a full scholastic year to put its educational house in order. In Trans-Jordan it only managed to re-open the Ottoman state schools, to arabicize their curriculum and to increase the total number of pupils to 1,247. Long-range educational planning and development fell to Abdullah and his British advisers.

The poverty of the country is reflected in the state budget which was in 1924 about £275,000 out of which some £15,000 was spent on education. In that year the state educational system consisted of 44 elementary schools with 3,257 pupils (including five girls' schools, with 353 pupils.) Secondary education had a slow beginning, some ten years later, in the addition of secondary classes to elementary schools. There was a shortage of trained staff, but within the limited resources of the country, some of the teachers and inspectors were recruited from neighbouring Arab countries, and a few students were sent for further education to these countries and elsewhere.

Progress was slow and during the Second World War there was even stagnation. In 1946, however, Britain agreed to terminate the mandate and to establish a new relation with what was re-named the Hashemite Kingdom of Jordon. The change is reflected in educational statistics: increase in financial allocation and rise in the number of schools, teachers and pupils. But these increases remained relatively small. Thus in 1947–48, before the Palestine disaster altered the character of Jordan, there was a total of 11,587 pupils in the country's elementary schools. Forty-four of these were in villages and did not provide more than four years of schooling for some 3,243 pupils. Only ten schools for boys and four for girls provided the full seven years course. The number of girls in all elementary schools was no more than 2,319.

The elementary schools were organized as for villages and towns.

Generally the duration of a village school was only four years, and the education of the majority of their pupils ended after the fourth year, except for the few who could go to higher classes in town schools. In towns the elementary school was of two cycles, lower extending for five years and higher for another two years.

Under the law, elementary education of boys and girls was free in village and town schools, and compulsory in centres to be specified from time to time by the minister of education. Making no doubt allowance for the prevailing social conditions, the age of first admission to school was between six and eight; secondary education was for four years open to pupils who passed a state examination at the end of the elementary school, and against payment of a small fee for those whose parents were able to pay it. In 1947–48 there were only 446 pupils attending secondary classes in five schools. Only 64 presented themselves for the state examination (the equivalent of matriculation) in June 1947.

The educational ladder, the syllabus and indeed the system as a whole, resembled the conditions prevailing then in Palestine, where the system of education was under more direct British control. The wasteful four-year village school, the promotion of pupils from one stage to another by examination which eliminated the "unsuccessful", the charging of fees in a poverty-stricken country, and the teaching of English from the fourth year were some features of questionable educational benefit.

There were, however, some redeeming features. In a number of schools in rural areas, and where the right teachers were available, pupils were taught what the syllabus calls "theoretical and practical agriculture", simple classroom instruction aided by observation and work in a school garden.

Perhaps of more utility was the opening in Amman of a trade school which taught only carpentry and the craft of the blacksmith. It admitted pupils from the two levels of the elementary school and provided facilities for boarders from distant places. On average about ten young men completed their training every year. There was furthermore provision for handicraft in boys' schools matched by domestic science in girls' schools.

Private schools, native and foreign, were compelled by law to teach Arabic, history of the Arabs and geography of the Arab countries. In addition they were required to submit for the approval of the ministry of education their syllabuses, textbooks and the nominal roll of their teachers. While admission of pupils to foreign elementary schools was not, as in Iraq, prohibited, these schools were strictly debarred from any attempts at proselytism or any teaching disrespectful to the beliefs of those of the pupils not professing the religion of the school authorities. There was furthermore explicit interdiction against mixed schools above the primary level and the employment of male teachers in girls' schools. This was no doubt a safeguard against possible discontent in a very conservative environment and an echo of a deep-rooted social prejudice.

Jordan lacked educational facilities higher than the fourth secondary year. A few students were sent by the government for training at institutions in neighbouring Arab countries and fewer to universities abroad. A limited number of other students sought higher education in different countries at the expense of their parents.

The above is a fairly complete picture of the Jordanian educational system when in 1948 the Palestine tragedy created a new political situation which greatly affected education in the two countries. It is therefore necessary to deal with Palestine up to that year before resuming the discussion of the changed conditions in Jordan.

PALESTINE

The theory of the mandate under the League of Nations has an element of benevolent and disinterested idealism in it, since its professed objective was to lead undeveloped countries to a better level of civilization and ultimately political independence. In the words of article 22 of the Covenant this task was "a sacred trust of civilization", and in the selection of a trustee the wishes of the people concerned was "a principal consideration".

However, in its essentials, the Palestine mandate was in direct contradiction of the principles of the Covenant. Its main provisions were not concerned with the promotion of the welfare of the indigenous Arab population, who then constituted over 90 per cent of the population, or with leading them to ultimate independence, but with putting into effect the British promise to establish a Jewish national home while giving no more than safeguards of the "civil and religious rights" of the Arab majority. Furthermore, Britain was appointed as mandatory contrary to the express wishes of the Arabs who refused absolutely to recognize this assault on their national rights which resulted in the denial of self-government simply because this would hinder the establishment and development of the Jewish national home.

The operation of the mandate with these terms was possible only by force as the repeated Arab revolts over thirty years amply testify. During this period Jewish immigration into Palestine, under British protection, raised the ratio of Jews from about 8 per cent to a third of the population, and correspondingly reduced that of the Arabs to two-thirds. Next to the denial of self-government this radical upsetting of the population ratio was the most obvious manifestation of a British policy that pervaded every other department of the country's life including education.

Even in this vital aspect of national life the seeds of future disaster for the Arabs were sown right from the beginning. British policy and might enforced the planting of over half a million Jews in Palestine, with the superior material and technical resources that world Jewry and Zionism could command. The immigrants led a separate existence as a colonist community with its own economy and education. The trustee made no tangible efforts, once Arab political rights were denied, to raise at least their economic and educational standards to the level of those of the Jewish colonists. To understand this circumstance fully it is necessary to begin from the end of the Ottoman period.

In 1914 Ottoman administrative divisions, which later formed mandatory Palestine had a total population of some 700,000 souls. They were served by 95 state elementary schools with 7,758 pupils (including 13 schools for girls with 1,480 pupils). In addition there were two lower and one higher (Sultani) secondary schools in the principal cities, with 471 pupils. During the war the Salahiyya College was established in Jerusalem as a modern institution that laid stress on Islamic studies, served as a centre for training teachers, taught partly in Arabic and partly in Turkish as a concession to Arab nationalists and employed a number of Arab scholars as teachers.

Many of the traditional Muslim schools, particularly the *Kuttab* type, were absorbed in the state system, but many more continued to operate on the usual lines. This was particularly true of higher schools, attached to mosques, which enjoyed income from special foundations. At the outbreak of the war Muslim schools of all grades had a total number of pupils greater by a thousand than that in all state schools.

The children of the various Christian denominations were served partly by church schools but largely by foreign schools of various national affiliations. The most prominent among them belonged to Russian, French, British and German organizations. The Russians and the Germans paid special attention to the establishment of teacher training centres. In 1914 the former had a centre for training men teachers at Nazareth and another for training women teachers near Bethlehem. The Germans had a centre for training men teachers near Jerusalem.

The British missionary schools, originally intended for Jewish children, had gradually and increasingly to divert their attention to those of the Christian Arabs. Just before the war the two largest English schools, Bishop Gobat School and St. George's School in Jerusalem, had pupils from all Christian communities but fewer Jewish pupils. The second school even attracted a handful of pupils coming from well-to-do Muslim families.

Christian missionary effort was resisted by the small Jewish community which insisted on maintaining its essentially religious education unchanged. However, philanthropic Jewish bodies of European origin, notably, the Alliance Israélite, the Anglo-Jewish Association, and the Hilfsverein der Deutschen Juden, succeeded in establishing modern schools that taught Jewish children through the medium of French, English and German respectively. Of particular interest was a farm or agricultural school established by the Alliance near Jaffa.

Although the language of ritual and literature, Hebrew was not the common spoken language. Hence other schools taught through the medium of Yiddish or Ladino or Arabic. However, in the last two decades of the nineteenth century there came to Palestine with refugees from Russia a number of Jews imbued with the new idea of Zionism. These Zionists were both against the conservatism of the rabbis and the assimilationism implied in the foreign schools. They were small in number but united in an ideal of Hebrew revival. They settled in new agricultural colonies away from the city ghettos. For the education of their children they opened small community schools that taught through the medium of Hebrew. In 1914 there were twelve such schools with about as many children in each.

These twelve schools formed the nucleus of the Zionist educational system in Palestine which by the grace of the British government was recognized as the Hebrew public system. The right of religious and racial communities to establish private schools for their children had, of course, been recognized by Ottoman law and practice. But the recognition of the schools of a minority within a community as its public system was peculiar to the Zionist policy of the British government which made it possible for the Zionists, still a small minority among the Jews in Palestine, to begin imposing their nationalist imprint upon and through education.

The mandatory administration agreed not only to leave the Zionist system independent of direct state control but also to allocate to it an annual block grant from the national education budget in proportion to the number of Jews in the country or their school age population. Ultimately most of the other Jewish schools belonging to different organizations joined the Zionist Hebrew system under guarantees of autonomy to each of three major "trends".

The system as a whole followed Swiss or German models. Excluding the kindergarten which was not universal, the elementary school was for eight years from the age of six, for boys and girls together. Such elementary schools were managed by municipal or local councils but parents contributed to the cost in the form of school fees.

Although loosely connected with the public system, secondary education was a private enterprise, and the schools charged fees. They varied considerably, but in general the course was for four years after the elementary school. Vocational schools, parallel to the secondary, were run on similar lines. Teacher training was under the control of the authorities of the "trends".

Facilities for higher education existed from 1925 at two independent institutions, the Hebrew Technical College in Haifa and the Hebrew University in Jerusalem. Although neither formed part of the public system they both constituted in practice its apex. The College offered against the payment of fees courses in architecture and civil, industrial and chemical engineering. The University began with institutes of Jewish studies and biochemistry as a research centre and had an academic staff of seventeen and 85 students. Not before 1928–29 did regular teaching begin in a new faculty of humanities. A great expansion followed the deterioration of the status of Jews in Germany, so that before the end of the British mandate there was added a faculty of science, a school of agriculture, a school of medicine and a school of Oriental studies. There was an academic staff of 150 and some 800 students.

The Arab public system had a different history. From the beginning it was under direct British control, and all Arab demands to relax or share it were in vain. Educational reconstruction began during the war in 1917 by the British military authorities with the modest sum of £15,000. Ottoman state schools in the major centres were gradually re-opened, and local authorities defrayed half the cost of re-opening or opening schools in smaller towns and villages. As in Iraq, British and Arab administrators and experts were brought from Egypt, and two centres for training men and women teachers were opened in Jerusalem. Again as in Iraq, the medium of instruction became Arabic where it had been Turkish.

But it was clear that the British authorities were responsible for two separate and distinct systems of education, directly and completely for the Arab, and indirectly and nominally for the Jewish. Having thus conceded in principle and in practice such separatism in education, on linguistic, racial and national grounds, during the formative years and even before the mandate's system was worked out, the British authorities had consciously or unconsciously made the ultimate political partition of the country inevitable. Nor were the Arabs prepared at least educationally by their rulers for this end, as the following description of the system will no doubt show.

In the majority of villages fortunate enough to have schools the standard type was the four-year school for boys, after which education came to an end except for the very few who could go to a town school. In towns and cities the elementary school, for boys and girls separately, was for seven years, divided into two cycles, the lower extending for five years from the age of six. Promotion to the higher cycle was not automatic, but by selection and fees were charged in these cycles as in secondary classes.

There were no secondary schools as such. During the first half of the mandatory period first and second secondary classes were added to town elementary schools (for boys earlier than for girls). These classes were formed again by selection, not automatic promotion. The formation of these two secondary classes was primarily designed to provide students for the two training colleges, first started by the military authorities. The course at these colleges was for two years and led to the matriculation examination.

The college for women did not develop beyond this level and continued to supply teachers for town schools. A new college for the supply of rural teachers was opened in 1935 and admitted pupils by selection from the top elementary class. At the college for men, since renamed the Government Arab College, there was added in the last years of the British mandate two post matriculation years of literary and scientific sides. A similar development took place at another institution, the Rashidiyya College. This is the highest academic level, approximately the sixth form at an English grammar school, that the Arab public system reached under British control.

Such vocational education as was attempted failed in its primary purpose. A trade school opened in 1936 which offered a two years course in carpentry, joinery, welding and car repairs admitted pupils by selection from the top elementary class. An agricultural school opened in 1931 which offered a two years course in theoretical and practical agriculture which admitted pupils by selection from the second secondary class. The first school was intended to produce skilled artisans and the second intelligent farmers. But neither fulfilled these expectations, and both were geared to producing teachers, when their buildings were not used as army barracks during the Arab revolt.

Attempts, first made in 1922 and repeated later on, to establish a British university were frustrated largely because the Zionists opposed the project as "a threat to Hebrew culture". Thus the Arab and Hebrew school systems continued to drift apart without the unifying agency of a neutral institution of higher learning. Adult Jews, coming as many of them did with European university education, did not need a British university, and the nationalists among them feared it as an obstacle to the development of the Hebrew University. The Arabs, on the other hand, welcomed the idea for they needed a local university. Wealthy students sought higher education in Cairo and Beirut and a few of them went to Europe and America. After a decade of inaction the government department of education began to award a few annual scholarships to students who were sent to the American University of Beirut or to the United Kingdom, with a view to future employment as teachers.

Arab dissatisfaction with the system was vociferous on many counts. Two deserve special mention here. The school syllabus never satisfied Arab thinkers, not because of its "modernism", which was here as elsewhere in Arab lands taken for granted, but because in content and tone it had too little Arab and Muslim character. This was particularly directed to the history syllabus which was beyond the average village and small town school teacher. How could he teach anything of value about the Greeks if he could not even pronounce Themistocles listed in the syllabus? Was it not more profitable and practical for those with his qualifications to concentrate on Arab and Muslim names?

But the loudest Arab protest was against the continued failure of the mandatory government to provide, failing compulsory or universal education, at least enough school places in elementary schools for those who apply for them. The major cause of this failure was publicly admitted. It was not lack of resources, but the diversion of nearly a third of the budget for "defence". There was, of course, no external enemy, and defence meant simply the maintenance of large military and police forces to subdue the Arab majority, often in armed revolt seeking to assert its right of political self-determination. Hence the force of the standard Arab complaint to the League of Nations that the mandatory power used the taxpayer's money not only to uphold a political injustice but in the process also to grossly neglect the education of his children. (Palestine was self-supporting, and Britain incurred no expense except on the army).

In the school year 1938–39, and after two decades of British administration, roughly half of those who applied for admission to state schools were, according to official reports, actually admitted. This does not take into account those of school age who could not apply because of the absence of schools in their neighbourhood. According to the last official figures issued for the school year 1945–46 the state schools accommodated then no more than a quarter of the school-age population.

This state of affairs was repeatedly criticized by British experts and successive commissions of enquiry. It was often deplored in strong terms by the League of Nations. The permanent mandates commission had to consider the annual reports of the mandatory government and petitions from Arab organizations. These petitions often charged the government with deliberately pursuing a policy of maintaining ignorance (*tajhil*), not one of educating (*ta'lim*). It is, of course, useless to speculate about political intentions, but the educational facts are undeniable. In 1938 the Norwegian member of the permanent mandate commission remarked that, given the natural increase of population and the inadequacy of school places, "there seemed to be a danger that illiteracy was no longer on the decline among Arab children."

In 1944–45 the educational ladder was as follows: In crude figures the first elementary class had 17,500, the seventh only 2,000; the fourth secondary class had 232 and only 58 in the fifth and sixth classes together. In a highly selective system the wastage was relatively great in order to allow only an élite to reach the top. Their quality was excellent in the academic sense. But the system produced no comparable élite in the technical field, and still less in female education.

This was the picture when before and after the British withdrawal in 1948 the Arabs and Jews began to fight for survival. With the military, economic and political aspects of the struggle we are not concerned here. As regards education the above discussion leaves little doubt that the Jews were better prepared than the Arabs. The former enjoyed almost universal literacy among males and females, better and more comprehensive technical education especially at a high level, and more men and women with higher education received in Palestine (not to mention the more numerous Jews who had had technical and higher education abroad).

One need not be an expert in military science to perceive the advantage of the one side over the other, or to detect in the Arab discomfiture a large element of educational deficiency. As a trustee and being solely responsible for Arab education, the mandatory power must accept responsibility for this deficiency. The reader will judge for himself on the facts cited above how far was "the sacred trust of civilization" executed, neglected or betrayed in at least the field of education.

The upheaval of 1948 brought about a great disruption in Arab education in Palestine. Henceforth the education of Arab children must be observed in four different states, partly as refugees and partly as citizens. Jordan had to shoulder a great share of the burden.

JORDAN

Although adopted sometime earlier, it was not before 1950 that the name Jordan was formalized after the incorporation of the central parts of Palestine. The original state of Trans-Jordan became known as the East Bank and the Palestinian districts the West Bank. Thus enlarged in territory and population, Jordan's educational responsibilities were correspondingly increased. Yet at the beginning the West Bank had a separate budget of which some £135,000 or 13 per cent was spent on education in 1950–51, and the education of the children of refugees in both parts of Jordan was entrusted to the United Nations Relief and Works Agency (which also operated for the same purpose in Lebanon, Syria and Gaza).

In the same year there were 262 state schools of all grades in the West Bank with 50,921 pupils, and only 138 schools in the East Bank with 39,079 pupils. These figures do not include private schools, native and foreign. The United Nations operated in both parts of Jordan and in the same year controlled 55 elementary schools with 16,948 pupils. Another 3,167 pupils were in private schools with grants from the Agency which moreover defrayed the cost of training 692 boys in various kinds of crafts.

It is clear that state schools in the West Bank were more numerous than those in the East. But they were also more developed in that they contained more secondary classes and more girls. They included moreover the only agricultural school established by the mandatory government and the centre for training rural women teachers. Higher education was sought abroad. In 1950–51 there were no fewer than 500 Jordanian students in the universities of the neighbouring countries and abroad. The majority of these were Palestinians whose claims on national and international assistance were irresistible.

The educational system made a remarkable recovery and even good progress. Particularly noteworthy was the increase in the number of pupils in secondary classes, the increased facilities for vocational training and the development of the colleges for training teachers. The United Nations Agency shouldered an increasing responsibility and made valuable contributions in all these and other directions.

By 1955–56 state schools had 157,101 pupils, native private schools 25,777, foreign private schools 8,501 and the Agency's 49,215. (The practice of publishing figures of state schools in each of the two parts of Jordan separately was now discontinued.) In the same year state schools alone had some 21,000 pupils in secondary classes, the trade school 94, the agricultural school 74 and 77 others received instruction in commercial subjects in secondary classes. There were twelve centres for vocational training at which 2,661 students from training colleges and secondary classes received instruction that year. There were three training colleges, two for men and the third for the training of rural women teachers.

Since facilities for higher education were still lacking, the system of sending students abroad was continued, now with considerable international aid. In the year under review the United Nations Agency assisted 160 Palestinian students, the state 85 Jordanians, and 202 others received assistance from such sources as Unesco and the American Point Four.

Reference must, at this juncture, be made to a new education law and an important cultural agreement. The new law was passed in 1955, and provided for free and compulsory education. The period of free schooling was six years, and could be prolonged if the five years assigned for secondary schooling was shortened. This meant in effect the maintenance of a combined period of eleven years as hitherto. The application of compulsion was, similarly, muffled by making it subject to the ability of the treasury to supply the necessary funds.

The special significance of the law is, however, the stiffer provisions it makes in respect of private foreign schools. They were, of course, still required to teach Arabic and other subjects as detailed above. But now the Iraqi precedent was followed in that no foreigner was permitted to open a new kindergarten or elementary school, though existing foreign schools were allowed to expand in secondary education.

There were political and religious, in addition to educational reasons for this stiffer attitude. This may be deduced from the clause which forbids the "imparting of any religious or national creeds contrary to those held by the pupils". Foreign and native private schools were given full freedom to develop religious education according to their particular creeds, but the law forbids the teaching of these creeds to pupils of other faiths. More specifically no missionary school may seek by teaching or otherwise to change a pupil's religion or denomination. This last stipulation must not be mistaken as a measure by a Muslim government against Christian missions. Its intention is clearly the protection of native Christians against foreign Protestant and Catholic proselytizing endeavours.

Equally important was the signing in 1957 by Jordan, Syria and Egypt of the Arab Cultural Unity Pact. The first sentences in the preamble appeal to general sentiment. "Believing", the preamble begins "that unity of thought and culture is a principal prop of Arab political unity; responding to the call by leaders of Arab thought and nationalism; desirous of upbringing and educating Arab citizens serving one Arab homeland . . .", and goes on to lay down concrete measures to be taken as from the beginning of the school year 1957–58 to streamline and co-ordinate the educational system in the three states. The most important provision was the adoption of a uniform educational ladder (six years primary, three years intermediate and three years secondary) and the equalization of standards at every level according to principles spelled out in a special annexe.

Other provisions of special interest include guidance on the development of vocational and technical education, and one article deals with the exchange of professors, teachers and experts and facilities for the admission of students to the various schools, institutes and universities. Another article states that the pact was a preliminary to a universal Arab cultural unity, and accordingly other states are invited to join it.

In accordance with the pact the Jordanian educational ladder became as follows: six years primary, three years intermediate (actually called preparatory) and three years secondary. The first secondary year had a general common syllabus, but the next two years had either a literary or scientific one. The vocational education ran parallel to these classes at different levels after the primary school. There were now four training colleges for men, providing a two-year course after the secondary school, and only one, with a special syllabus, for the training of rural women teachers. The number of colleges and centres has since risen to seven, two of which belong to the United Nations Agency.

The University of Jordan was established by a royal decree in 1962, but it was decided to begin with a faculty of arts. In that year the total number of pupils in the top secondary class in state schools, native schools, foreign schools and schools controlled by the U.N. Agency was 5,739 including 1,200 girls. Those who passed the equivalent of matriculation, and thus became eligible for higher education, numbered 3,547 boys and 787 girls.

However the College of Arts began with 149 male and 18 female students and three full-time teachers. Three years later a college of science and another for economics and commerce were started, and the number of students rose to 1,763 and the number of teachers of all grades to seventy-eight. Students pay no fees except about £10 p.a. The University is independent of the government, even financially. Out of a budget of nearly a million pounds sterling the government contribution was only a hundred thousand. In 1965 Kuwait contributed double that amount. Other generous contributions were received from wealthy Jordanians, and foreign foundations. (There were, according to official sources, over twenty-one thousand Jordanian students in universities abroad.)

EGYPT

We last mentioned Egypt to say that in 1919 the country was in revolt seeking the end of the British occupation and protectorate. The revolt was quelled by the British army, but the protracted negotiations that followed led in 1922 to a British unilateral declaration, terminating the protectorate and recognizing a conditional Egyptian independence to be regulated by a treaty with Britain.

The national government under the new dispensation inherited an oddly constructed state educational system. It was odd not only because of lack of co-ordination with the large number of traditional schools at the apex of which stood al-Azhar, but because of a divorce between two types of schools within the state system at the first step of the educational ladder. In 1922, these two types were firstly 719 elementary (*awwali*) schools, partly controlled by the ministry of education and largely, by provincial councils, with 74,219 pupils (including 21,500 girls) providing a minimum of schooling for four years after which formal education ceased. A great many of these schools were of the *Kuttab* type taken over by the local or central authorities with the minimum of change. Thus the curriculum was little more than the Koran, the three R's and some hygiene. A limited number of pupils completing this type of school had access only to some vocational training, itself very limited at this level.

Secondly, there were 103 primary (*ibtidai*) schools controlled by the ministry of education, with 20,207 pupils (including 2,040 girls), providing education for four years of a better standard than the elementary school. Unlike the elementary school which as a rule admitted pupils who had had no previous instruction, the primary school admitted pupils only after they had received grounding in the three R's. In practice therefore, the primary school was for a minimum of six years. The primary schools were better housed and furnished and enjoyed a larger proportion of educated and trained teachers than the elementary schools, and unlike the latter led to the secondary schools. The link between the primary and secondary school was facilitated by the teaching of a foreign language, usually English, which was absent from the curriculum of the elementary school.

There were only ten secondary schools in 1922 with 3,882 pupils (including no more than 43 girls). The number of pupils in vocational schools (trade, commercial and agricultural) was then 2,738 of which only 189 received agricultural training. The specialized high schools had 2,570 students.

The training of teachers was, at the lower stages, rudimentary. Thus an intending teacher for an elementary school was admitted for training after the completion of such a school. Those intending to teach in primary schools were similarly trained. Only secondary school teachers and some of the primary school teachers received more advanced training. The number of those under training was 367 men and 106 women, the latter in what is called "intermediate" institutions.

Out of a state budget of some £38 millions the share of education was about one million.

Thus was the picture when Egypt assumed full control over education without British advice, direct or indirect. It is right to enquire what successive Egyptian governments did for education during the thirty years before the turning point of the revolution in 1952. Their action was governed partly by a century of a utilitarian school system and partly by the provisions of the new constitution. The application of these provisions resulted in complicating an already complex first stage of education. It made elementary schooling compulsory for boys and girls, and free in state schools (*makatib, sing. maktab*). The outcome was the compulsory elementary school which provided a minimum of education for six (later reduced to five and then to four) years from the age of seven.

With a curriculum not much better than that of the existing elementary school, and under similar handicaps of poor buildings and equipment and unqualified teachers, the new compulsory school was robbed of much of its educational value by the adoption of the system of half-day teaching. The official rationalization of the system was on grounds of making the maximum use of buildings and teachers and, at the same time, affording the children of the poor the opportunity to work or learn a trade in the other half of the day. But only after years of wasted money and effort did it become clear that such a school, which in practice taught for a maximum of three years, failed to achieve permanent literacy.

Egypt never lacked the educational experts and thinkers, but the ministry of education was the prisoner of a long tradition of educating only an élite, military and civil. The education of the masses was not seriously considered before the days of Muhammad Abduh. As we have seen he was a pioneer in this as in other matters, but his ideas lacked official support for application. Apart from a faint murmur in 1868, the earliest official reference to the education of the

masses was made in 1880 by the minister of education who con-
templated its "gradual spread among all sections of the population
from towns to villages". The prime minister, however, still linked the
desirability of more education with the government's need for civil
servants. The idea was never put into practice.

The compulsory school was a feeble, and in the end, an unsuccessful attempt. More successful were the government's efforts in the
field of higher education. It is curious that the top of the educational
pyramid should be built before the safety of its base was ensured.
The dual, or rather triple, system of an elementary school was with
its serious defects tolerated and the establishment of a state university was proceeded with. For soon after independence the control
of the Egyptian University was transferred from private to official
hands. The University was in 1925 established by law with four
colleges: the original school of arts, a new college of science, the old
school of medicine established in 1827 and the old school of law
established in 1868. Within two decades the University expanded to
embrace ten colleges with over ten thousand students. A branch was
opened at Alexandria and in 1942 constituted as a separate university. A third state university was established in Cairo in 1950,
now known as Ain Shams University. In 1957 another university was
opened at Asyut.

But the major problem of a uniform primary school, leading to
secondary and higher education continued to elude the authorities
who simply fumbled for a solution without real success. It would
take too long even to mention the changes, devices and expedients
adopted or abandoned with astonishing daring. All were indicative
of a lack of a consistent and persistent policy. The utmost that
was achieved was the scrapping of the compulsory school and the
adoption of some measures to equalize the primary and elementary
schools with a view to ultimate unification. After some fluctuation
the period of elementary schooling was fixed as six years, and the
standard of the elementary school syllabus was raised, at least in
theory, to that of the primary school, except in the teaching of a
foreign language which remained a monopoly of the latter school.

Much of the travail in education was due to the nature of Egyptian
politics under the monarchy manifested in party political strife and
frequent change of government. A change of government did not
simply result in the change of the minister of education but sometimes also in the change of senior officials. This led to some lack of
continuity in the direction of education. Matters were made worse
by ideological and even personal antagonism among the leading

educationists. Their controversies are now of mere historical interest, and need not concern us here. But the politicians must accept a large share of the blame, since from the days of the national rising in 1919 student political demonstrations and strikes were among the weapons in the armouries of the political parties and individual politicians. Inevitably the teachers and administrators were, at least indirectly, drawn in with unfortunate results.

Yet the quantitative expansion of the educational service was extraordinary. On the eve of the revolution in 1951–52, the number of pupils in state primary and elementary schools was 1,092,816 (including 410,502 girls), in secondary schools 126,091, in vocational schools 28,250, and in training colleges 20,446. The state universities had 37,648 and the independent al-Azhar University 3,777 students. The number of students in universities abroad was 167. Figures for private schools, native and foreign, are not included.

The provisions of Egyptian law concerning these schools are milder than the laws of Iraq or Jordan, but there is little difference in their spirit. All private schools were required to teach their pupils, whether Egyptian or of other nationality, a standard of Arabic equal to that in state schools, and no private school was allowed to give religious instruction to any pupil other than that according to the religion of his parents. Two foreign institutions for higher education deserve specific mention: the French law school, established in the nineteenth century, and affiliated to the college of law in the University of Paris, and the American University at Cairo, established in 1920 as a culmination of missionary endeavour.

The 1952 revolution had a socialist philosophy favourable to the cause of education. It introduced radical political changes accompanied and followed by an ambitious programme of social and economic reform in which education figured very prominently. Following an established Egyptian custom every stage of education was regulated by a separate law. At long last the Gordian knot of the first stage of education was cut by the law of 1953. (An attempt in 1950 remained ineffective.) Without making any specific mention of the elementary school, the new law abolished it by instituting a national primary school, free and compulsory for boys and girls from the age of six to twelve. Children were, moreover, to be served with free lunch.

But compulsion was to apply only to those areas where the ministry of education had the necessary facilities. The curriculum, adaptable according to circumstances, included the Koran and religious instruction (with alternative instruction for non-Muslim pupils), Arabic, patriotic education, arithmetic, practical geometry, history, geography, nature study and elementary science, hygiene, drawing, physical education, manual work for boys, and domestic science for girls, and singing.

This was regarded as the "indispensable minimum" for the education of the future citizen. In the curriculum special stress was laid on religious and patriotic education and the Arabic language. The teaching of a foreign language was abolished. It was impossible to make its teaching universal, and to continue its random teaching in some schools was tantamount to perpetuating a social and educational injustice by restricting the admission to secondary schools to those who had had instruction in the foreign language.

Until adequate resources could be commanded this "indispensable minimum" was regarded as a substitute for universal primary education. But it was not regarded as sufficient for intelligent citizenship. Hence the creation of a three-year primary high school intended to train young men and women not destined for higher education for future employment in agriculture, crafts, commerce and domestic science. Gifted pupils could proceed to vocational secondary schools, or the appropriate training colleges, or al-Azhar, if they had received the necessary instruction in the Koran.

Inadequate resources was also one of the reasons for providing secondary education only by examination. The law of 1953 envisaged it in two stages: (a) preparatory or intermediate of four years duration (two overlapping with the last two of the primary school and two corresponding to the first two in the primary high school). The curriculum stressed religious education, Arabic and history, and included science and English as a foreign language; (2) secondary proper of three years divided after the first into literary and scientific sides, with provision for two foreign languages, usually English and French, though in theory pupils in the literary side could choose German, Italian, Spanish or Russian. From this type of secondary school, the universities recruited their students. Very few students climbed up any other ladder.

The one or two remaining awkward corners were soon to be smoothed. Indeed, many an educational development in the first decade after the revolution reflects its social and economic aims. Two deserve particular mention here. The first is the great increase in the number of mixed schools in the state primary system. This is very significant since the law stipulates for either mixed or separate schools "acccording to circumstances". The second development to be noted was a marked shift in secondary education to the vocational or technical side. This is interesting when related to the ambitious long-range programme of industrialization. From 1956, there were instituted, after the primary school, preparatory and secondary technical schools, each of three years duration, and leading under stringent regulations to higher education. (The four years general preparatory school was now for three years, and little was heard of the primary high school).

Within five years of thus raising the status of technical education the number of pupils in technical preparatory schools rose from some eight-thousand to forty-two thousand, in technical secondary schools from some twenty-two thousand to seventy-five thousand, and in higher technical institutions from 1,485 to 15,881.

Looking at both ends of the educational ladder as in 1961–62 the state primary schools had 2,968,211 pupils (including 1,044,123 girls), the state universities had 96,941 students (including 15,356 girls) and al-Azhar alone 7,140 students. For the same year the total number of pupils in secondary schools (excluding technical schools) was 140,733. Admission to university was open to holders of the secondary school certificate in order of merit.

Facilities for higher education are mainly centred in Cairo. Upper Egypt and the Delta remained, until recent years, dependent upon the capital and Alexandria. Accordingly in 1957 the fourth state university was established, and is still expanding, at Asyut. In the early 1960s Alexandria University opened a branch of its medical faculty at Tanta, and Cairo University opened a branch of its medical faculty at Mansura. Nor was this all. To relieve pressure on existing universities, institutes, some with powers to grant first degrees in such disciplines as agriculture, commerce, industry, music, drama and art were established. In 1961–62 there were no fewer than nine such institutions with 6,479 students (including 1,370 girls).

However, the most revolutionary change took place in al-Azhar. In 1961 it was by law brought into the national system and its curriculum radically widened. The language and terms of the explanatory memorandum accompanying the law are highly conciliatory to that ancient bulwark of conservatism and clearly solicitous of enlisting the co-operation of its erstwhile defenders. "Al-Azhar", the memorandum begins, "has long played a great role in the history of learning, in the history of Islam, in the history of the Arabs, and in the national struggle throughout the ages. . . ." Then it goes on to explain that this unique role itself occasioned some conservatism which in modern times debarred the institution from performing its meritorious functions. Thus its graduates were steeped in religious and Arabic sciences but knew little or nothing of modern science.

While preserving its essential character, and without diminishing its place in Egypt and in the Arab and Muslim worlds, al-Azhar was accordingly in need of renewal by bringing it into harmony with other Egyptian universities. Article 34 of the law directs that, in addition to the traditional colleges of Islamic and Arabic studies, four new colleges be established for agriculture, business administration, engineering and medicine, and empowers the minister for Azhar affairs to open other colleges and institutes. One of these was itself an innovation—a college of Islamic studies for girls in that hitherto impregnable fortress of the male. It may be added that modernization applies equally to institutions affiliated with al-Azhar and to secondary and primary sections.

The Shaikh (Rector) of al-Azhar kept all his privileges, but he was now assisted by a director (*mudir*) for all academic, administrative and financial affairs. To emphasize that the new university, like the old, was for all Muslims, the law gives students from all Islamic countries an equal opportunity for admission to any of the colleges subject only to the availability of places and financial provisions.

Here it is necessary to explain that while legally the universities are controlled by the state, in practice they enjoy a large measure of autonomy, so much so that the government almost automatically ratifies their decisions within the law and financial provisions. Not only that each university is an autonomous entity but each constituent college of any university also enjoys its own autonomy. The organization, government and curricula are on the whole modelled on European lines, largely French or British. Recently some American influence may be discerned in new colleges such as those at Asyut.

The reference above to the academic hospitality offered to Muslim students at al-Azhar is of course in keeping with an established custom. Another and larger form of academic hospitality developed since the end of the Second World War. With the formation of the League of Arab States in 1945, Egypt assumed some political leadership in Arab affairs in addition to its already acknowledged leadership in cultural affairs. Under the monarchy, but more particularly since the revolution and the establishment of the republic, Egypt consolidated its leadership in the political and cultural fields. The pact of cultural unity between Egypt, Jordan and Syria has been noted above. A year later in 1958 it was followed by a political union between Egypt and Syria as the United Arab Republic, which though short-lived left a permanent mark on education in both countries.

Some of Egypt's educational aid to other Arab countries has too often been misunderstood and even misrepresented by journalists in England and America. They regard it as political opportunism and overlooked its idealism of Arab national and cultural solidarity. Thus Egypt was ready to send experts, professors and schoolteachers to all parts of the Arab world, and at the same time to receive in its schools and universities students from most Arab countries. Both involved the state in considerable expense with no visible material return. In 1961–62 the number of school teachers sent was 3,232 and the number of students received was 20,878 (including 6,874 in the universities).

Only an expanding system can absorb so many students from abroad and still maintain its equilibrium. In a decade the numbers in state primary schools have tripled and those for the universities nearly tripled also. We have noted that in 1951–52 there were 167 bursary students in universities abroad. In 1961–62 their number was 1,587. In addition, 808 were on study leave and 3,275 went as private students whose studies were nevertheless directed by the government. Here again it is necessary to explode a myth created by sensational journalism that the Soviet bloc was attracting the majority of Egyptian students. The truth is that West Germany had the greatest number of Egyptian students, that the United States had double the number of those in the Soviet bloc, and that Great Britain had 300 more than in the Soviet bloc.

Students were carefully distributed among different countries, for educational not political reasons, and according to the needs of the Egyptian development plans. For these science and technology are indispensable. Hence the direction of students for specialization in these fields must be to the best institutions wherever they happen to be. But no state can ignore offers of scholarship to its students from a friendly country. Such offers were accepted indiscriminately from the United States and the Soviet Union, and from East and West Germany, with no political concessions. (France's lead in the nineteenth century had gradually declined to a vanishing point at present.)

Without going into many of its byways, the above is a fairly complete description of the essential fabric of the Egyptian educational system from the primary school to the university. Reference to administration and teacher training was purposely delayed till now, so that both could be related to the final shape of the school system with the minimum of words. The standard of the old institutions for the training of teachers had been raised and their facilities expanded and diversified. For the training of primary school teachers there were now general as well as specialized colleges for such subjects as art, music and physical education. The training of secondary school teachers became the function of university colleges of education or specialized high institutes for such subjects as art, music and domestic science. Among the university colleges the veteran Dar al-Ulum became a constituent college of the University of Cairo. The other universities also have their colleges of education. Ain Shams has two, one mixed for postgraduates and the other for women undergraduates. In 1961–62 there were altogether 57 lower and 13 higher colleges and institutes for teacher training, with 21,899 (11,063 women) and 6,830 (4,574 women) students respectively.

Educational administration is now rather complicated and distributed among several ministries and higher councils. But since this study is concerned mainly with the schools and universities, only the two ministries of education and higher education are directly relevant. There is a third ministry of culture that controls, among other activities, broadcasting, the stage and music, and at least three other ministries with participation in educational affairs: the ministry of scientific research, social affairs and youth. Thus the tradition of a highly centralized system has been varied by the distribution of responsibility, and by some devolution of authority on central and local bodies. It was first introduced in the local government law of 1960, and is now evident in the development plans, the first completed in 1965, and the second to run for seven years up to 1972.

Need it be pointed out in conclusion that the curriculum from school to university was now in substance European, though a great deal of Islamic and Arabic spirit is infused in it? "Science is international" is a phrase often heard in educational circles in Egypt and elsewhere in the Arab world. What remained undoubtedly national in the curriculum is religious instruction, the Arabic language, Arab history and Islamic civilization. These are studied also at university level and pursued on a more specialized basis at al-Azhar.

Viewing developments over a century and a half the observer cannot fail to be impressed by the achievements of the last fifteen years. From its early days the Egyptian educational system was the privilege of the few. During the British occupation the limited state primary education became the preserve of those who could pay fees. The national governments after independence greatly expanded the educational facilities at all levels, but as we have seen their measures lacked spirit and philosophy. Only since the overthrow of the monarchy did the way towards democratizing the system begin to be clear. Gradually the educational ladder was rationalized, and sector by sector was made free. From being the privilege of the few, education was made legally the right of the citizen. Progressive lifting of economic barriers led finally in 1962 to making higher education, like the elementary and secondary, completely free. Equality of opportunity was at last guaranteed in a diversified system that is hopefully on the way to becoming universal.

THE SUDAN

Egyptian expansion into what is now the Republic of the Sudan was begun by Muhammad Ali and extended and consolidated by Ismail. The British occupation of Egypt involved Britain in the Sudan. It was thus an Anglo-Egyptian force that defeated the followers of the Mahdi in 1898 and restored the Sudan not to sole Egyptian control but to a joint Anglo-Egyptian *condominium*.

Behind the façade of this novelty of "joint sovereignty" British control was paramount. The Sudan was governed and administered by high British officials with Egyptians as subordinates. The future of the country was not settled when Britain recognized the independence of Egypt, and the Sudan question continued to embitter Anglo-Egyptian relations till the early 1950s when the two sides agreed to recognize the right of the Sudanese to self-determination. After a transition period, the Sudan emerged as an independent state on New Year's day, 1956.

During the greater part of the nineteenth century when Egypt alone was responsible for the administration of the Sudan, the country's educational facilities were according to the familiar traditional pattern. At the lower level there was the *Khalwah* (literally "a place of retreat" where the pious retired for meditation) which performed the functions of the *Kuttab* in other countries. At a higher level there was either the mosque or the *Zawiyah* which performed functions similar to those of the *Madrasah* elsewhere.

The Sudan lacked educational institutions higher than this level. A notable exception was a short-lived establishment at ad-Damir which was thriving before the Mahdi's revolt. It gave instruction in religious science of a high standard and prepared some students for further education in Hijaz or at al-Azhar. This institution owes its origin to the initiative and religious zeal of a native shaikh. It was here that al-Mahdi received his formative education. Unfortunately the institution did not survive, or, if it did, degenerated after its shaikh's death into an ordinary *Khalwah*.

The teachers of the traditional system were roughly two types according to previous education: those initiated locally by mystics and taught in the schools of their respective orders, and those educated by other means either locally or at al-Azhar. In the Sudan, as elsewhere, the mystic orders played an important part in education as well as in the general religious revivalist movements. As we

124

have seen, this revival was represented in the first half of the nineteenth century by the Wahhabi movement in Arabia and in the second half of the century by the Sanusi movement in North Africa. In the last decades of the century it was represented by the Mahdi movement in the Sudan. Each of these movements had an essential educational ingredient, with the teacher playing a part just as important as the preacher, if the two were not combined in one.

Teachers, other than members of orders, were perhaps less disciplined both in the pursuit of their own education and in the conduct of whatever school they taught in. On the whole it may be said that the *Zawiyah* was peculiar to the mystics. On the other hand, the *Khalwah* was not the preserve of any particular teacher though generally associated with the *faki*, a corruption of *faqih*, which means one learned in jurisprudence. In fact, many teachers of this type were learned in little more than reciting the Koran, but the stories about their general ignorance are somewhat exaggerated.

There is no evidence that Muhammad Ali extended his modern school system to the Sudan. But there is no doubt that many Sudanese conscripts in his army learned the elements. Some of them, together with sons of Sudanese notables, were trained in the specialized schools and most of them were later sent back to their country as clerks in the Egyptian administrative service. There is, however, some vague mention of early modern schools in a few administrative centres. This probably refers to *ad hoc* arrangements made for the instruction of the children of Egyptian officials and army officers, with opportunity for sons of Sudanese notables to profit from these arrangements.

The first official Egyptian effort was a boys school which Abbas decided in 1850 to open in Khartoum with Tahtawi as headmaster. The school was "to save the sons of the Sudan from the hell of ignorance." Whether, as Tahtawi and almost all who subsequently referred to it suspected, the school was a mere device for his banishment from Cairo is of little importance. What is important is that while it remained open the school had both Egyptian and Sudanese pupils.

Under Ismail in the 1860s five official schools were opened in administrative centres with similar mixed pupils. As in Egypt these schools served the needs of the government by producing a few junior clerks. A number of former pupils were later employed as such in the Mahdi administration.

At the beginning of the *condominium* the traditional school system was more or less intact. The official Egyptian schools seem to have disappeared, but two Egyptian community schools at Wadi Halfa and Suakin survived. These were probably the only "modern" schools in the Sudan when in 1900 a British director of education took charge. Imbued with Cromer's spirit, under whom he worked in Egypt, he conceived a very limited school system, with equally limited objectives, at the very minimum cost. The three objectives he formulated were really one centred round the needs of the British administration. The schools must, through their product, promote understanding of the orders of the government and produce the clerks and artisans the government departments required.

Imagination was reserved for Kitchener who soon after his victory over the dervishes conceived the idea of Gordon Memorial College to be established with money raised by public subscription in Britain. The fund was raised very quickly and the College was opened in 1902 as an elementary school. But Kitchener was a great soldier not an educational planner. The planning was left to the director of education who also became principal of the College.

Two years before the opening of the College the first elementary school was opened at Omdurman with some 120 Sudanese and Egyptian pupils. It was an exact copy of the four-year Egyptian school. Its teachers were seconded Egyptian teachers and its textbooks were imported from Egypt. But the often quoted statement that a training school for elementary teachers was at the same time opened at Omdurman requires an interpretation. Less than half a dozen pupils in the new elementary schools, probably with some previous schooling, were singled out for training by their own teachers. That was not a "training college", even an elementary one. Its very name, "the school or class of prefects", confirms this view.

At any rate, the Omdurman establishment was transferred to form the nucleus of the College to which was added an "industrial school". This term also requires some explanation. During its first year the College had some 150 pupils, more than a third of whom were Egyptians and Syrians. In conjunction with the elementary course some pupils were taught handicraft and others "trained" as future teachers. In 1906, after the end of the four year course, some seventy boys were employed in government departments, but far fewer were ready for employment as artisans or school teachers.

Apart from the College a handful of elementary schools were opened in administrative centres. Gradually higher elementary classes up to the fourth were formed so that each of the elementary and higher elementary cycles was four years. (The higher elementary cycle was later officially termed intermediate). Gradually two new sections were added to the College until 1920 when it began to develop as a secondary school relying on higher elementary classes elsewhere to supply the pupils.

It is clear that these modern schools were established beside the traditional schools, similar to the procedure adopted in Egypt and other countries. A faint attempt to improve the traditional schools through a system of grants and inspection proved unsuccessful. Yet the British administration was responsible for the rise, under provincial authorities, of what was called "sub-grade schools", as a doubtful improvement on the *Khalwah*. A sub-grade school offered a three-year course. To the authorities it was a cheap school, but low cost apart, the permanent educational value of such a school must have been negligible.

The schools so far discussed were boys schools, all located in the northern provinces. Nothing has been said on female education or the education in the southern provinces. It is on record that in 1906 the British authorities received a formal request for a girls school at Khartoum. And yet the earliest initiative was taken by a native shaikh at Rufa'a where he opened about 1907 a school for the daughters of his family, relatives and friends. The authorities were content for the time being to encourage this native effort, but not yet to second it. The first government school for girls was established in 1911 in Omdurman. By 1920 there were five schools for girls.

The rudimentary school system in the northern provinces served a population whose language was Arabic and whose religion was Islam. The three provinces in the south, inhabited by pagan and multi-lingual tribes, were not touched by the official educational programme. Education in these provinces was deliberately entrusted to Catholic, Presbyterian and Anglican missions, each denomination with a specified sphere. Despite their different national and denominational affiliations the missions adopted a similar approach to education: teaching at a lower level through the medium of tribal dialects written in Latin characters, and at a higher level through the medium of English. Naturally the ultimate aim of all Christian missionary work is conversion to Christianity.

Experienced administrators might have foreseen the political if not the educational consequences of this abdication of responsibility in favour of different missions. None seems to have thought of the difficulties their action would create for the independent Sudan. Their confidence in the permanence of *Pax Britannica* must have represented such a development as unlikely in the forseeable future.

Fortunately, missionary activities in the north were regularized on a different basis: missions were free to open private schools, but they were given no responsibility for national education.

National education in the Sudan remained, during the first half of the period of British administration, simply embryonic, not only in quantity. It scarcely performed functions other than supplying government departments with a number of junior clerks, teachers and other government employees. For this purpose the schools were geared to supply Gordon College with a corresponding intake of new pupils. The educational value of three or four years at a lower elementary school was negligible, if not followed by attendance at higher elementary schools. But the number of these was not more than eleven in 1920, and remained almost stationary for the next twenty years. English was taught in these schools largely for the purpose of admission to Gordon College where the language of instruction was English except in Arabic and Islamic subjects.

From 1920, the College began to develop as the first and only secondary school, and its elementary sections were discontinued. When the four-years secondary course was finally established it was divided into two years of general education, followed by two years of vocational specialization for the training of clerks, accountants, teachers, surveyors and Islamic lawyers. The emphasis was still on utility and the needs of the government. There was no post-secondary education till 1924 when the Kitchener school of Medicine was opened in Khartoum. A report of graduates after four years indicates the standard of the school in its early days.

Teacher training remained haphazard for two decades. Any mention of training schools or colleges before the 1930s must be interpreted with some imagination. Reference has been made above to such training of men teachers at Gordon College and elsewhere. It may here be added that in 1921 a "training college" for women teachers was opened at Omdurman when there were only five elementary schools for girls.

In 1924 the fragile school system suffered a serious staffing difficulty when, in consequence of a crisis in Anglo-Egyptian relations, Egyptian teachers and staff had to leave. For several years to come the schools and the College stagnated. The latter in particular was now viewed in a different light. The British authorities were anxious lest it became a breeding ground of political agitators. The English staff adopted a supercilious attitude not only towards their pupils but also to their non-English colleagues. However, it must be said in favour of the British educational authorities that about this time they sent the first batch of Sudanese students on scholarships to the American University of Beirut.

On the whole, more educational advance was achieved during the second half of the period of British control. Particularly important was the establishment in 1934 of Bakht ar-Ruda as a training college for men teachers. By the end of the British era the number of institutions for training men teachers was four with 632 students, and for training women teachers, two with 277 students.

Gordon College began from the 1930s to develop as a post-secondary institution. It now shed its secondary classes as it had previously shed its elementary classes. Its various sections were up-graded as high schools of arts, science, law, engineering, etc., and it became a college in fact after having been one only in name. In 1951 it became, jointly with the Kitchener School of Medicine, the University College of Khartoum, affiliated with the University of London. One of the first acts of the Sudanese Parliament was to make it the University of Khartoum. The number of students was then 722 (including 22 girls). Up to the time of writing English is still the medium of instruction except in the Arabic and Islamic departments.

Female education made small but significant advances. In the last school year of the British era, and excluding sub-grade schools, there were 30,439 girls in elementary schools; 1,255 in intermediate schools and only 190 in two or three secondary schools.

British policy regarding education in the south began to change when in 1927 grants-in-aid were paid to mission schools. This gave the government more say in the conduct of the schools. But active intervention came only after the Second World War when the government itself opened some schools in the south. In these schools, as well as in some of the mission schools, the teaching of Arabic was introduced. Further evidence of the realization of their early mistakes was shown by the British authorities when instead of sending on the Sudanese students to Makerere College in Kampala they began to send a few to the University College of Khartoum.

That, after independence, the Sudanese should express dissatisfaction with the British record in education is not surprising, for they did express similar sentiments while still under British rule. However, the Sudanese, like others liberated from foreign control, found it difficult to effect desirable changes in the educational structure bequeathed by the British. The sub-grade school is still part of the system. Nor was it possible to raise to six years the period of elementary education, much as the Sudanese planners insisted on its imperative necessity. The language of instruction in secondary schools remained English until 1965 when Arabic became the language of instruction in the first class, so that in four years' time Arabic would replace English. There were in practice financial, administrative and educational considerations which hindered a speedy solution of this problem.

There was, however, a remarkable quantitative expansion of elementary and all levels of education. At the end of the fifth year after independence, the total number of pupils in state elementary (primary according to present official usage) schools rose in crude figures from 106,000 to 177,000, in intermediate schools from 9,000 to 25,000. While the number of pupils of both sexes in secondary schools doubled, the number of girls alone increased fourfold. In vocational schools the number for both sexes rose from 910 to 3,574.

More important than statistics is the new spirit that has been infused in the curriculum. The Sudan is perhaps the only state outside the Arabian peninsula that seeks to make the Koran and Islam the pivots of teaching at the elementary school. And above the elementary school the educational ladder includes a distinct religious side. There are thus intermediate and secondary religious schools leading to four years of higher religious education at the Institute of Islamic Studies, now the Islamic University, in Omdurman. (This is distinct from the study of Islamic law and history at the University of Khartoum.)

This University had in 1966–67 over three thousand students in nine faculties. In addition there were several hundred students in universities abroad, either as government scholars or receiving assistance from foreign governments and international organizations. Several hundred more Sudanese students were at al-Azhar and other Egyptian universities. Furthermore, a branch of the University of Cairo in Khartoum had in 1961–62 three colleges of arts, law and commerce with a total of 1,318 students.

It is not proposed to go into more details or to attempt to cover all aspects of educational development. But teacher training and education in the south are two subjects that deserve further notice. Since its establishment during the British era Bakht ar-Ruda came to play an important part not only in training elementary and intermediate school teachers but also in devising the syllabus and supervising its application in the schools, holding refresher courses and generally leading in educational experimentation. Apart from its different sections at the centre, Bakht ar-Ruda is now an institute of education with branches at Shendi and Dilling, Kassah and al-Fashir.

The Higher Institute of Teacher Training in Omdurman has since been responsible for the training of secondary school teachers. In 1967 the Institute became part of the University of Khartoum.

The national government took an early opportunity to assert its right to educate the children of all its citizens, in the south as in the north. Accordingly it conferred, in 1957, with the heads of missions operating in the south and a scheme was worked out whereby the government takes over elementary boys schools forthwith, and girls schools to be taken over as soon as feasible. Under this arrangement, local dialects, written in Arabic not Latin characters, were to be used as media of instruction in the first two years. But thereafter Arabic was to be introduced both as a language and as the medium of instruction. Special provision was, however, made for religious freedom, so that pupils would not be taught a religion other than their own.

To show that they are in earnest the Sudanese authorities held special courses for teachers in missionary schools in order to acquaint them with the syllabus and the textbooks. The intention of controlling all elementary education was further emphasized by a declaration that no new missionary schools would be licensed. Furthermore the government established a special training school for teachers at Meridi in the South.

The British army, which in collaboration with the Arabs in Trans-Jordan defeated the Turks in Palestine in 1918, included a French contingent. Its presence symbolized a secret Anglo-French agreement dividing greater Syria into British and French spheres of influence. In accordance with this agreement the French were almost immediately placed in charge of the administration of the north Syrian littoral including Lebanon. But they claimed under the same agreement special administrative and other rights in the interior where an Arab government based on Damascus had been recognized by the British commander-in-chief.

In the two years after the war, Britain and France agreed on the extent of their respective spheres: French in the north and British in the south. The two powers had their arrangements sanctioned by the peace conference and later legalized by mandates from the League of Nations. But while France could from the beginning establish her authority in Lebanon, it could do so in the Syrian interior only by war with the Arab government. And with the military occupation of the interior in the summer of 1920, France controlled the territories of what became later the two republics of Lebanon and Syria.

France came to these Arab countries with nearly a century of experience in governing another Arab country, Algeria. But in international law the status of Algeria differed widely from that of Lebanon and Syria. Algeria was then legally part of metropolitan France with no prospect of political independence. On the other hand, Lebanon and Syria were under the terms of the mandate potentially independent states, and France was a trustee whose task was to lead them to independence. Yet France sought to introduce such methods of administration, including educational control, as were similar in spirit to those adopted in Algeria.

LEBANON

Lebanon had been for long an important centre of European missionary activities. Those of the Catholic, and particularly French, educational missions were the most prominent. Indeed, the French claim to the political control of the country's destiny during and after the First World War was based in part on educational grounds, and the French administration set up in 1918 began with the assumption that Lebanon was its minor child. This administration was to start with military, and French army officers were appointed as advisers to native officials. In the choice of such officials the French naturally preferred members of the Catholic minority which came to wield relatively more influence than any other religious or national group, Muslim, Druze or other Christian.

In two years' time the League of Nations appointed France as the mandatory power to lead Lebanon (and Syria) to ultimate independence. Meanwhile the administration, including that of education, was placed under direct French control, and gradually this control became indirect, exercised through a native government. One of the first acts of the French was to enlarge the territory of the pre-war Turkish district of Mount Lebanon. This fact alone makes it very difficult to estimate the size of the state educational system inherited by the French.

It is safe, however, to generalize that at the primary level the state schools were outnumbered by various native private schools and foreign schools. At a higher level it is possible to be specific concerning the city of Beirut, where as the capital of a province the Turks had established a number of important institutions. These included a higher secondary school (*sultani*), a school of arts and crafts, a training college and a higher school of law. Apart from their positive function in the public system, these schools were intended to discourage at least Muslim pupils from patronizing the numerous foreign missionary schools, American, British, French and other.

The French made no immediate attempt to revive any of these schools, not even the training college. They only sanctioned the revival of the state primary schools. In 1920–21, the first year of the mandatory regime, there were 129 such schools with some 16,000 pupils, roughly one-fifth of the pupils in all schools. This is a singular abnormality which the French neglected to remedy. Nay, they made it worse by concentrating most of the effort on the French schools giving them the primacy in fact, if not in law, so much so that these schools and not the state primary schools were in reality the national system.

It must be explained that the state primary schools were almost entirely attended by Muslim pupils. For Christian pupils had the various foreign missionary schools to go to, and the French schools now were the most favoured by parents mindful of the future of their children. Inadequate financial resources was the excuse repeatedly offered not only for neglecting to develop the state primary schools but also for frequently reducing their number. In 1919 the share of education of the national budget was 200,000 Syrian Liras: in 1924 it was reduced to 124,712 with the result that the number of pupils was reduced to some eight thousand from double that figure five years earlier. This was done at a time when the French schools had in round figures thirty-five thousand pupils. (The French schools had a special budget controlled by the French High Commissioner and the money came from France.)

The state primary schools were then no more than a sop to Cerberus. They were the beginning and end of the educational ladder, since secondary and higher schools did not exist in the state system. Pupils who completed a primary school and desired to proceed to secondary education had to seek and often compete for admission to some foreign, including French, or native school, with payment of fees.

Nominally controlled by the native government but actually by a French *conseiller* and his staff, the state primary schools were for five years expected to put into practice a modern syllabus without the benefit of trained teachers. The syllabus was devised by the French Adviser. For a village school it included religious instruction, Arabic, French, arithmetic, history, geography, elementary science, manual work, drawing and singing. For a school in a large or urban centre, the syllabus included, in addition, Arabic and French literature, algebra, chemistry and hygiene.

After thus putting the cart before the horse for five years the French came round in 1925 to the right idea of opening a training college for men in Beirut with the assistance of two French teachers. In the following year a training college for women was opened also in Beirut with the assistance of two French teachers. These establishments were quite elementary, and provided a two-year course, the first for general education and the second for professional training. To aid the process of improving the teaching profession three school inspectors were appointed, directly controlled by the French Adviser.

France was accountable to the League of Nations. In 1924 its accredited representative made an altogether misleading explanation for an obvious failure. He began by saying that "the number of schools can only be increased very slowly", thus hiding the fact that the number had actually decreased. "For financial reasons", he said "it has unfortunately been impossible hitherto to do all that could be desired for public education". The financial reasons were really political, since a considerable portion of the revenue was assigned not to public education and health but to public security.

The neglect and the prevarication in explaining it continued down to the end of the French mandate. In 1933 the Norwegian member of the permanent mandates commission, a lady of high academic qualification and mature educational experience, asked the French accredited representative to explain the "very considerable cut" in expenditure on education in South Lebanon, despite unsatisfied demand for school places. His laconic reply was that in Lebanon "public education only supplemented the private". The lady did not press her point. Had she done so, she might have said that South Lebanon needed more public education particularly as it had relatively less private schools than other parts of the country.

In Lebanon, and more specially in Syria, the Muslim population accused France of following a policy of retarding the education of their children for political reasons. A question on this subject was in fact put to the French accredited representative in 1939, but he dismissed it with two words: "nationalist propaganda". But politics apart, the accusation had at least educational justifications.

Briefly the French were more interested in the diffusion of their culture and the imposition of their language on all schools than in the promotion of indigenous culture or the cultivation of the Arabic language. They brought practically all schools in the country under their direct or indirect influence. The skeleton of state primary schools was, of course, under direct French control; so were the French schools. The other schools, native and foreign, were required to teach French. None escaped one or the other of the French methods of exercising influence on their syllabus.

Among these methods employed according to circumstances were the following: (a) professional inspection by the French Educational Adviser or his staff; (b) the issue or withholding of grants-in-aid; (c) the official banning of textbooks, especially in history, unfavourable to the French mandate; (d) and above all,

the institution of French examinations from the *baccalauréat* down
to the primary school certificate, which was the most effective method
of imposing the French syllabus on all the schools that, in the interest
of the future of their pupils, offered candidates for public examination.

Nothing of importance was changed in this pattern down to the
end of the French era. The last report submitted to the League of
Nations in 1938 marks the end of this era, even though it antedates
the legal end of the mandate by five years. Unlike most of the
previous reports its tables are fuller and more informative. It gives
the number of state primary schools as 177 with 18,306 pupils
(including 5,288 girls) plus 43 students at the two training colleges.
It also gives the number of French primary schools as 344 with
31,429 pupils (including 19,323 girls). Other primary schools,
private belonging to various communities, numbered 1,180 with
76,196 pupils (including 21,095 girls).

These figures speak for themselves. It is impossible to draw a
similar comparative picture for secondary and higher education.
Both were entirely in foreign hands, chiefly French, American and
British. The apex of the French schools, and the schools teaching
through the medium of French, was the Université Saint-Joseph
established in Beirut in 1875 by the transfer from a mountain village
of a Jesuit seminary and secondary school. To these two departments a new faculty of philosophy and theology was immediately
added. A faculty of medicine was later added with assistance from
the French Government. In 1902 a faculty of Oriental Studies was
founded, and just a year before the First World War, which resulted
in the closure of the University, a school of law and a school of
engineering were opened in affiliation with the University of Lyon.

The Syrian Protestant College established in 1866 was the culmination of some forty years of American missionary endeavour. It
also began as a modest literary department, but in the following
year a medical department was added. For fifteen years the two
departments taught through the sole medium of Arabic before the
change to English took place. Gradually the two departments grew
into what became the school of arts and sciences and the school of
medicine, each with its subdivisions. But not until 1920 was the
name changed to the American University of Beirut.

Nothing comparable to the American or French institution was
developed at the top of the British schools. These were started in
1860 as philanthropic and missionary establishments. By the turn
of the century they had developed into a complete school system

from the primary to teacher training. But depending as it was on the support of voluntary societies the system began to decline and shrink. It managed, however, to maintain its lead in the valuable field of training women teachers.

It was thus a legacy of educational and cultural chaos that the French left for independent Lebanon in 1943. The comparative abundance of schools of all affiliations is deceptive. One has only to consider its dividing influence on the community to realize that it was a mixed blessing. It is fair, however, to say that the French only contributed, by commission and omission, to aggravate the educational chaos, but did not create it themselves. Foreign cultural competition, in which the French took active part and for which the sectarian communal structure of society provided a fertile soil, was a major factor. Nor was it easy for independent Lebanon to re-shape the legacy or to see clearly at once how to do so.

The programme of the first national government after independence included an important statement of educational policy and future reform: strengthening the status of the Arabic language in all schools in the country; endeavouring to make primary education universal; and introducing a unified syllabus in all secondary schools. Within five years the number of state primary schools was more than double that during the last year of the French mandate: it rose from 23,116 to 54,663. The other objectives were necessarily long-range, but the ministry of education took the preliminary steps of issuing syllabuses for primary and secondary education as well as regulations for public examinations at both levels. The ministry's explanatory note is a most significant, if indirect, assessment of the French administration by making the new aims perfectly clear:

"Until the first quarter of this century all the schools in Lebanon were private, whether native or foreign. They followed different syllabuses with a different cultural spirit and different educational methods. We should have no quarrel with a different culture or a different educational method, but we cannot tolerate conflict of aims in education. For we are a nation that must make the maximum effort to mould and unify all its elements."

Although Arabic was the language of instruction in the primary school, the simultaneous teaching of a foreign language, begun by the French, was continued after independence with one difference. Under the national system the pupil could now choose either French or English. However, the shortage of qualified teachers in English made the choice of French inevitable for many years to come. In higher primary and secondary schools the pupils were also given the choice between French and English. Whilst history and geography were to be taught through the sole medium of Arabic at these schools mathematics and science were to be taught in French or English, theoretically according to the pupil's choice.

Secondary schools were all still outside the national system, and official control over them was practically confined to the control of public examinations. These remained essentially the same as during the French mandate. After the five years of primary education, all schools, state and private, offered candidates for a public examination. Only those who passed it could proceed to higher levels in state schools. They could either follow the *course complémentaire* for four years and then sit for the *brevet* or follow secondary education at various schools for seven years and then sit for the *baccalauréat*.

The Lebanese secondary school has general, technical, agricultural and teacher training sides. In the fifth and sixth years the courses are either literary or scientific, while in the seventh they are either philosophy or mathematics. The *baccalauréat* is taken at the end of the sixth year (part I) and at the end of the seventh (part II).

Before assuming some responsibility for secondary education the state made a small but significant move in the vocational and professional fields, in post-primary or *moyen* (intermediate) education. By 1947–48 there were nine vocational, including one agricultural and five trade schools with 949 pupils. On the professional side there was one training college for both men and women, probably a successor to the two separate training schools that existed under the French.

The preponderance of the private educational institutions, native and foreign, remained. In 1947–48 the native schools alone accommodated 68,947 pupils, considerably more than the state schools. Private foreign schools of all grades accommodated 48,794. Of the native private schools forty-two were secondary and only one higher institution with 300 students. This was the Lebanese Academy which then specialized in fine arts and political science. On the other hand the foreign private institutions included twenty-eight secondary schools, one French centre for higher studies established in 1946 in affiliation with the University of Lyon and the two veteran institutions, the Université St. Joseph and the American University of Beirut.

No radical change in this distribution of the burden between state and private institutions took place except in the primary schools where in 1951–52 the number of pupils in state schools exceeded for the first time that in native private schools, but this lead was not maintained. The Lebanese state primary school was mixed, for boys and girls, unless the number of girls of school age in a given village or a quarter of a town was fifty. Then a separate school for girls becomes legally imperative. Complementary classes were added to these primary schools where the number of deserving pupils warranted such action. This was the manner in which the *moyen* stage of schooling was developed.

Before the development of state secondary schools there grew a popular demand for a state university. In answer to this demand the Lebanese ministry of education proposed the establishment of higher institutions specializing in subjects not taught at the two foreign universities. Accordingly it was decided to begin with a college or institute for the training of secondary school teachers as well as an institute of statistics. A decree issued in 1953 regularized all stages of education and officially created the Lebanese University in Beirut with these two institutes as a nucleus.

The period of training at the institute was to be three years followed by a fourth year of professional specialization. Admission was by a competitive examination. An indication of the language question is given by a stipulation that Arabic was the language of instruction "except where it is impracticable." The same stipulation applied to the departments of the state university and even to the training college for primary school teachers.

The same decree provided for the institution of free state secondary schools at which the number of places would be decided by the ministry of education at the beginning of every school year, just before eligible pupils compete for the available places by examination. Needless to say this was a very limited secondary education. For a variety of reasons, including financial and educational, the state remained unable or unwilling to depart from custom and assume more than a symbolic share of the burden of secondary education.

But the Lebanese University, having begun as a pigmy beside the two French and American giants, rapidly expanded by the addition of an institute of public administration and finance, a branch for modern languages, a college of arts, a college of law and a college of science. By 1961–62 it had a total of 2,423 students (compared with 3,055 at the American University and 6,891 at the Université St. Joseph). In that year the state maintained seventeen secondary schools with 3,454 pupils, including 707 girls.

However, the most dramatic development in higher education was the rise in 1960 of the Arab University in Beirut. Founded according to Lebanese law by a native Muslim society, which had laboured in the fields of philanthropy and education since 1936, the new institution was closely connected with the University of Alexandria for the purpose of the grant of degrees and the secondment of professors. It began with colleges for arts, law, commerce and civil engineering. In 1966–67 the total number of students in the four colleges was 9,501 (including 1,159 girls). It is commonly assumed, because of the academic connection with Alexandria, that the Egyptian government bears a large part of the financial burden.

Although still dependent upon private and foreign enterprise, Lebanon allocates a fair share of the national income for education. In 1967, out of a national budget of some 689 million liras, 97 millions were allocated for education, or 14.1 per cent.

In January 1968 a decree redefined the steps in the Lebanese educational ladder: five years of primary education from the age of five followed by four years of "middle school" for orientation and finally three years of diversified secondary education. In practice, however, the majority of secondary school pupils still prepare for the academic *baccalauréat*. The number of those who train to be teachers is necessarily small, and the number of those who enter the field of technical education is even smaller. In 1966–67 the numbers were 1,861 and 1,482 respectively.

Another recent development is the revision of the curricula which remained virtually the same as the French had left them a quarter of a century earlier. As officially explained the aim of the revision was to render the subjects taught less abstract and to lay more stress on science and general "lebanonization". Undertaken by special committees the revision was thorough and comprehensive. The new curricula were due to be introduced in 1969.

Finally mention may be made, among the private institutions, of the Beirut College for Women which owes its origin to American missionary effort. Run on American college lines it offers courses leading to a first degree in arts and science, and caters for some four hundred students.

In Lebanon, as in Jordan, the United Nations Agency maintains schools for the children of the Palestine refugees. These schools are noted in Appendix 1.

In the first years of the mandate the French treated Syria more as a conquered territory than as a League of Nations trust. Next to having imposed the mandate by force of arms the French antagonized the Syrians by their educational policy. They inherited from the Turks and the Arab government a state educational system with primary, secondary, teacher training and high schools. They placed this system, or such of it that had survived the war, under direct French control through a *conseiller*. The private schools, Muslim, native Christian and foreign missionary, were as in Lebanon brought under indirect control through inspection, grants-in-aid and public examinations.

From the beginning the French forced the teaching of their language, as the *première langue vivante*, in all state schools from the first year in the primary school upwards, and gave the curricula throughout a French bias. But as in Lebanon they failed to revive the two training colleges that existed under the Turks in Aleppo and Damascus. Of the four high schools established by the Turks in the latter city only two were revived, the schools of medicine and law, which in 1924 had 141 and 111 students respectively. These were the only educational institutions dispensing higher education. The Arab Academy was a semi-official body established during the short-lived Arab administration and devoted its activities to the advancement of Arabic learning.

During the first year of the mandatory regime state primary schools had a total of some seventeen-thousand pupils. Secondary classes had yet to be formed; in 1922–23 such classes had a total of 250 pupils (including 38 girls). There was no evidence of a determined effort to expand the educational system in a manner and at a scale commensurate with the needs of society. Indeed the French record in Syria is even poorer than theirs in Lebanon. Each of the annual reports which France had to submit to the League of Nations contained a section on education. These sections are best read in conjunction with the remarks thereon by the members of the permanent mandates commission and the replies by the French accredited representative.

These replies followed on the whole the familiar lines of all unimaginative and neglectful administrations: "financial reasons" hindered the opening of more schools, "a teaching staff could not be formed in a single day", and grants-in-aid to native private schools were withheld on political not educational grounds since "vilification" of the mandate was enough cause to debar a school from financial assistance from the state funds. When in 1936 the Swedish member remarked that "the schools were insufficient in number, the classes overcrowded and too many applications for admission had to be refused", the French representative ascribed it all to inadequate financial provision. In the polite atmosphere of the meeting none asked why such provision was inadequate, or why in an Arab Muslim country French secondary schools contained nearly four times as many pupils as state secondary schools.

The truth is that the French were more interested in the advancement of their schools than the native Syrian schools, whether belonging to the state or to private organizations. This tendency was pushed to such absurd lengths as to attempt to frenchify the pupils. Count Sforza, the Italian nobleman and statesman, visited Syria in 1935 and he saw some fifty dark-skinned and black haired young Arab boys stammering together: "*nos ancêtres les Gaulois étaient blonds!...*"

On the whole the French record in education was poor. They failed to provide in state primary schools places for at least those prospective pupils who sought admission. They allowed state secondary schools to be dwarfed by the French schools. Their attitude to teacher training and higher education was not much different. Apart from one training school at Aleppo and another at Damascus, there were only "sections" or classes for training teachers at one or two lycées. The annual report for 1938 states that the teaching staff *n'a pas encore toute la valeur professionnelle désirable*. If this was true who except the French trustees was to blame?

Higher education never developed beyond the two schools of medicine and law in Damascus, inherited by the French from their Arab and Turkish predecessors. From the beginning these two schools were placed under French control, so that in the end they were conducted virtually as French schools. The school of medicine, for example, admitted only students with French qualifications and had French teachers who taught through the medium of French. This circumstance was the subject of a question by the Norwegian member of the permanent mandates commission: was it not discriminating against those who did not attend French schools? There was no direct answer to this question, but the French representative asserted that the appointment of French teachers at this school was intended to raise its standard.

Small though the number of students at the schools of medicine and law remained during the period of the mandate (371 in 1939–40), the French annual reports speak against the creation of "an intellectual proletariat". Syria had in fact too few, not too many, of them coming out of the two schools in question. The truth is that the French for political reasons, distrusted all Syrian intellectuals, even those who had been educated in French institutions.

One of the subjects of dispute between the Syrian intellectuals and their French rulers was education. In particular the Syrians took exception to thorough-going methods of controlling the curriculum and textbooks. Questions of principle were decided by the *conseiller*. As in Lebanon the primary school syllabus was devised under his direction. The secondary school syllabus was practically French, if only because of the *baccalauréat* examination at the end.

Closely connected with the control of the curriculum was the method of adopting or banning textbooks in schools. Mention has been made of the French practice of withholding grants from private schools where the mandate was allegedly vilified. More schools were affected by another measure. Textbooks in history unacceptable to the French were banned from state schools. In 1937 a member of the permanent mandates commission asked the French representative to explain. The answer was evasive; in general, said the French official, textbooks in use showed enough regard to "the prevailing opinion" in Syria.

It is difficult to square this assertion with the facts. From the beginning the French sought to make their own opinion prevail. Thus, with their blessing, the Jesuit father Henri Lammens, then professor at the Université St. Joseph, wrote a controversial textbook entitled *La Syrie*: *précis historique* to which Syrian intellectuals, including the president of the Arab Academy, took strong objection as anti-Arab and anti-Islamic. Their protest averted its use in state schools, but it was used all the same in French schools and the schools that were obliged to take French examinations.

Such was the educational situation on the eve of the Second World War. Owing to the collapse of France, and the political and military situation in Syria during the war, there was little change in the last years of the French mandate. The French record may therefore be closed with their last report to the League of Nations in 1938. In that year the number of French schools of all grades was 85 with 19,843 pupils, and the number of state schools of all grades 472 with 58,867 pupils. Most of the latter were primary schools in villages.

Once more the figures may be left to tell their story. But it is important to point out that in 1938 the state budget showed a surplus of over three million Syrian liras. Why was not a fraction of it spent on providing places at state schools for at least those who applied for admission?

France never had another chance to redeem her reputation as a civilized trustee. Despite misfortunes in the war she clung to her position in Syria (and Lebanon) to the bitter end. And before leaving these two countries sought to perpetuate by treaty special privileges including safeguards for the French schools and the position of the French language. It is ironic that the cause of the last conflict with Syria was educational. For in December 1944 the Syrian chamber of deputies passed an education law with a clause which though educationally sound was regarded offensive by the French. This clause stipulated that "no foreign language will be taught in state primary schools". This was, of course, an indirect way of discontinuing the questionable practice of teaching French to Arab children from the age of six simultaneously with Arabic. The French challenged the law and the last bloody clash with the Syrians took place before the French "civilizing mission" came formally to an end in April 1946.

The government of independent Syria paid special attention to education, and carried out spectacular expansion of the service. Within three years admission to state primary schools was more than doubled. Expenditure on national education was now second only to that on national defence in the state budget. After performing distinguished services in Iraq, a leading Arab educational expert moved to Syria to direct its new educational policy.

However, financial allocation and expert advice cannot alone create a new educational system overnight. It was easy enough, with these benefits, to open new primary schools. But long-range planning was required in order to develop secondary education, teacher training and higher education. To do so time was just as important an element as money. Hence it was not possible to achieve as spectacular an advance as in primary education. Thus in 1947–48 there were 13,380 pupils (including 3,460 girls) in state secondary schools, 365 students (including 231 girls) in four training colleges, and 2,221 students (including 284 girls) receiving higher education. Only 955 pupils (including 132 girls) were then receiving some vocational training, mainly commercial and crafts.

In educational legislation and curriculum Syria adopted the broad principles already tested in Iraq. The French system was modified

to a greater extent than in Lebanon. Under the law, primary education was free and potentially compulsory for boys and girls from the
age of six. But as elsewhere in the Arab states at the time, the
ministry of education decided where and when to apply compulsion
according to its resources. The primary school syllabus was a uniform
one, but adapted for boys and girls as well as for rural and urban
areas.

Provision for the teaching of foreign languages was made after the
primary stage. In the intermediate or lower secondary and in the
higher secondary classes, the foreign language was now either
English or French. The syllabus as a whole was inspired by liberal
principles. Thus if we consider the sensitive subject of history we
find a directive insisting that it must be tackled in secondary schools
with a humane attitude of mind.

The aim of the study of history was to understand the human past.
Within this frame the history of the Arab nation should occupy a
prominent place, with special attention at the same time to the past
and modern history of other nations. The part played by the Arabs
in the history of civilization must be emphasized, but not at the
expense of covering up their failures, since the history of no nation
is without its ups and downs.

In dealing with private schools, native and foreign, the Syrian
educational authorities also followed the general Arab policy. All
schools were subject to state supervision, and foreign schools were
required to teach Arabic, Arab history and geography of the Arab
world according to the official syllabus. Their certificates were not
recognized unless they submitted their pupils to public examinations
conducted by the ministry of education for all schools.

The traditional Muslim schools were either ancient foundations
or private establishments. The former were attached to the ministry
of religious foundations, and the latter remained unattached as
private schools. To this category also belonged the schools maintained by the various native Christian communities. Those of the
private schools that satisfied certain conditions were eligible to receive grants-in-aid from the state. In 1947–48 native private schools,
Christian and Muslim, had 40,122 pupils, and foreign schools
6,561 (including 4,763 in ten French schools).

Higher education had a modest beginning under the Turks and the
short-lived Arab government in the two schools of medicine and
law at Damascus. Under French control the two schools were,
with the Arab Academy and the state museum, constituted by decree
as the Syrian University. It remained in an embryonic state till the

French withdrawal in 1946. In that year the national government established four new colleges of arts, science, engineering and education. Together with the two old schools of medicine and law they formed the new Syrian University at Damascus. Other colleges were added later on, notably one for Islamic law and another for commerce. The college for engineering was located in Aleppo, and formed a nucleus of a new university in that city. Two other colleges of agriculture and law were added in the 1960s.

Expansion of the Syrian educational system was paradoxically advanced not retarded by frequent change of form of government. For Syria successive rulers of whatever political persuasion vied with one another in the development of the social services, chief among which was education. In the 1950 constitution education is declared as a right of the citizen, and primary education, according to a uniform syllabus, as free and compulsory in state schools with a view to making it universal in ten years time.

Viewed superficially as a whole, the Syrian educational system was, despite a centralized control and a written syllabus, fairly diversified to suit the different stages of social development. There was thus provision for beduin schools, the teaching of the elements of agriculture in rural areas and technical and professional subjects in urban centres. In addition there were a few secondary schools specializing in Muslim religious instruction. But relatively few pupils at this stage benefited from these specialized services, and the great majority followed what might, for want of a better term, be called "academic education".

From the late 1950s some change began to take place. A cultural agreement was signed between Syria, Egypt and Jordan in 1957, and in the following year a political union between the first two states was effected. The Syrian educational ladder was now like the Egyptian, formed of six years of primary school followed by three years intermediate and another three years secondary education.

Henceforth comprehensive planning was adopted for state services, particularly education. According to an official report issued by the ministry of planning in 1963 places were provided at state primary schools for *all* children of school age for the first time in Syria's history. While state schools continued to expand, private schools of all types began to contract. Even the traditional Muslim schools became fewer in number, partly because of the increased facilities for free schooling at state schools.

Secondary education was re-organized and its abstract content somewhat mellowed. In 1962–63 five million Syrian liras were allocated for the development of the University of Damascus, and another five million for the expansion of the newer University of Aleppo.

The expansion of primary and secondary education naturally increased the pressure on the two universities. To relieve this pressure, and more specially to provide higher technical and vocational education not available at the universities, three institutes were opened. These were for agriculture, commerce and fine arts. The period of training at each of the three institutes was four years after obtaining the secondary school certificate. The aim was to train agronomists, accountants, surveyors and architects.

Another concomitant of the expansion was the attention paid to the training of teachers. Of the nine colleges for men and women, the highest was the college of education at the University of Damascus. Founded in 1946 for the training of secondary school teachers, it gradually changed its character to a post-graduate college, granting a diploma in education after one year and providing instruction and supervision for higher degrees. The number of students taking these degrees remains, however, very small. The total number of students at the college as a whole, about 300, is indeed very small and inadequate to meet the chronic shortage of teachers.

More and more students were sent for training abroad. In 1960–61 those sent to European countries and the United States numbered 363 students. Because of previous commitment to French, and because of a desire not to depend too much upon France, more students were sent to French-speaking universities in Belgium and Switzerland and less to France. Contrary to journalistic reports the number of students sent to Russia and the countries in East Europe remained relatively small. It was in 1962 smaller than the number of students sent to the United States. There were then 101 students in the Soviet Union and 151 in Britain. The greatest number of Syrian students went, however, to Egyptian universities which in the same year received a total of 1,057.

One of the recent developments is the creation in 1966 of a new ministry for higher education with the task of co-ordinating the work of existing and future institutions, and contributing towards the success of the state policy of economic and social development. The autonomous institutions brought by law within the ministry's purview include the two universities of Damascus and Aleppo, the Arab Academy, the Higher Council for the Advancement of Art, Literature and Social Science, the Higher Council of Science and the Higher Technical Institute.

This Institute was established in 1963 with the assistance of Unesco in order to meet the growing need for mechanical and electrical engineers as well as instructors in the technical schools and trainers of skilled workers. Admission to the Institute is after the end of secondary education and the length of the course is five years, the first being for general orientation. Successful students are granted the B.Sc. in the branch of their specialization. In 1967–68 the Institute had about 600 students.

The creation of the new ministry was soon reflected in a large increase in the budgets of the two universities, the planning of new colleges for science, and the despatch of junior professors to foreign universities for further training. The new ministry paid special attention to the college of agriculture in the University of Aleppo whose buildings and installations were "designed to be the most up-to-date in the Middle East." Attached to the college is a sizeable farm with buildings for lectures and experiments, dairy products and enclosures for poultry and cattle breeding.

While the University of Aleppo is still growing, that of Damascus is continuously improving its facilities. An important development is the preparation for the grant of higher degrees which had hitherto been restricted to medicine. There are now facilities for students to proceed to higher degrees in education and law.

New lecture halls and laboratories are rapidly rising, both at Damascus and Aleppo universities. In addition new buildings are erected for the accommodation of men and women students in the *cité universitaire*, against payment of modest rent. While tuition fees are still charged, there is ample provision for remission or grants to deserving students, whether on grounds of academic merit or poverty, or both.

Aleppo University has now colleges of engineering, agriculture, law, commerce, languages, medicine, and science. The colleges of law and commerce were discontinued in 1967 and replaced by a single college for economic science, which includes a department of commerce. In 1966–67 the total number of students at Aleppo University was 4,337 including 724 females.

LIBYA

Most of the Arab lands in Asia and Africa fell at one time or another in their modern history under British or French control. Apart from a Spanish zone in Morocco, Libya, was the only exception. In 1911 Italy invaded the country when it was part of the Ottoman Empire.

From the beginning of the last decade of the nineteenth century modern state schools were established in the territory as elsewhere in the Empire side by side with the traditional Muslim schools. In the year of the Italian invasion there were seventeen primary schools in urban centres with some 1,500 pupils, including 175 girls. No figures are available for other schools of which an authoritative source lists one secondary school, one school of arts and crafts, one training college and one military school. The traditional Muslim schools were much more numerous in urban areas, villages, oases and tribal settlements. The most organized of these belonged to the Sanusi order, and the highest of the Sanusi schools was at Jaghabub where Arabic and Islamic studies were pursued.

For a long time Italian control remained confined to the coast, and extended inland only as far as the range of the guns of their warships. Indeed, Italy had to fight the beduins, and particularly those led by the Sanusi, intermittently for nearly a quarter of a century before establishing a firm control.

In the meantime Italian policy was taking shape. In broad outlines, it was similar to that of France in Algeria: colonization and italianization. The entire coast from Egypt to Tunisia, including the main urban centres and most of the settled population, was ultimately incorporated in metropolitan Italy as the *quarta sponda*. The first education law was published in 1914 but the war intervened and Italian control shrunk to the few coastal towns. After the war the Italian minister for the colonies declared that primary education should be so conducted as to achieve "a progressive and efficient penetration of the native minds by the Italian language and spirit".

Before the Italian conquest there were a few Italian private schools that were mainly patronized by Italian, Maltese and Jewish children. After the conquest and increased Italian settlement in the country, a dual school system was developed. The Italian schools for Italian and foreign children, with a handful of Arab pupils, were conducted as the schools in metropolitan Italy. The state primary schools for

Arab children were bilingual, taught Arabic and religion by native teachers and Italian and the other subjects by Italian teachers.

None of the Ottoman state schools survived the change of rulers, and many of the traditional Muslim schools, particularly those belonging to the Sanusi order, disappeared as a result of the Italian repressive measures. Nor did the state primary schools meet this deficiency or their pupils represent more than about eight per cent of the school-age population. In the first year of the occupation under one hundred pupils were admitted to school. On the eve of the First World War it was about 1,200; on the eve of the Second roughly 9,500. (These are official Italian figures).

Secondary education for native Arab children did not exist. Very few Arab children were allowed into the Italian secondary schools. Thus after more than a quarter of a century of Italian rule the secondary school population of 1,789 pupils included only 102 Arab pupils.

Female education was likewise neglected. Only four schools with 650 pupils are mentioned in 1931. Their teachers were sixteen Italians and eight Arabs. Nor was there any provision for the training of teachers, male or female. They were recruited by examination in Arabic, arithmetic and general knowledge from among those who offered themselves. The guide in professional questions was the Italian teacher who never saw the need for textbooks suitable to local conditions. One of the books favoured by the authorities included such slogans as "O God! help me to be a good Italian" and "O God help me to love Italy, my second fatherland".

Higher education under these conditions was impossible. Students who lived nearer to Egypt sought it at al-Azhar and those nearer to Tunisia at Zaitunah. But the product of these institutions, particularly the former, were feared by the Italians on political grounds. However, the Italians needed some religious judges, junior Muslim officials and teachers. Political perhaps more than these practical considerations led to the establishment in Tripoli in 1936 of a high school for Islamic and Arabic studies. It never had more than thirty students carefully selected for future government employment. So were the handful of the sons of "collaborators" who were sent to Italy for further training.

Taken as a whole the Italian achievements in education were very poor indeed. Here is a statistical picture at the outbreak of the war in 1939. According to official reports there were then 6,754 Arab pupils in state primary schools and schools subsidized by the state, only 134 in secondary schools and 636 in vocational schools. The corresponding number of Italian pupils was 5,297 primary, 1,417 secondary and 383 vocational.

Vocational training was discriminatory in that Italians were trained for skilled and managerial posts while the Arabs were trained as semi-skilled artisans working under the former. Such private Muslim schools that survived the Italian measures accommodated in the same year four hundred pupils more than the total in state schools.

For more than three years from the autumn of 1940 Libya was a major theatre of war. Many school buildings were destroyed or damaged and all schools were closed for the duration. After the end of the fighting the country was occupied largely by British and partly by French forces. Under military administration some educational reconstruction was started in the British and French zones with personnel and apparatus from Egypt and Algeria respectively.

Uncertainty about the political future played havoc with educational planning. Thus not a single educational system but virtually three systems were allowed to develop. The major and more settled part of the country from Egypt to Tunisia was under British control, but educationally two rather different systems were maintained. In the east the schools were modelled according to the Egyptian system and the teaching of English was introduced from the fifth year. In the west concessions were made to the Italian community to the extent of making Italian the second foreign language in secondary schools. In the largely deserted zone under French control the school system was modelled on that of the French schools in Algeria. In administration, teachers, curricula and textbooks there was little to unite the three zones, except that in the two under British control the divorce was not very pronounced.

It was feared that this educational division was a prelude to a political one. But the United Nations recognized the right of Libya to independence which was proclaimed in December 1951 with a Sanusi as the first king of a federal Libya. While the federal state embraced the three zones it inherited three educational systems each controlled by a separate education department. It is important to note the humble beginning of education in a country that needed educated men to carry on the work of government. In 1950–51 there were only some 32,000 pupils in primary schools and 300 in post-primary classes in a country with a population of just over one million. There were as yet no secondary schools.

Huge in territory, small in population and poor in resources the country's optimism was reflected in its constitution which guaranteed free and compulsory primary education to all children in urban, rural and desert areas. Before the discovery of oil which converted a poor country into a rich one there was little cause for optimism. The small foreign aid and United Nations technical assistance were not enough. Yet by the use of hired buildings, recruitment of teachers in other Arab countries and the resort to teaching by shifts the number of pupils in primary schools was quadrupled in ten years.

The problems remained, however, colossal: unity between the three regions was to start with artificial, and disparity of the levels of social advance between their respective populations was matched by another between the urban, rural and nomadic population of each region. In the purely educational field there was a great shortage of teachers, buildings and equipment. Egyptian curricula and textbooks were readily adopted, and the authorities were eager to employ trained personnel from other countries. Yet despite these and other difficulties a small if sometimes only symbolic advance was made.

Regionalism in education was somewhat overcome by the adoption of a uniform school syllabus. This was an important step for the primary school, the base of the educational pyramid that was being built. The new syllabus differed little from those of other Arab countries. Its emphasis on elements of agriculture in the fifth and sixth years of the primary school was a belated but welcome step. It was, however, like similar steps taken in other Arab systems, little related to the needs of society in that it failed to produce better farmers.

Another significant step was the increase in the number of girls in state schools, though with the natural increase in population and the tendency of pupils to leave school prematurely this step did not always result in an improvement in the ratio of female literates. In the year of independence some five thousand girls were admitted to primary schools and about fifty to secondary and teacher training classes. The figures for boys were then thirty-three thousand and 167 respectively.

The main obstacle to more progress in female education was the shortage of teachers. It was not simply an educational or even financial problem; it was also and perhaps more so a social one. In a conservative society custom was against unmarried women living away from their parental homes, whether for the purpose of attending a training college or taking up teaching in a small town or village. There is evidence that these scruples are now being overcome. Thus the more conservative Cyrenaica has now boarding sections for girls, similar to those first introduced in Tripolitania. Parents are taking into consideration the addition to the family income from teaching and the social prestige a literate female brings.

Nor were the special needs of the nomads, a large proportion of the total population, overlooked. From the beginning boarding facilities were provided at selected primary schools for the children of nomads in the area. This experiment was first introduced in the eastern provinces, the traditional home of the Sanusi. A few boarding sections were developed as boarding schools, primary and secondary including technical.

As was to be expected under a Sanusi monarch, religion figured very prominently in the curriculum of the state schools, and no pupil could be promoted to a higher class without passing the prescribed examination in religious knowledge. Then special attention was paid to the traditional schools, both those affiliated to the Sanusi order and those conducted by private teachers. Teachers at the former were paid by the state and grants-in-aid were given to the latter. To both categories of schools books and material were supplied free.

The site of the oldest Sanusi *Zawiyah* at Baida was made the headquarters of a new Institute of Religious Studies, established in 1952. Two qualified teachers were delegated by al-Azhar to launch the Institute which was designed, to start with, as a boarding preparatory school training pupils with a view to completing their education at al-Azhar University in Cairo.

As finally developed the Libyan educational ladder is six years of primary school, theoretically compulsory, followed by three years of preparatory and another three years of secondary education. Post-primary education is largely general (or "academic") with parallel technical and vocational sides. But while the general continues to grow the technical continues either to stagnate or even decline as regards the number of pupils. This is the more unfortunate in view of the country's accession to considerable wealth and its need for skilled personnel in several new development projects.

Measured by this need the number of personnel trained at school is very small indeed. Thus in 1961–62 only 44 pupils completed technical training at preparatory and secondary levels, and 49 completed agricultural training at the same levels. What is more unfortunate is that a large proportion of these small numbers found employment not in industry or agriculture but in clerical and administrative sections of government departments. No doubt a deep-rooted tradition despising manual work and respecting office employment does obviously take a long time to mellow and longer to overcome.

Secondary education, teacher training and higher education had to develop against the background described above. The first secondary schools were modest. In the year of independence fewer than one thousand pupils were in secondary classes, including some fifty in an agricultural and eighty in a technical school. Five years later the total was 2,806 and five years later still 3,891 (including 583 girls).

Teacher training was an uphill struggle. It was a regional responsibility, each of the three regions training its own teachers. But in 1963 the federal system was replaced by a more central authority and thus the ministry of education became responsible for teacher training throughout the land.

At the very beginning recruitment of native unqualified teachers followed roughly the Italian method of public examination in Arabic, arithmetic and general knowledge. Qualified teachers were, however, recruited from other Arab countries, notably Egypt. The training of native teachers began at a centre in Tripoli in 1940 and four years later at another in Benghazi. The two centres were quite elementary; they admitted pupils with a minimum of five years of primary schooling, and the course of training lasted four years.

Gradually the requirements for admission became stiffer, for men more than for women and the number of centres was ultimately increased to ten. While a girl could still be admitted after finishing a primary school, a boy was now required to have had eight years of primary and preparatory education.

The above training centres were for primary school teachers. Secondary school teachers came mostly from other countries. In 1965, and with the help of Unesco, a higher training college was established in Tripoli with a first intake of 91 students, all holders of the secondary school certificate. This institution was intended primarily for the training of teachers of science, mathematics and foreign languages in secondary schools. This function was also performed by the new University of Libya, of which the higher training college now formed a part.

Some of the new universities in the Arab world were established more as a result of popular pressure than of normal educational development. The state University of Libya is one of these; it opened in 1956 when the number of pupils in state secondary schools was only 2,806, and when almost all its teachers had to be recruited from Arab and other countries. The University began with a faculty of arts and education based at Benghazi with 34 students. In 1958 a faculty of commerce was added also at Benghazi with the same number of students. In the same year a faculty of science was started at Tripoli, the centre of the country's major industries, with 32 students. In 1962 a faculty of law was added at Benghazi with 72 students. By 1965–66 the four faculties had a total of 1,440 students about one-fifth of them in the faculty of science. There was a demand for graduate teachers as well as for civil servants. The oil industry and foreign enterprise increased the demand for science graduates. And yet the growth of the University was not spectacular, despite the fact that tuition was free and every student, irrespective of academic performance, received books free of charge and also a monetary allowance.

Associated with the University, and now regarded as part of it, are two institutions: the Higher Training College mentioned above and the College of Advanced Technology established in Tripoli in 1961. In 1965–66 the two institutions had 90 and 217 students respectively. The college of Technology like the Training College owes its origin to the initiative of the Libyan government and the assistance of Unesco. In 1966–67 a college of agriculture was added with only 43 students. In that year the total number of students in all colleges was 2,254 including 213 girls.

The most obvious anomaly about the Libyan University at this juncture is that it has only fourteen Libyans, none of whom is a professor, among an academic staff of 277. This total includes 29 British and 150 Egyptians. The rest are from other Arab countries, Pakistan, India, America and Germany.

The King remained, however, faithful to his upbringing. In 1961 he reconstituted by decree the Institute of Religious Studies as Muhammad Ibn Ali as-Sanusi University to serve as the apex of the traditional Muslim schools. In 1968 there were 109 of these all over the land with a total of 5,264 pupils. As well as supervising these schools for boys and girls the Sanusi University conducts separate schools for girls which emphasize domestic science. In the same year these schools had a total of 1,020 pupils. At higher level the University had three colleges of Islamic studies, Islamic law and Arabic. In 1968 the three colleges had 287 students. In addition there are other schools and institutes attached to the University with over a thousand students, including a large number from other Muslim countries.

For still higher specialization in Islamic and Arabic studies students continued to go to al-Azhar in Cairo. More students from Libya went to other Egyptian universities and institutions. Indeed

Egypt continued to attract more than half the students who went for higher education abroad. The rest went to Britain, the United States Italy and other countries. It is noteworthy that the majority followed courses in medicine, engineering, science, agriculture and commerce and rather a minority pursued arts studies.

During the first decade of independence, and before the sudden wealth from oil revenue, Libya received generous aid, both material and technical, for educational development from the United Nations, the United States, Britain and Egypt. In recent years American and British assistance diminished almost to a vanishing point. But the United Nations' various agencies are still active, and Egypt continues to be a major source of supply of teachers and to provide a considerable number of scholarships in its universities for students coming from Libya.

It must not be forgotten that an Italian community still lives in the country, mostly in Tripolitania. This community has its schools; so has a small native Jewish community. In addition there are a few foreign schools. According to a law passed in 1958 all these schools must be licensed and inspected by state authorities. They must teach Arabic and the history and geography of Libya according to the official syllabus. Those schools not following the official syllabus in other subjects must not teach anything calculated to create disharmony between the different inhabitants of the country. Those attended by native Muslim or Christian pupils must teach them their own religion and no other.

Finally the huge oil revenue made it possible for the government of Libya not only to dispense with foreign aid but also to embark on large-scale development schemes. Libya began her independent existence with a very large deficit, and its national income was then about £L 12 million. Five years after the discovery of oil at the end of 1958 this figure was increased twenty-five times. It continued to increase with the rise in oil production.

A five years plan of economic and social development was theoretically completed in 1968. It began with a budget of £L 170 million, but the projects envisaged at the beginning were so expanded that by the final year another £L 65 million was spent. Education ranked fourth after agriculture, communications and public works in the plan. Briefly stated the educational part of the plan made provision for an all round expansion from the primary stage to the university.

It is still too early to assess the results. The operation of the plan is officially taken to be a rehearsal for a new twenty-years plan which will carry development up to 1988. This is frankly stated in the draft of the new plan: "Since the five years plan is the first of its kind in our modern history, we must regard it as an experiment in the light of which we shall better plan progress in the extended plan".

TUNISIA

When in 1881 France imposed a protectorate over Tunisia the country had been ruled by a semi-independent Turkish dynasty that owed allegiance as vassals to the Ottoman sultan. As elsewhere in the Ottoman Empire and Arab and Muslim lands, Tunisia had then its own traditional school system with its apex at the Zaitunah Mosque College in the city of Tunis. There were a few Catholic mission schools principally for the education of the children of foreign residents, chiefly Italian and French.

In 1875 the Sadiqi College was established in the city of Tunis. Its curriculum combined the traditional Arabic and Islamic subjects with modern languages and science. The aim was to train the cadre for modernized state services. On the eve of the French protectorate this modern college had about two hundred students, while Zaitunah, together with the primary *Kuttab* schools below it, had some twenty-thousand.

The French assumed full control of state education. In 1885 the Direction de l'Instruction Publique was established with a French head and French senior and executive assistants. The traditional school system was regarded as private though subject to French legislation and supervision. Gradually two other types of state schools were developed: the French schools that functioned with the same syllabus and teachers as in metropolitan France, and the Franco-Arab schools that functioned on the same lines except that Arabic and religion were taught by native teachers. The first type of school was for the education of the children of the French *colon* and of other European residents and led directly to the French lycée. The second type was intended for Tunisian Muslim children and led to the Sadiqi College as re-organized by the French.

At the turn of the century there was a total of 78 state primary schools, one French lycée and the Sadiqi College. In only 19 of the state schools were Tunisian children educated together with those of the Europeans. The single lycée had then 338 French pupils, 160 Tunisian Jews and only 10 Tunisian Muslims.

Apart from these glaring inadequacies perhaps the most deplorable aspect of the system was the neglect of native female education. Thus there were only nine girls in state schools in 1889, and thirty years later only 1,433 girls.

Naturally thoughtful Tunisians were dissatisfied with the French educational policy, particularly the initial neglect of the traditional schools and the imposition of a French imprint upon the state schools. They perceived the cultural and even religious dangers of educating young Arab Muslim children on almost exclusively French lines. They noted, on the practical level, that those educated at French schools were favoured by the French authorities for employment over those educated at Zaitunah. They took positive action to redress the balance in favour of native tradition and education. In 1896 the Khalduniyyah School was established with a view to giving Zaitunah graduates additional training on modern lines. Some ten years later a movement to reform the *Kuttabs* was launched; it continued to grow during the entire period of the protectorate, with remarkable success.

In French official reports the reformed schools are called *écoles Coraniques*, while in loose terminology the traditional *Kuttabs* are called mosque schools because many of them were conducted in mosques or in the precincts. The presence of three or rather four types of schools naturally produced three or four different types of citizens. That was the real danger in such an educational policy. In pursuance of such policy the French withheld material support from the majority of the "national" schools, gave limited grants to the koranic schools, exercised great economy in the opening and development of the Franco-Arab schools, and lavished money, staff, equipment and advice on the purely French schools.

General dissatisfaction with the French Protectorate assumed an organized form in the first decade of this century. It became a force to reckon with after the First World War when first autonomy and then independence became the objective of the Tunisian national movement. Education was one of the main grievances of the nationalists against the French. There was a genuine fear not only of frenchifying the future generations but also of weakening their Islamic faith and tradition. The future first president of the Tunisian Republic, himself educated in the Franco-Arab schools and later in France, claimed that it was the Eucharistic Congress held in Carthage, with its aura of Christian education in a Muslim country, that precipitated him into a career of agitation for national independence.

It must be acknowledged that in the three decades after the First World War there was a great advance in public education in Tunisia under French control. But it is evident from even a casual perusal of the reports that the advance was much greater in the French sector than in the native sector. This trend continued down to the outbreak of the Second World War during which Tunisia became a major theatre of military operations with great disruption and destruction of its educational establishments.

During the last decade of the protectorate education was influenced by the changed position of France after the Second World War coupled with the universal movement for the emancipation of colonial territories. While there was little change in the established pattern of the educational system it was considerably expanded for the benefit of larger proportion of Tunisian children, and it was symbolically liberalized with regard to the teaching of Arabic and Islamic history.

The state primary school, French as well as Franco-Arab, was now for eight years from the age of six. The Koranic schools, the reformed traditional schools, were brought more under official control and required to teach French. They were given grants-in-aid, usually in the form of teachers' salaries.

Secondary education was an exact copy of the French lycée and college, with Tunisian sections in a number of such institutions where the Arabic language and the Islamic religion and history were taught. In 1950 there were two lycées and ten colleges.

Technical education was likewise French and principally for French or French-speaking pupils. Tunisian pupils had a shorter course of three years, after the primary school, consisting of some training in arts and crafts.

The training of native teachers—for French teachers had French training—was restricted to one school for men and another for women. Their courses of study corresponded to whether they were intended for the French or the Franco-Arabic schools. In the school for the training of men teachers, however, there was a class for the graduates of Zaitunah who were exempt from learning French.

Apart from Zaitunah higher education was also French or French-inspired. Thus there was a higher school of commerce, another for fine arts and a third for music, all for French or French-speaking students. In 1945, however, there was established in the city of Tunis L'Institut des Hautes Etudes originally designed for Tunisian students. It had sections for (a) law, economics and administration, (b) science with preparatory studies for medicine and engineering, (c) sociology and history, (d) Arabic studies, (e) archaeology. Five years after its establishment this Institute of Higher Studies had only 176 Tunisian Muslim students among 702. The number of French students was 413, of Tunisian Jews 82 and of Italians 28.

For a population which in 1950 was estimated at three million Muslims, the schools of all grades, state and private, accommodated only 116,261, including 19,053 girls, of their children. Only some eighty-thousand pupils attended state schools. Many more were in private schools or at Zaitunah and its dependent schools. Excluding Zaitunah, the number of Muslim pupils in post-primary schools was then as follows: 5,023 (technical), 3,245 (secondary) and 604 (higher). The two training schools for men and women had 198 and 181 students respectively.

In 1950 a gesture was made by the French authorities to meet the criticism of teaching Arab children through the medium of French even at the primary level. It was then decided to begin the teaching of the subject of arithmetic gradually through the medium of Arabic. This small change was greatly accelerated by political developments. France was forced to recognize first the autonomy and finally the complete independence of Tunisia in 1956. One of the first acts of independent Tunisia was to make Arabic the language of instruction instead of French and to revise the syllabus so that a greater share was given to the teaching of Arab and Islamic history.

An important step was taken towards the unification of the schools. All the Koranic schools, reformed or otherwise, were incorporated in the national system. So also all the primary and secondary schools associated with Zaitunah, with the result that this institution became solely concerned with higher religious education. But the same measure could not be so easily applied to the French schools. These were protected under the Franco-Tunisian protocol of 1955 recognizing the autonomy of Tunisia.

As to the arabicizing of the educational system it was one thing to proclaim the intention by decree, but quite another to put it into practice. The French language was so entrenched that the process of replacing it must be very slow, if only because of insufficient supply of teachers and textbooks. Thus independent Tunisia could do no more than extend, subject to these and other limitations, the symbolic beginning of teaching arithmetic through the medium of Arabic, and then extend the measure further to the subjects of history and geography, but not so easily or quickly to science.

Five years after independence the number of pupils in primary schools was more than doubled. Particularly noteworthy is the increase in the number of girls which rose from 73,948 to 182,165. But it is necessary to say that this great rise in the number of all primary school pupils was largely due to the device of half-day attendance during the first few years so that teachers and classrooms could be utilized for double the number of pupils. Even as a temporary measure this device is of course educationally indefensible because it cuts by half the time for primary education. For the first two years the lesson periods were reduced from thirty to fifteen, and for the next four years from thirty to twenty-five per week.

While the ministry (secretariat of state) of education is responsible for the educational system from the primary school to the university there are other government departments in control of important educational services. Thus vocational education is controlled by the secretariat of state for youth, and agriculture and health education by the secretariats concerned.

The Tunisian educational ladder is six years of primary school followed for the less gifted pupil by three years intermediate with general industrial and commercial sides. The term intermediate is, however, misleading because for this type of pupil that is the end of education and the beginning of employment.

The secondary school proper is also for six years of which the first is for orientation, after which pupils follow either general or technical or economic sides. In the last three secondary years there are nine divisions of subjects between arts and science including teacher training.

In 1960 the University of Tunis was established by decree, and in 1961–62 instruction was started in colleges for arts and science, law, politics and economics. Zaitunah became a constituent college for Islamic law and religious studies. A teachers' higher training school also formed a constituent college of the University. There were also associated institutes and schools.

The French schools, from the primary level to that of the Institut des Hautes Etudes, were under the Franco-Tunisian agreement of 1955 outside the national system and controlled by a French cultural mission. The agreement made some concession to Tunisian nationalism in that the French schools were ready to adapt their syllabus for those of their pupils who desired to follow the Tunisian system with a view to taking a Tunisian rather than French certificate, and in that the mission was required to hand over gradually certain schools or sections thereof. The exodus of the French settlers altered the situation and greatly reduced the number of pupils in the remaining French schools.

However, the problem of tunisification or arabicization in education remained. The national system depended to a great extent upon the services of French teachers. The change from French to Arabic as the medium of instruction depended upon, among other factors, the progress in the training of native teachers and the preparation of suitable textbooks in Arabic and on the arabicization of secondary and higher education.

To start with it was not possible to give Arabic more than equality with French in the primary school timetable. In secondary schools the share of Arabic was only one-third of the time. Under this arrangement French teachers were indispensable. Thus when the University was opened in 1961–62 it was necessary to engage 64 French with the 59 Tunisian teachers.

An important element in the present and future educational plans in Tunisia is the educational background of the country's foremost leaders. From the president to the minister of education the men were the product not of the traditional system and Zaitunah but of the French or the Franco-Arab schools. Under a declared policy of arabicization these men seem to be for secularism and bilingualism in education. If this is so French seems to be destined to continue to play an important part in Tunisian state education as a powerful rival to Arabic.

In 1958 a ten-year plan was drawn up which aimed, *inter alia*, at universal primary schooling by 1969. Apart from the need for large-scale school building (or renting, as it is, other buildings) this aim required for its achievement the tripling of the number of teachers. With the language difficulty, the inadequate equipment and the insufficiency or absence of suitable textbooks the plan implied, if carried out, a tacit sacrifice of quality to quantity, excellence to speed.

In 1962 it was officially claimed that 90 per cent of the boys and 50 per cent of the girls of school age were actually at school. To achieve these results the country devoted 24.47 per cent of its budget for education. Tunisia was obviously for speed. Ten years after independence the country began to claim the highest percentage of literacy in the Arab world. This is a claim which cannot be accepted without examination of the facts on which it is based. From the description of the Tunisian primary school given above it is clear that it was manifestly ill-equipped for the achievement of permanent literacy.

Official reports are notorious for their brevity and vagueness. The figures are generally given with little or no background material. We are told that in 1960–61 there were 777,686 primary pupils, 27,851 intermediate pupils, 70,756 secondary pupils and 6,830 students in the University. In addition there were only 1,918 pupils following vocational training and 5,505 training to be teachers in all grades of schools. In considering these figures we must not lose sight of the crippling handicaps including the half-day primary school and the strains of bi-lingualism.

In 1968, while this account of education in Tunisia was first written, it was very difficult to obtain certain information. For example the Tunisian Embassy in London was three times asked to substantiate the claim of highest literacy rate, but would neither itself reply nor obtain a reply from Tunis. Moreover, the Embassy and certain academic authorities in Tunis were evasive concerning the suggestion of a visit for personal observation. There was at the time some serious unrest among university students and young intellectuals which led to trials and the sentencing of scores to long terms of imprisonment.

ALGERIA

When in 1830 France occupied Algeria the rulers of the country had for a long time acknowledged the suzerainty of the Ottoman sultan. But if a remote sovereign could do nothing to prevent France from imposing her rule over Algeria, the Algerians themselves offered heroic resistance for almost four decades. France suppressed the resistance with great severity, and at the same time confiscated millions of hectares of common and tribal land which was given to French colonists. Then Algeria was by law incorporated with metropolitan France, and consequently greater numbers of colonists settled in the country.

Even according to French sources there was a flourishing school system at the time of the occupation. Thus a military report dated 1834 states, probably with reference only to those areas then under French control but still not without some exaggeration, that all villages had schools and that all Arabs knew how to read and write. There were also higher schools of the *madrasah* type in the three principal cities.

The declaration of the country as part of metropolitan France subject to French law, and the mass settlement of French *colons*, led inevitably to an educational policy that was bound to be inimical to the traditional Islamic education and the Arabic language. But rather than abolish the native traditional school system the French proceeded in practice to undermine and supplant it. The schools established for the children of the French settlers were a replica of those in metropolitan France. The schools established for Algerian children were called Franco-Musulman, even though they followed French curricula and used French as the sole medium of instruction. Arabic was taught in such schools only as a foreign language. The first of this type of school was established in the city of Algiers in 1836.

As if this cultural assault was not enough the French authorities, on the whole anti-clerical in France itself, encouraged *la société missionaire d'Afrique* and also *les soeurs missionaires de Notre Dame d'Afrique* to establish schools for boys and girls respectively which aimed not merely at the diffusion of the French language and culture but also the Catholic faith.

Gradually the French schools, official and missionary, began to monopolize such education as was favoured by the authorities. The

165

native schools began, for lack of official material and moral support if not also for active obstruction, to dwindle. This was calamitous because the French schools of all affiliations catered for only a small fraction of the children of school age. At the time of the French occupation the population of Algeria was estimated at three million. According to French official figures only 194 Algerian Muslim children were in French schools in the first years of the occupation. Fifty years later their number was just over three thousand. At the outbreak of the First World War it was 48,570. The proportion of girls in this total was about one in fifty.

Here it is necessary to emphasize the discrimination maintained throughout the period of French control, against the native Muslim children and the favour shown to the children of the *colons*. In theory both categories of children were entitled to equality as French citizens. In practice, however, it was otherwise. Comparatively more schools were opened in areas inhabited by French settlers. Native children could not be admitted to such schools until all French applicants had been accepted. Furthermore, a great many of the schools established in purely Algerian districts were poorly equipped and staffed, and some of them opened for half a day only. Such schools seldom had upper primary, still less secondary classes.

The French system began in 1833 with one school in the city of Algiers which had twenty pupils. Fifteen years later the school became a lycée. Some forty years after the French occupation state primary schools accommodated some 57,000 pupils of whom only some 1,500 were Algerian Muslims, and state secondary schools some two-thousand pupils of whom only 226 were Algerian Muslims. Thus the vast majority of pupils were French together with a small proportion of native Jewish children whose parents became naturalized French citizens *en masse*.

Very little change in this educational set-up was made till the end of the Second World War. The French system steadily gained ground as the native system became depressed. The development of higher education was primarily for the benefit of French or French-speaking students. In addition to the lycée in the city of Algiers, schools of medicine, law, science and letters were gradually established. In 1909 these schools were made faculties and constituted as the University of Algiers. It had then a total of 1,605 students, the vast majority French.

By 1930, or a century after the occupation, the number of French settlers had reached one million. They were strongly opposed to equality in educational opportunity with the *indigènes* whom they preferred to keep ignorant and a permanent source of cheap labour for French enterprise.

Algerian resentment took various forms. In the educational field there was a positive reaction led by the ulema from the early 1930s. They established, without French approval and indeed in the teeth of official opposition, private "Koranic" schools which, using mosques and similar buildings taught in addition to the Koran and the Arabic language all modern subjects through the sole medium of Arabic. French was studiously excluded. The spirit of these schools is represented by their general motto: "Islam is my religion; Arabic is my language; Algeria is my fatherland".

This was, of course, a far cry from the French slogan of *L'Algérie sera faite à l'image même de la France, cet enfant de la France*. Hence the Koranic schools were subjected to all sorts of restrictions, including the trial of their teachers on charges of teaching—teaching, that is, what was not in accordance with the Franco-Muslim curriculum.

By 1950, and despite French opposition, the Koranic schools had a total of 16,286 pupils (including 5,696 girls). As an apex to the system there was the Ben Badis Institute in Qasantina (Constantine) which in that year had 720 students. Graduates of this Institute proceeded to higher Arabic and Islamic education at Zaitunah in Tunis or at al-Azhar in Cairo.

After a century of French occupation and the prosecution of an educational policy which sought to frenchify the Algerian Muslim and assimilate him in the French system it was abundantly clear that the attempt had failed. Even some of the products of the French schools became disenchanted. In the words of one of them: "the French educated Algerian may be attracted by the rationalism, logic and poetry of France, but he can find spiritual solace only in the principles of Islam".

The French have undoubtedly underestimated the force of Islamic and Arabic culture. They also underestimated the latent strength of the religious fraternities like the Tijaniyyah which played a great role in upholding the ulema's drive for Arabic and Islamic education. Indeed, there was a religious fervour in the programme and fight of the *Front de Libération Nationale*. The national movement, first for autonomy and finally for independence, had as one of its aims the restoration of the Arabic and Islamic character of education.

But not until the upsurge of national sentiment after the Second World War, and not until she was chastened by the humiliation of defeat and Nazi occupation, did France respond to the loud Algerian protests against the inadequacies, in quantity and quality, of education. In 1944, a plan was drawn up for "the schooling of Algerian Muslims". Three years later an organic law recognized Arabic as "one of the languages of the French union" and accordingly provided for its teaching throughout the educational ladder.

When the 1944 plan was drawn up the number of children of school age was estimated at 1,250,000, but only 110,000 of these were actually at school. The task, representing over a century of colossal neglect was clearly formidable. It is not surprising that the execution of the plan barely managed to keep pace with the natural increase in the population so that the number of admissions to school remained in practice infinitesimal. Matters were made worse by the fact that the plan made woefully inadequate provision for the training and supply of teachers.

That this plan needed radical improvement is clear from a few figures relative to the school years 1950–51. State primary schools had then 188,678 Algerian pupils (population eight million) and 111,403 European pupils (population one million). In the primary schools there were 6,227 teachers of whom only 509 were Algerians.

Such glaring disparity is noticeable at every step up the educational ladder. Its top, the University of Algiers, had then some five-thousand students of whom only 213 were Algerians. And when in the last days of French rule two new universities, each called *centre universitaire*, were created in 1961 at Oran and Constantine with faculties of letters, science, law and medicine, the vast majority of the students were French and the number of Algerians was negligible. At Oran it was no more than one-tenth of the total.

It was estimated that, when the Algerian revolt broke out in 1954, only one-tenth of the Algerian Muslim children of school age were actually at primary school. The number of pupils at secondary schools was seven-thousand and the number of those receiving higher education was 685.

At the height of the revolt in 1958 the French authorities recognized that the provision of the 1944 plan of educational expansion was inadequate. Under a new plan admissions to primary schools were considerably increased, but it was too late. The great disruption of seven years of war and the French repressive measures almost wrecked the school system particularly in rural areas.

France recognized the independence of Algeria in July 1962. Education was in a sad state indeed. It was rendered much worse by the destruction of schools caused by the French elements that opposed the Algerian independence by violent means. The task of the Algerian Republic was not merely educational reorientation but also reconstruction. She received foreign aid from Russia, China, France and the Arab states, the latter in the important matter of the loan of teachers.

Under the agreement with France, the French schools were protected under a French cultural mission. In 1967 these schools comprised 57 primary, with 9,137 pupils (of whom only 4,046 were Algerians) and six colleges with 526 pupils (including 327 Algerians) and six lycées with 5,903 pupils (including 2,518 Algerians). The primary schools were in the process of passing under Algerian control.

From the beginning the Algerian Republic was anxious to assert the Arabic and Islamic content of its tradition. In education the aim was to make Arabic the language of instruction and to revive Arabic and Islamic values in educational establishments. In practice, however, the educational pace could not be forced. Arabicization had to begin modestly with the first year of the primary school. Even here its application was limited by the acute shortage of teachers. Thus in 1963 the primary schools had 16,546 teachers who taught through the medium of French and only 3,452 through Arabic.

By 1967 it was possible to extend the process of arabicization to the second primary year. The number of teachers in all primary schools was then some thirty-thousand of whom thirteen-thousand taught in Arabic and seventeen-thousand in French.

The problem was tackled by the opening of six Arabic training colleges and the addition of Arabic training classes at a number of lycées; the sending of bursaries abroad including 1,079 students to Arab countries; the institution of an Algerian *baccalauréat* under which an examination in Arabic composition was obligatory; the recruitment of teachers in other Arab countries notably Egypt which sent almost immediately one-thousand graduates of al-Azhar, and Syria where an equal number of teachers was recruited from the top secondary class and given special training before joining the Algerian teaching force; and finally the continued employment of French teachers.

Despite all difficulties a vigorous drive was made to increase admission to school. Nearly a quarter of the national budget was devoted to education. Hired buildings, even garages, were used for classrooms. Monitors had sometimes to do for teachers. Under such circumstances lowering of standards was inevitable. Yet the efforts bore at least numerical fruit. In 1967 there were 1,409,391 pupils in primary schools of whom only nine-thousand in French schools. In that year fifty-thousand applications for school places had to be rejected. In a country where the natural increase of the population is 2.5 per cent it is very difficult, considering the initial disadvantages, to achieve universal education.

Apart from the French schools, private education is under the control of the ministry for religious foundations. This comprises the strictly Koranic schools as well as newly established Islamic institutes attached to lycées which teach through the medium of Arabic. There is a project for establishing a faculty of theology at the University of Algiers to serve as the apex of this school system. In 1967 a maximum of thirty-thousand Algerian pupils were at schools classified as private.

Except as indicated above state secondary education is still run as under the French. Like the primary school the secondary school is also for six years, the first three cover general, technical and agricultural sides. In 1967 the total number of pupils in secondary schools was 134,697 (including 38,659 girls). The technical and agricultural sides are the weakest in the system and are still far below the needs of a developing country.

The University of Algiers still follows, on the whole, the French system. Perhaps the most significant change is that now Algerian students (about 20 per cent of whom are girls) form the majority, while foreigners (French and others) are no more than one-fifth of a gross total of some ten-thousand. Another significant change is in the content and spirit of a number of "sensitive" subjects such as Arabic literature and Islamic history, philosophy and law. These are now taught in Arabic. Other courses are being adapted to the needs of students coming from other African and developing countries. The Ecole Normale Supérieure which forms a college in the University had in 1967 only 234 students (including 52 girls).

There is no doubt that since independence Algerian education made giant strides forward. The inadequacies and the short-comings should right themselves in time. But the most difficult problem remains that of arabicization—its rate of progress has been relatively slow and the time and degree of its successful completion is very hard to forecast.

MOROCCO

Alone among the North African states to escape falling under Ottoman suzerainty, Morocco could not in the end escape foreign domination. In 1912 France imposed a protectorate over the country except for a small area in the north which was reserved for a Spanish protectorate.

The Muslim schools that were then in existence were all of the traditional type. The koranic or *msid* (a corruption of *masjid*, mosque) school, very much like the *Kuttab* elsewhere, was the typical primary school, followed by the *Madrasah* as the next and final step in the educational ladder. Distinguished among this higher type of school was Qarawiyyin at Fez. It was established over a century before al-Azhar in Cairo though it remained regional and never acquired the universal character of the other institution. Needless to add that in curriculum, teachers and methods these schools differed very little from their type elsewhere in the Arab world.

With their experience in Algeria and Tunisia as a guide for an educational policy in Morocco, the French had no difficulty in applying their well-tried methods. They left the traditional Muslim schools alone, and introduced two types of French schools and patronized two others.

The strictly French schools, which were a replica of those in France, were attended almost entirely by the children of French residents. The Franco-Musulman schools, intended for Moroccan children, were also open to French children in those localities where their numbers did not justify the opening of separate schools. The Franco-Musulman schools followed much the same syllabus as the strictly French schools, taught through the medium of French right from the first primary class, and taught Arabic only as a foreign language.

There was also a French attempt at what might be called a cultural cleavage between the two sections of the Muslim population. A minority of the population spoke Berber and had some peculiar customs. The French sought by educational and administrative means to encourage and emphasize these linguistic and social variants, thus promoting national division instead of cohesion.

A smaller minority than the Berber were the native Jews who settled in the country after their expulsion from Spain. Before the French protectorate the Alliance Israélite Universelle based on Paris

171

had established French schools for this Jewish community, and under the protectorate these schools received grants from the state treasury. More schools known as the Franco-Israélite were established as state schools under the protectorate.

The first decade of the protectorate produced little or no educational advance. If anything it resulted in the eclipse of the traditional Muslim schools which declined in number and prestige. The internal disorders at the beginning of the protectorate were soon followed by the outbreak of the First World War from which France emerged victorious but very exhausted. At the outbreak of the war all state schools had no more than 794 Moroccan Muslim pupils.

The first French Resident General, with a reputation for conciliation, was the author of a most damaging principle for the education of at least the Berbers under French rule:

"It is not our business to teach Arabic to populations which have hitherto got on without it. Arabic is a factor in Islamization because it is acquired with the Koran. It is our interest to make the Berbers develop outside the framework of Islam".

In pursuance of this policy between the two wars the Franco-Musulman system, though serving a relatively insignificant proportion of the school-age population, was diversified by the French to include the so-called Franco-Berber schools, schools for the children of native notables, schools in towns and in rural and beduin areas. Some of these schools had industrial or agricultural classes. All were of a symbolic character, and far below the needs of the country.

On the whole Spain followed a policy in its zone similar to that adopted by France in Algeria, Tunisia and Morocco: grant of land to settlers, encouragement of Catholic missionaries, promotion of the language and culture of the protecting power, and neglect of Arabic and Islamic schools. Less efficient than the French, the Spaniards were not less damaging to native education. Without going into details the damage may be seen in two figures for school attendance. In 1948 the state schools had 9,300 Spanish pupils taught according to the Spanish system through the medium of their mother tongue, and only 4,200 Moroccan pupils also taught through the medium Spanish, while Arabic was taught to them as a foreign language. In the whole zone there was only one and incomplete secondary school.

Under both the French and Spanish systems there was a woeful neglect of female education in the state system. Want of detailed statistics precludes precise judgement, but such education as the daughters of wealthy families had received was either at the hands of private teachers or in establishments conducted by Catholic nuns.

It was after the First World War, and under the spell of the liberal ideas it generated, that protests against French (and Spanish) educational and other policies began to take shape. The national rising in the Spanish zone, which spread to the French zone in 1925, assumed the character of war and proved in fact the first signal for movements of national and cultural liberation. In the cultural field the movement was significantly started in 1927 by students from Algeria, Tunisia and Morocco in France who launched the Association of Muslim Students.

Back in the three countries under French control the movement for educational reform adopted a positive and almost identical method, the only one possible under foreign laws and administrative restrictions. They opened Koranic schools designed both to counteract the French (and Spanish) schools which treated Arabic as a foreign language, and also to reform the traditional schools by teaching all the modern subjects through the medium of Arabic.

In Morocco the task was undertaken by the *Istiqlal* (Independence) party with active encouragement from the palace. A small beginning had already been made in 1925. The movement gained momentum in the next decade, stagnated during the Second World War and was resumed with increased vigour after it. In 1948 the *Istiqlal* had more than a hundred schools with a total attendance greater than at all the state schools. It undertook the writing of textbooks in Arabic, the training of teachers in that language and the sending of bursaries to other Arab countries as well as Europe.

This creditable effort coincided with a radical change in the objectives of the national movement. In 1944 it sought negotiations with France to end the protectorate and restore to the country its complete independence. The cry was for political as well as cultural independence. France had in the end to recognize the independence of Morocco and Spain followed suit in 1956.

The agreement with France provided for a cultural mission to supervise the education of French and French-speaking children. The agreement also provided for the retention of some of the French schools as well as for the maintenance in the state primary and secondary schools of "European sections". In the first school year after independence the European sections had 46,700 primary and 16,691 secondary pupils. The first figure included 6,700 and the second an unknown number of Moroccan Muslim pupils who presumably had started in the French schools and their parents were unwilling to subject them to an abrupt change.

Abrupt change was in any case impracticable. The Moroccan ministry of education had three broad aims, all qualified with the adjective "gradual"—unification of the school systems, arabicization of the syllabus and language of instruction, and admission of all pupils of school age. In 1958 the Speech from the Throne put these objectives succinctly when it stressed the need for "an education that was Moroccan in thought, Arabic in language and Islamic in spirit".

But the difficulties were formidable, and the most formidable of these was perhaps the shortage of teachers trained to teach in Arabic, especially in secondary schools where almost all the teachers were French (or Spanish) or Moroccans trained to teach in French or Spanish. Another serious difficulty was the paucity of suitable textbooks in Arabic which delayed the introduction of a new syllabus to replace the essentially French one. Nor must the difficulties of accommodation and equipment be forgotten.

The Moroccan authorities were determined to tackle these problems without much regard for speed. They tried to make a cautious advance on all fronts at the same time. New classrooms were built and the local authorities in rural and beduin areas contributed generously towards building new schools. Ignoring the risks of employing unqualified and untrained teachers and of the resort to half-day shifts, the authorities were able to more than double the annual admission to the first primary class.

Under these circumstances, figures can be deceptive, particularly that the manner of their reporting is not uniform from year to year. In November 1958 the total number of pupils in primary, secondary and technical classes was 658,000, exclusive of those in classes controlled by the French mission. In November 1962 the total number rose to 1,160,216 pupils exclusive of those in French schools.

The educational ladder consisted at first of five years primary (raised to six in 1963). This led to an orientation year (*année d'observation*) counted as the first secondary year. This was followed by two years of intermediate (*moyen*) diversified into general, industrial, commercial, agricultural and female sections leading to certificates and employment for those not destined to continue their schooling. The upper secondary cycle is three years with literary, scientific, mathematical and economic sides leading to the *baccalauréat*, as well as industrial, commercial and agricultural sides leading to a diploma.

From the beginning the interrelated problems of arabicization and the supply of teachers engaged the attention of the authorities.

In 1960 an institute for the scientific study of arabicization was established in Rabat with the task of producing textbooks and the coining, in consultation with the Arab academies in Damascus and Cairo, of scientific terms.

The application of arabicization in schools began in the first and second primary classes. It was for these classes that textbooks in Arabic were prepared covering such subjects as arithmetic and geography. In the upper primary and secondary classes it was still as late as 1962 impracticable to arabicize on a large scale, if only because there were then 7,767 indispensable French teachers. The magnitude of the problem would appear from the fact that out of some eighty-thousand Moroccan pupils in secondary classes only twelve-thousand were then taught in Arabic.

However, confidence that things will right themselves in the course of time led in 1957 to the establishment by decree of the University of Rabat (later known as Muhammad V University) with faculties of letters, law and science based on three French establishments: Institut de Hautes Etudes Marocaines, Centre d'Etudes Juridiques, Centre d'Etudes Supérieures Scientifiques. To these was added immediately a faculty of Islamic law and then a faculty of medicine. Needless to say that, to start with, this national university could not function without the French language and French professors. In 1962 the University had branches at Fez and Casablanca. The total enrolment was over four-thousand students including some 600 girls, three-quarters of whom were in the faculties of letters and law, the first to be arabicized. There was also added to the University a higher training college with an initial enrolment of 300 students. Other additions, with insignificant enrolments, included a school of administration, a school of agriculture and, with Unesco's assistance, an institute of sociology.

Qarawiyyin in Fez remained as hitherto an institution devoted to Arabic and Islamic studies. It now received the dignified name of a university, and branches belonging to it were opened at Tetuan and Marrakesh, with a total number of some 450 students in 1962. In that year Morocco had some fifteen hundred students receiving training in the West (two-thirds in France) in addition to those similarly placed in Arab universities.

A campaign for the training of primary school teachers gradually reduced the dependence on French or French-speaking teachers. The number of training colleges was doubled. In 1961 they produced 1,100 teachers, but the need was for 3,536. Another plan provided refresher courses for untrained teachers and several thousands were thus covered. Then large numbers of teachers were, and still are being, recruited in other Arab countries.

By 1967 significant developments had taken place. Firstly, expenditure on education was tripled within ten years after independence and constituted twenty-one per cent of the national budget. Secondly, the cultural agreement with France was revised so that Arabic had to be taught to Moroccan pupils in French schools whose number had in any case greatly diminished. Under the same agreement a gradual transfer of French schools to national control was continued.

Thirdly, arabicization made slow and sometimes faltering progress. All teaching in the first primary year was now in Arabic, and arithmetic and observation lessons (*leçon de choses*) were taught also in Arabic throughout the primary school. However, a provision made in a ministerial circular in 1967 for the arabicization of the first (orientation) secondary class for pupils entering it from primary schools where Arabic was the medium of instruction had to be abandoned. The necessity was described by the *Istiqlal* party as a educational "catastrophe".

The situation in sections of the primary and secondary school, where teaching was conducted through Arabic and French, led to some confusion and even lowering of standards as may be deduced from the following official Moroccan statement made to the XXXth session of the International Confernce on Public Education:

"In the majority of cases, classes in the second-year intermediate course are taught by two teachers: one, monolingual, teaches in Arabic for fifteen hours each week, devoting most of this time to the Arabic language, while in a parallel class the other teacher, who is bilingual, gives instruction in French for ten hours a week and in Arabic for five hours a week, the lessons being devoted to arithmetic and observation.

"Nevertheless, and contrary to the arrangements made for the courses mentioned above, when it was decided to teach arithmetic in Arabic, simultaneous classes according to the old timetable were arranged for those pupils who were obliged to spend two years in the same class. Thus, pupils who have been taught arithmetic in French for several years can finish their primary studies in the same way and present themselves a second time for the secondary school entrance examination without being handicapped by a change of language in arithmetic. The timetable for these special classes remains fifteen hours teaching in Arabic and fifteen hours teaching in French".

Finally mention must be made of two development plans which were applied consecutively from 1959 to 1967. The aims were broadly to increase admission to school without a specific mention of universal or compulsory application; to unify the school systems into a national one; to arabicize the syllabus and the language of instruction; to train the necessary cadre for the administration with a view to its morocconization.

In the words of the authors of the second plan the need was for "a reform of primary education with a view to strengthening it and basing it on a better system of civic and religious instruction", as well as for "the training of secondary school teachers and the improvement of agricultural education".

Lack of precise information at the time of writing precludes accurate assessments of the actual results achieved. There is no doubt that a remarkable quantitative advance has been achieved, but the same cannot be said without reservation regarding the qualitative achievement particularly in arabicization. As in other former French dependencies there is a danger that foreign cultural domination may linger too long under the guise of the liberal notion of bilingualism. The use of a foreign language for educational purposes is one thing but its toleration as a rival to the native tongue is quite another.

SAUDI ARABIA

The Kingdom of Saudi Arabia was formed in 1926 mainly of two dissimilar territories at different stages of social development: the former Ottoman province of Hijaz to the east of the Red Sea with the two holy cities of Mecca and Medina, and the independent principality of Najd which stretched eastward across the Peninsula to the shores of the Persian Gulf and acknowledged the nominal suzerainty of the Ottoman sultan before the First World War.

The rulers of the kingdom belong to the puritanical "Wahhabi" movement which enjoins strict observance of Islam according to the Koran and prophetic tradition. The ruler is both king and imam whose function is to apply the principles of Islamic law throughout the land. Following the Arab Revolt against the Ottoman Turks in 1916 Hijaz became an independent kingdom until its conquest by the Wahhabis and its amalgamation with Najd to form the present Saudi kingdom.

Such educational facilities as existed in the two parts of the kingdom before the First World War were a reflection of their respective administrative, religious and social conditions. Hijaz had, in addition to the traditional Muslim schools and the specialized religious circles in the mosques of the two holy cities, a rudimentary school system introduced by the Turks during the last decades of their rule. According to official figures published in 1915 the province of Hijaz had 78 state primary schools. The independent Arab kingdom of Hijaz inherited those of them that survived the war. They were, with the help of Syrian administrators, converted into Arab schools. A few new schools were also established as a nucleus of a modern system.

There were also a few private schools sponsored by individual benefactors such as al-Falah schools, or supported by the voluntary contributions of resident Muslim communities such as the Indians and Indonesians. These private and community schools, if only because they were in the cradle of Islam, stressed religion. Some of them added to their curriculum such modern subjects as history, geography and mathematics.

In Najd the educational facilities were governed by a more tribal and nomadic life as well as by the missionary fervour of the Wahhabi preachers who monopolized teaching. It is difficult to label their activities as an organized system before the introduction from the first decade of this century of a state plan to settle the beduins on the land and to educate them in the Wahhabi tenets with a view to making them farmers and soldiers. An agricultural settlement of this kind was formed of carefully selected members from different tribes. They were given land, seeds and implements, and provided with the material for building dwelling houses, a school and a mosque.

When Hijaz and Najd became united under the Saudi monarchy, the new state was very poor in resources. Its main source of income was from the annual pilgrimage to Mecca and Medina by Muslims from all over the world. Yet an attempt was made to create a new school system soon after the conquest of Hijaz, and the task was entrusted to a new directorate of education. It was at once apparent that the apparatus of government required trained personnel which the traditional schools alone could not supply.

The move was opposed by the Wahhabi ulema who questioned both the need for and the legitimacy of a modification of the traditional curriculum. They did all they could to obstruct the first cautious moves towards modernization. Partly to allay the fears of the ulema and partly because of the high cost of new schools, the movement remained on a very limited scale. However, the pressing need for trained civil servants, teachers and school inspectors prompted the directorate of education to send selected pupils for study in the neighbouring Arab countries, particularly Egypt.

Since this was for some time the only source of supply of trained personnel a special preparatory school was established in Mecca in 1937 staffed with Egyptian teachers who prepared pupils for the equivalent of the Egyptian secondary school certificate. In this way pupils could follow courses in the various colleges of Cairo and Alexandria universities. In 1950 there were 192 Saudi students undergoing training at the different colleges of the two universities.

A great change came in the 1930s with the discovery of oil and the new wealth its production brought to a poor country. Checked during the Second World War, it increased by leaps and bounds after it. Around 1926 the average state annual income was about £5 million. It rose during the next twenty-five years to £100 million, and has continued to rise ever since.

Factual and statistical material on education before the 1950s is scanty and fragmentary. Within its limited resources and freedom of action the directorate of education made some significant moves. One of these was the establishment in Jiddah in 1948 of an industrial school with Egyptian staff and curriculum. The school taught the

12

usual theoretical and practical subjects appropriate to a trade school as well as English.

Another move was the establishment in Mecca in 1949 of a college of Islamic Law for the training of judges and preachers. The third important step was the opening also in Mecca in 1952 of a teachers' college on Egyptian lines and staffed largely by Egyptians.

At the end of its twenty-five years' life the directorate bequeathed to the ministry of education the above institutions as well as 326 primary schools with 43,734 pupils, all boys.

In 1953 the directorate was replaced by the ministry. By then the economic and social consequences of the discovery of oil were apparent. They constituted a challenge to the traditional school system in that demands were made upon it which it was not geared to meet.

It is important to bear in mind that, unlike other Arab countries, Saudi Arabia was not seeking to relegate the traditional system to an inferior position, or even to isolate its subject matter to a fixed position in a combined syllabus. There is, on the contrary, a studied effort to cast the new system in an Islamic mould.

It is also important to bear in mind that nearly three-quarters of a population, variously estimated from five to eight million, are nomads and that the urban population in the western region was more advanced, at least materially, than the eastern. The oil industry upset this balance. Concentrated as it is in the eastern region, it revolutionized the economic and social life, not only of the settled but also of the nomad population. The greatly improved communications by road, rail and air, the sudden availability of modern amenities and even luxuries, the ever increasing demand for labour, and the immense opportunities for learning technical skills, have all created new tastes for educational facilities of more direct bearing on life in the modern world.

Yet the traditional system with its spirit, methods and even curriculum survived in the modern Saudi system as nowhere else in the Arab world. There is a virtually complete system run on religious lines under the control of the Mufti. There are schools devoted to memorizing the Koran, and there is a religious besides the "secular" trend in secondary education. There are post-primary institutions wholly concerned with Islamic and Arabic disciplines. The college for Islamic law in Mecca inherited by the ministry from the directorate was modernized in that, in addition to law and Arabic, it now teaches history and Islamic civilization. As if to counterbalance this modest "secular" trend there was established in Riyad in 1953 under the Mufti's control another college of Islamic law devoted to the subject.

The effort to preserve tradition in the new educational system may be seen not only in the recognition of trends but also in placing strictly religious education under the Mufti, not the ministry. Another evidence of the care taken not to challenge tradition is that when in 1960 it was decided to introduce new state schools for girls the matter had first to be considered by a committee under the chairmanship of the Mufti and the control of these schools was vested in a special directorate under his supervision. (Hitherto such formal education of girls as existed was sponsored by resident Muslim communities in Hijaz).

Even with such division of responsibilities the new ministry of education had to face immense difficulties. The most immediate was the lack of trained personnel. Here again assistance was sought from other Arab countries, particularly Egypt. At the same time Saudis trained in Egypt or elsewhere were given accelerated promotion to senior posts in a centralized and hierarchical system. The initial budget of the ministry was twenty million Saudi Riyals; it increased ten-fold in ten years.

It is now necessary to consider briefly the syllabus that was formulated in the 1960s, because it is almost unique in the special stress it lays on the Koran and Islam. The syllabus is written and with detailed instructions for the three stages of the educational ladder: six years primary, three years intermediate and three years secondary.

Roughly two-thirds of the periods are reserved for religion and Arabic, and one third for arithmetic, history, geography, elements of science, hygiene, drawing and physical education. While memory still plays a great part there is a welcome stress on exposition by the teacher and understanding by the pupil. It is of course difficult to discover how this works out in practice.

Take as an illustration the syllabus for the sixth primary year. The pupils are expected to learn to read aloud, with correct chanting, certain suras of the Koran and to learn by heart certain others. For "theology" three Wahhabi tracts by the founder of the movement are prescribed; for "jurisprudence" some twenty items on prayer, fasting, alms-giving and pilgrimage; and for prophetic tradition twenty authentic texts on steadfastness in belief, good morals and general conduct.

Next to the Koran, Arabic is given the pride of place, not simply as the national language and the key to the national heritage, but, in the words of the official syllabus, because "God has chosen it as the vehicle through which He revealed His message to mankind in the Koran".

Because of its novelty in Saudi Arabia, female education too deserves to be considered briefly. A generation ago, state schools for girls were unthinkable; now they are a vigorous reality. The economic and social change alluded to earlier was bound to lead to this development sooner or later. But to use official terminology again, the female education introduced was of a type "compatible with the country's religious position and Arab tradition".

To start with, the directorate of girls' education opened with a relatively small budget seven primary schools with 5,204 pupils, and initiated a programme for training some twenty teachers. These schools were, like other state schools, free. But in deference to the suscepti-bilities of parents pupils are given free transport to and from school. The syllabus is an adaptation of that for boys' schools to allow for the teaching of domestic science, dressmaking, embroidery and cookery.

Enrolment was so encouraging that within three years the number of schools rose to sixty, the number of pupils to 19,139, and the number of teachers under training to 261. In 1962 the schools had about 900 teachers and headteachers; roughly one-sixth of them Saudis; the rest Palestinians, Jordanians and Egyptians in this order. Some Saudi teachers were Egyptian trained, mostly daughters of Saudis resident in Egypt.

There is a programme for constructing new school buildings; meanwhile reconditioned dwelling houses are used. Even with these provisions the demand for more schools is growing. Therefore the state recognized that private girls' schools shoulder some of the responsibility and generous subsidies were allocated to them from public funds. In 1967 the number of state schools for girls was 201 with 67,953 pupils.

Parallel to the schools for boys, and following a modified form of the syllabus for these schools, girls' schools soon began to develop intermediate and secondary classes. The government authorized the ministry of education to regard the primary, intermediate and secon-dary school certificate for girls as equal to those for boys.

Although the general syllabus is overloaded with Islamic and Arabic subjects, the religious authorities still prefer to conduct a parallel system of their own. Thus the Mufti has exclusive control over religious institutes which in 1965 numbered twenty-seven. They teach for five years, after the primary school, Islamic and

Arabic subjects, and serve as recruiting ground for the faculties of Islamic law and Arabic language under the same control. The faculties in turn train religious functionaries. In 1965 their graduates numbered 314.

Post-primary modern education has at the intermediate level, in addition to the general side, industrial, commercial, agricultural and teacher training sides. Only the general leads to the secondary where, after the first orientation year, there are two years of either literary or scientific sides. No foreign language is provided for in the primary school syllabus. English is provided for in the intermediate and secondary classes, and a syllabus for French is printed with the general syllabus for secondary classes.

Teacher training began under the directorate of education when in 1931 an elementary training school was established in Mecca, followed eighteen years later by another at Medina. No more was done until the ministry of education established in the year of its own creation three new elementary training schools. By 1961–62 the number of teachers was 4,940 of whom less than half were Saudis. This fact shows the magnitude of the task and the slow progress towards achieving it. Yet the ministry did its best to open more new training schools including some for teachers in intermediate and secondary classes.

The development of teacher training was a natural growth brought forth by necessity. Not so was the state university at Riyadh which was created by decree in 1957 when, academic standards apart, the total number of pupils in all intermediate and secondary classes was around five thousand. Hence the first college of arts had no more than twenty-seven students. In the following year a college of science was added with ten students. A year later a college of commerce was opened with 83 students. In 1960 a college of pharmacy was started with seventeen students. In that year the four colleges had a total of 985 students.

It must be explained that in the schools of arts and commerce more than half the students were registered as "external". A welcome feature of this system was the symbolic opening of higher education to girls. In 1961–62 one girl was registered in the school of commerce and three girls in the school of arts, as external students.

The University was modelled, like the entire educational structure in Saudi Arabia, on the Egyptian system. Indeed, most of its teachers were, to start with, Egyptians together with Syrians and others from Arab and Muslim countries.

While there is no direct religious control over the University of

Riyadh, the Mufti controls directly the Islamic University established in Medina in 1961. It is the apex of the religious institutions, and serves moreover as a link, through teachers and students, with other Islamic countries. In 1964–65 it had 286 students.

The Mufti also controls a college of Islamic law established in Riyadh in 1963. It must not be confused with the college bearing the same name in Mecca which is controlled by the ministry of education. This college had a variegated life and was more than once re-organized. It finally developed into two colleges, the one devoted to Islamic and Arabic disciplines with some modern subjects, and the other became concerned with teacher training. The Mufti also controls a college of Arabic at Riyadh.

As mentioned above there is provision for technical education at the intermediate and secondary levels. In addition, Aramco had been since 1948 training craftsmen for employment in its own oil industry. At a higher level a college of engineering was established in Riyadh in 1962 with technical assistance from Unesco. It had then seventeen students; by 1967 their number increased to 234.

The comparatively sudden flourishing of these and other institutions of higher education resulted in a modification of the principle governing the sending of students for training abroad. Government scholars are now sent to pursue the study of subjects that cannot be studied at home, particularly science and medicine. For a long time Egypt was the only country to which scholars were sent. Later on some were sent to Lebanon and Syria, and after the Second World War to Europe and America. Thus, in 1964–65 there were 360 students in the United States, 309 in Egypt and 287 in Germany, out of a total of 1,324.

Finally, a word about King Abdul Aziz University which was established in Jiddah in 1967–68 as a private institution supported by voluntary contributions. In accordance with the recommendations of Arab, American and British advisers it was decided to make five years the length of the first degree course. This was a wise decision in view of the standard of secondary education.

The University began with 98 students (including 30 girls), all in the preparatory class which concentrated on English and mathematics. In 1968–69 a college of economics and administration was launched with 53 students (including 11 girls), presumably selected from the preparatory class. In the following year a division for English was established as a nucleus for a school of arts. The two dozen teachers come from other Arab countries, Britain, U.S.A., India and Pakistan. But over thirty Saudi students were sent by the

University to Britain and America to study for higher degrees with a view to assuming teaching posts on return.

Taking the system as a whole the latest available figures are significant in that they indicate that there is a sharp decrease of numbers from the primary to the intermediate and secondary, and consequently the relatively small numbers at colleges and universities. Perhaps the most serious imbalance is to be noticed in the still fewer pupils following courses of technical education at intermediate, secondary and higher levels. Thus in 1967 there were 212,674 primary pupils, but only 1,600 following industrial, commercial or agricultural courses at intermediate or secondary levels. Then while the University of Riyadh had 1,352 students, the university colleges of Islamic law and education at Mecca and that of engineering at Riyadh had together 541 students. The institutions of higher religious education had between them 7,364 students.

There are, however, some healthy signs. One is the growth of female education; in 1967 there were 71,160 girls in government schools. Another healthy sign is that fifteen hundred students were in that year studying abroad including 246 in Arab countries, 561 in America and 251 in West Germany.

KUWAIT

Before the discovery of oil Kuwait was relatively a poor desert country with its small population concentrated in the capital and engaged in overseas trade and pearl fishing. In 1899 the ruler signed an agreement with Britain whereby his country became a British protectorate. This arrangement continued till 1961 when complete independence was proclaimed.

There is no evidence of the extension of the modern Ottoman school system to Kuwait, despite the fact that maps show the country as part of the province of Basra before the First World War. Facilities for learning the elements were in private hands, and at any rate, there was nothing higher than an ordinary *Kuttab*.

With the initiative of leading merchants and the encouragement of the ruler, al-Mubarakiyya school was established in 1912 on somewhat modern lines. Its main purpose was to train clerks for the management of the business of its founders who contributed to the cost by subscription. But the school differed very little from the traditional *Kuttab* except perhaps in the stress on letter-writing and commercial arithmetic. Otherwise the Koran and religion formed the main centre of attention. In 1931, however, the sharp decline in the pearl trade led to loss of interest in the school and its closure.

When the merchants felt again the need for clerks it was decided this time to establish a department of education with powers to levy an education tax and to initiate a nucleus of state schools. The new department invited the Supreme Muslim Council in Jerusalem to send a mission to organize the new schools. The result was the establishment in 1936-37 of four primary schools, three for boys (600) and one for girls (140), and the starting of a secondary school with the best of the pupils of the old Mubarakiyya. The syllabus was almost identical with that followed in the Muslim schools in Palestine, and most of the teachers came from Palestine, Syria, Lebanon, Iraq and Egypt. Further education was sought by a few Kuwaiti students in the neighbouring Arab countries.

The progress of the new system was necessarily slow commensurate with modest resources. But after the Second World War, when a huge revenue from oil made Kuwait one of the richest countries in the world, the state invested much of the new income in large-scale economic and social development. Educational development plans were drawn up and revised in the light of reports by experts coming from Egypt and other countries.

The expansion of the system was now dependent upon technical not financial limits. Among these was the supply of teachers, particularly women teachers. Until then the vast majority of the staff came from the other Arab countries, and the Palestinians constituted a sizeable majority. Some observers regard the pace of educational development as too fast and the expenditure lavish. Not only is education free, but also books, meals, clothing and transport. In the organic law of the state, education is one of the "rights" of the citizen.

The department of education (which became a ministry in 1962) had in 1949–50 a budget of half a million pounds sterling; it rose to six million in 1955–56. For a population of 180,000 the number of schools in 1951–52 was 33 with 8,111 pupils (including 2,516 girls). There was then only one secondary school with 230 boys including 55 training to be teachers and 8 in a commercial section. But in the same year 151 students were under training abroad, including 97 in Egypt and 32 in England.

By 1961–62 the number of schools rose to 148 and the number of pupils to 50,687. The educational ladder is composed, after two years of kindergarten, of four years primary, four years intermediate and four years secondary. Parallel to these three stages there is a "religious institute" for boys, and parallel to the general secondary stage for boys and girls there is a commercial side for boys only and teacher training side for both sexes.

In 1966–67 the "training institutes" produced 361 teachers for kindergarten and primary classes. Qualified teachers for higher levels are still recruited from other Arab countries. Nearly 95 per cent of the total teaching force is thus recruited. Native teachers are still very small in number.

By other standards the idea of a university would have been regarded premature. Yet in 1960 a commission was set up to study the project. There were then exactly 2,730 pupils in secondary schools. Eventually the University was inaugurated in the academic year 1966–67 with two colleges, one for arts, science and education (242 students) and one as a university college for girls (176 students). In that year primary and intermediate (but not secondary) education was made compulsory by law. In 1967–68 two new colleges were added: one for Islamic and civil law (40 students) and one for commerce, economics, and political science (103 students). The rector and most of the staff are Egyptians with a few others from Arab countries.

The University was envisaged for Kuwait as well as for the neighbouring shaikhdoms, where Kuwait had established at its own cost some three dozen schools supervised by inspectors sent from Kuwait. This generosity is matched by another whereby scholarships are granted to students from other Arab countries to study in Kuwait at all levels from the primary to the university. In 1967–68 there were 463 such scholars. In the same year 1,218 Kuwaiti students (including 273 girls) were pursuing higher studies in Arab and foreign institutions.

Equally generous and imaginative is Kuwait's participation in the development of other Arab countries, including the establishment of schools. Of particular interest is the building of twenty schools and one training college in the Republic of Yemen. Equally significant from an educational point of view, is the financing of "Arab Heritage", a series of classical texts edited by well-known Arab scholars and printed in Kuwait. The series include a classical dictionary in several volumes.

According to a report issued by the ministry of education in November 1967 the budget for education was nearly £25 million. Excluding the University the number of educational establishments in 1967–68 was 194, with 11,036 pupils in kindgergarten classes, 54,349 (including 23,689 girls) in primary classes, 33,689 (including 14,293 girls) in intermediate classes, and 8,847 (including 3,103 girls) in secondary classes.

There is clearly a progressive drop-out which is not easy to explain in a welfare state. Another matter which is worthy of attention is the small numbers in industrial (803) and commercial (260) classes. Even the "religious institute" has only 286 pupils. The teachers "institutes", however, seem to be relatively well-attended with 1,149 male and 1,264 female students.

YEMEN

For centuries Yemen was held precariously as a province of the Ottoman Empire. After the First World War the country assumed full independence under native rulers, the imams. In 1962 a revolt deposed the ruling imam and established the present republic.

Each of the two main sections of the population, the Zaidis and the Sunnis, had their own traditional primary schools of the *Kuttab* type maintained from special pious foundations. The imams were of the Zaidi persuasion, but while they naturally encouraged the schools of their sect there is no evidence that they obstructed the operation of the other schools.

Above this primary level, where pupils learned part of the Koran by heart and were taught reading and writing, there were the mosque circles where the future teachers, preachers, judges and state functionaries learned the essentials of their profession. For the Zaidis little contact with educational institutions outside the country was maintained, but the Sunnis had recourse for higher education to the mosque of Mecca and to al-Azhar in Cairo where Yemeni scholars could maintain themselves from special endowments.

The Ottoman Turks made no attempt to alter this set-up till the introduction of modern state schools towards the end of the nineteenth century. Even this remote province was covered by the new system. According to official figures published in 1915 Yemen had then 96 modern state schools. Many did not survive the First World War, but a few were kept alive by the imam in the main centres.

Yemen had until very recently the reputation of being one of the most secluded countries in the world. Hence the contradictory accounts on the subject of education. An English traveller who visited the country a few months before the outbreak of the First World War testified that free Turkish state schools were maintained in the principal centres. He himself saw one, "a substantial building", in San'a with a section for boarders. He also saw in Hudaidah a well-equipped technical school but poorly attended.

In 1924 a Lebanese Christian Arab visited the country and spoke to a former pupil of the Turkish schools. "We had organized schools under the Turks," he said, "where geography and arithmetic were taught. They gave us books, slates, paper, ink, pens, exercise books and chalk all free. . . . Today we have no [modern] schools and no teachers except the *faqih* (i.e. teacher in a traditional school) and he charges eight riyals per month".

Three years later a Syrian Muslim Arab visited Yemen, and he has a somewhat different story to tell. He saw in the capital and other large centres not only schools of the *Kuttab* type but others of higher standard. An interesting observation by this writer is that some of the traditional schools had girls as pupils. While he found the technical school at Hudaidah in ruins as a result of a local war, he saw in the same town the Rushdiyyah school with 200 pupils under a Syrian headmaster and four teachers. Not only the Koran and Arabic but also geography and arithmetic were taught. The highest school he saw was al-Mutawakkiliyya in San'a. Its syllabus was largely traditional, but it taught geography and arithmetic and had a section for boarders and another for the sons of the ruling family.

The disparity between the above accounts is perhaps best explained by a remark made in 1952 by another observer. "The education available", he wrote, "is not the kind that is shown to strangers". The last word means, of course, non-Muslims. Although Yemen became a member of the Arab League, and took part in general Arab affairs, its reluctance to "advertise" itself remained even under the republican regime.

Native accounts published after the Second World War seem to indicate the existence of a flourishing educational system. There is no doubt that the traditional system continued to prosper, and that there was a minister of education among the imam's ministers. But there is insufficient evidence to suggest the actual re-creation of the Turkish modern system or the creation of a new system parallel to the old as in other Arab states.

These accounts mention a secondary school, a school for arts and crafts, an agricultural school, and a military school. Were these part of a co-ordinated system starting from the primary level or isolated and haphazard ventures?

A clue was found in a report on teacher training published in 1958 by the cultural department of the Arab League. The inspector general of the Yemen ministry of education attended the conference which produced the report. But while there are lengthy replies from other delegates to the written questionnaire prepared by the committee, the one from the Yemen delegate was two pages of tables with very few explanatory words. According to him, Yemen had in 1957 fifty primary schools (six years) in towns with 13,301 boys, four intermediate schools (four years) with 321 boys, three secondary schools (three years) with 221 boys and one training college for men with fifty students. In addition there was one trade school (carpentry, blacksmithery and weaving) with 200 pupils, one agricultural school with 38 pupils and a "health" school with 100 pupils who received some training at hospitals.

This was presumably the state system for towns. There were 663 other state schools in villages (four years) with 36,350 pupils. It is clear from a note that the state had no schools for girls, but in towns there were private schools for them which taught the Koran. religion, morals, handwriting and arithmetic.

The traditional system appears under two heads: (a) Fifteen religious (*'Ilmiyya*) schools with 814 pupils (the length of the course was six or seven years except for the school in San'a where it was thirteen. The curriculum consisted of the usual Islamic and Arabic subjects); (b) private (*Ahliyya*) schools which numbered 1,438 with 53,117 pupils.

However, it is certain that apart from the trickle of students who went for further training to Mecca and Cairo, educational contact, even with Arab countries, remained till the proclamation of the republic rather small. It included inviting some teachers from Syria and Egypt, sending a few students to the military college in Baghdad and a few others to schools in Lebanon. It is, however, on record that despite this policy of isolation one or two students could, via Cairo, reach higher education in Europe.

Nowhere is isolation more regrettable than in the field of education. Here is a country with nearly five million inhabitants, with a glorious past history and rich national resources, which cannot manage to emulate at least other Arab states in the Arabian Peninsula. It is very curious indeed that the Arab Cultural Annual, edited by a leading Arab educationalist and published under the auspices of the Arab League between 1949 and 1963, contains nothing about education in Yemen, except half a page of figures in the last volume. The present writer had occasion to discover the real reason. He tried to stir San'a and its diplomatic mission in London but without any success.

Some facts culled from press reports are reproduced below, together with scanty figures supplied by a friend at the cultural department of the Arab League. They represent the sum total of our knowledge on the present educational system in Yemen.

The republican regime, with socialist intentions, paid special attention, despite the civil war, to education. It was claimed that the budget for education was increased fourteen-fold, and that Yemen received extensive aid for education from the socialist Arab states of Egypt, Iraq and Syria and from Kuwait. As mentioned elsewhere, Kuwait contributed the funds for the building of twenty new schools and one training college. Egypt helped to build two preparatory and two secondary schools and three training colleges in addition to seconding 300 teachers and donating a mobile school broadcasting unit and thousands of textbooks and offering some forty scholarships to Yemeni students at al-Azhar and other Egyptian institutions. Iraq and Syria likewise seconded some teachers and contributed textbooks.

In 1964 the number of primary schools was 67, preparatory schools nine and secondary schools four. These must be assumed to be "modern schools", and it must also be assumed that, save as a consequence of the civil war, the traditional schools remained intact.

In 1967 the desirability of establishing a state university was considered. Communist China, who had undertaken some major public works in Yemen, promised substantial aid towards an engineering faculty in the projected university.

How the above and other institutions fared in the last few years is a matter for conjecture. The figures given below were supplied without any background information or explanatory notes. In 1967–68 there were 749 primary schools of which only forty had the full complement of six classes. The rest had classes varying from the second up to the fifth. The total number of all pupils in primary schools was 66,830 (including 4,638 girls). The eight intermediate schools (three years) had only 2,007 pupils (including 22 girls), and the three secondary schools (three years) had 711 pupils, all boys. Teacher training is for three years and comprised in 1967–68 ten classes attached to secondary schools and attended by 215 pupils (including 30 girls). The six "religious institutes" (three years) had 629 pupils, all males.

SOUTH YEMEN

The People's Republic of South Yemen was formed in 1967 of the former British colony of Aden and the sultanates beyond it inland. Britain occupied Aden in 1839 and gradually extended her influence over the hinterland by concluding agreements with native rulers who accepted British protection. The national ferment after the Second World War in the area led to an unsuccessful attempt to form a viable federation of the colony and protectorates, in treaty relation with Britain. This did not work, and in the end Britain had to relinquish her position and a fully independent republic comprising the former colony and protectorates was proclaimed.

Traditional schools existed in the area long before there was any attempt to introduce a modern system by the colonial or protecting authorities. Most of the traditional schools were of the *Kuttab* type, and mosques provided more advanced if informal instruction. In addition, there were, especially in Hadramaut, a few institutions which specialized in more formal instruction and had moreover amenities for lodging scholars coming from distant lands. An institution of this type is called locally *ribat* (i.e. a place of retreat and meditation for the mystic, which is elsewhere called *zawiyah*).

Not before 1935 did the British authorities take action to develop modern education. In that year a "college" for the sons of chiefs was established in Aden with accommodation for a maximum of 38 pupils. The staff came from the Sudan and Palestine, both then under British control. The "college" was, however, little more than a preparatory school; it admitted boys from the traditional schools with hardly any qualification more than a working knowledge of the three Rs. The construction of a modern system of primary schools to be followed by secondary was still to come, first in Aden and then in the protectorates.

From the middle 1930's a few primary schools were opened in the protectorates, inspected by the department of education in Aden which also gave grants-in-aid to the well-conducted traditional schools. To assist the British authorities an Arab adviser was seconded from the Sudan education service. At the same time a handful of teachers were sent to the Sudan for training. Much of the work was, however, improvization, often with poor equipment. An English writer with long residence in the area stated that in some of these "modern" schools "chalk and pieces of Kerosene boxes painted black take the place of pencils and exercise books".

Post-war development was sometimes retarded by shortage of funds and sometimes by political unrest. For the colony of Aden the figures for 1958 were: 4,159 pupils (including 1,545 girls) in government primary schools, 1,591 (including 370 girls) in government intermediate schools and 811 pupils (including 131 girls) in government secondary schools. Only 300 boys received vocational training, and teachers under training were 26 males and 15 females.

Primary and intermediate education was free, but moderate fees were charged for secondary education. In 1965–66 the number of pupils for Aden alone were 14,595 primary, 7,106 intermediate, 3,443 secondary, 685 technical and 430 teacher training. For the other states of the federation combined the figures were 16,635 primary, 1,772 intermediate, 3,656 secondary and 80 teacher training. The only technical school was at Aden. Higher education was obtained overseas, in the Sudan, at the American University of Beirut and in Britain. (The population was estimated at one million for the states and a quarter of a million for Aden).

Since independence South Yemen was beset with shortage of funds aggravated by diminished income from the port of Aden and several political difficulties. In consequence educational progress was not as great as might be expected from a socialist regime. Here again there is no background information or notes to explain the meagre educational statistics. These were supplied through the cultural department of the Arab League. But despite their inadequacy these figures are reproduced below as the only available information.

For the school year 1967–68 there were 370 primary schools (length of the course four years) with 53,983 pupils (including 10,651 girls), 59 intermediate schools (length of the course not stated) with 12,227 pupils (including 2,610 girls), and 12 secondary schools (length of the course not stated) with 2,998 pupils (including 785 girls). No information or figures are available concerning vocational or teacher training. There is no mention of either in the official tables summarized above. Here again the author's efforts to obtain more information from official sources proved unsuccessful.

PART III

Interpretative Review

[1]

Viewed from the vantage point of the present, Islamic education is a mere shadow of its past. Its modernization has in the end led to its complete transformation. The modern systems have not simply supplemented it as was intended by the early modernists; they have in fact supplanted it, even though not always by the conscious effort of the modernists. Indeed, some of these still pay more than lip service to the Islamic educational tradition as may be observed in certain state constitutions, in national laws and also in the curricula. But there is no mistaking the radical shift in educational thought and practice from religious to national orientation.

The shift was from a religious philosophy, consistent and intelligible, to a national one that has yet to be formulated. There is little doubt that to the average Arab Muslim, Islam is still more intelligible, intellectually and emotionally, than Arab nationalism, or at least that the latter has little meaning to him without the former. Even to the average educated Arab, whether Muslim or Christian, the notion of Arab nationalism is still imprecise though emotionally strong. He does not know, for example, what Islamic and Arabic elements constitute its force and in what proportion. Nor can he find much guidance in the works of the intellectuals. For it is very difficult indeed to find in contemporary Arab literature an intellectual formulation of Arab nationalism that would readily command general approval.

That is not to say that there are no common elements in the current notions of Arab nationalism acceptable to Arabs of different religious, social and educational backgrounds. These elements are undoubtedly the ingredients of a philosophy, but they require time to acquire the cohesion and validity of a religious dogma. However, so long as they are not knit together in a form universally recognized, the philosophy of Arab nationalism is bound to remain in the making. So will, *ipso facto*, a philosophy of modern Arab education.

Without in any way detracting from the value of notable contributions by a number of thoughtful Arab educationists, it must be said that one searches in vain in their works for a consistent philosophy of education. There are indeed numerous glimpses of it here and there, but on the whole modern Arab education has not yet produced its modern Ghazali.

Nor is the discussion in this part of the book a pretentious attempt

197

at formulating such a philosophy. It merely seeks to throw light on aspects, mostly chosen at random, of contemporary Arab education from the primary school to the university, and to share with more learned colleagues ideas formed through the disciplines of history and education and tested in the course of long experience in educational administration and university teaching and research.

A few significant problems arising from the portrayal of the educational ladder in the fourteen educational systems discussed in the second part of this book will now be pointed out. Without being comprehensive in the treatment of these particular problems the aim is to call attention to lessons that may be useful for general applications.

Experienced workers in this sphere will readily agree that educational problems are not solved by the simple device of legislation, or even by adequate financial provision. In addition to professional and technical questions, such problems are often complicated by obstinate social conditions, which require generations to change or at least adapt to suit the introduction of educational measures. Take for example the question of educating the nomads. Laws, school buildings, children to teachers and equipment do not automatically bringings, children to school and keep them there. The raising of the living standards through settlement on agricultural land, improved communications and health services may be more profitably tried first, or at least in conjunction with any scheme for opening schools for nomads.

In discussing some of the problems of primary education therefore care must be taken not to be immersed in technical matters to such a degree as to forget the social background which, of course, varies from country to country, and also from one section of the population to another in the same country. Nor must we lose sight of the fact that constitutional and legal provisions, say for compulsory or universal education, represent the ideal and leave its realization for the near or distant future according to circumstances.

Some Inadequacies of the Modern Educational Ladder

[2]

Leaving aside kindergarten classes as forming an integral part of only a few school systems, primary education is now taken by the majority of Arab states to require six years of schooling. But this does not mean in practice that all primary schools in all states provide this minimum, still less that the provision is sufficient for all children of school age or at least for those who apply for admission.

Where the years of primary schooling are below the minimum, and where more particularly that schooling represents the end of the child's education, the problem of attaining and retaining permanent literacy is of such social and national importance as to deserve careful examination. Here again the problem is closely related to the social environment. Is the school in question for boys or girls or mixed? Is it in urban, rural or beduin areas? At what stage does the drop-out begin before the sixth year of school? How does this form of wastage vary from one socially and economically backward district to a more advanced one? There is clearly no educational remedy for the seasonal or permanent withdrawal of pupils from school for social and economic reasons. The remedy must depend upon social and economic development, and this is more in the hands of politicians than educationists.

Given the same number of years at school the chances of attaining and retaining permanent literacy depends to a large degree on whether the environment is literate or illiterate. Experience has shown that, again depending on the environment, the minimum of schooling required for permanent literacy is about five years. Ministries of education, which allocate money from public funds for schools giving less than this minimum and leading their pupils to no higher school, must satisfy themselves whether they are not wasting their resources on an unproductive service, and whether they are not required in the national interests to reconsider their policy. For surely if their aim here is to educate useful citizens in the lower grade of the labour force, and if such citizens do not receive enough training to make them permanently literate, then the present policy needs a radical change.

This is particularly urgent in those parts of the Arab world where the half-day primary school is still in vogue, and where such schools are to a great extent staffed with untrained teachers often working under such crippling conditions as poor accommodation, insufficient equipment and overcrowding. In addition to similar disabilities, the primary school in three states in North Africa, formerly under French control, is still suffering from the after-effects of teaching through the medium of French as well as by the present shackles of "bilingualism".

A random study of the educational statistics for most Arab states will readily show that the number of pupils who proceed, or are allowed to proceed, from the primary school to preparatory and secondary education, or from the former to the latter, is too small. If universal primary education seems to be a possibility in the not too distant future, "secondary education for all" must on the present showing remain a pious hope for a long time to come.

No doubt there are social and economic reasons for early withdrawal of pupils from school even before the completion of the primary cycle. But there are also deliberate official measures designed through successive and often excessive examinations, to weed out pupils at the end of every cycle. Statistics are lacking to show the type of employment, if any, which those who voluntarily leave school find. There is even less information on the future employment of those who are officially weeded out and are unable to pay for private schooling.

Both processes of early discontinued education involve considerable wastage of talent, and perpetuate a state of semi-literacy among a majority of the young generations. The wastage is surprisingly seldom noticed by educational authorities. But it is undeniable that it is as serious if not more serious than the provision of primary education that is insufficient to ensure permanent literacy. Surely the raising of citizens with a minimum of education is as important as the raising of a well-educated leadership. The present system clearly lays more stress on the latter than the former, on tolerably sufficient education for a minority and an insufficient one for the majority.

This insufficiency applies, in a different way, to the education of those who are fortunate to remain in school through the preparatory and secondary cycles. Although the general quality of education leaves much to be desired and the quantity is perhaps too abstract in intent, it is some lack of balance between general, vocational and academic sides that requires urgent adjustment. Here again the figures are most revealing as we had occasion to point out when discussing individual state systems in the second part of this book.

On the whole, and with possibly one or two exceptions, vocational and technical education is still little more than decorative on the fringes of the national systems. In an area where the majority of the population derive their livelihood from the soil, it is perplexing for the observer to note how few results the so-called agricultural education produced. Is it not disappointing that so many of the few who receive it tend to work not on the land but in offices? Is it not astonishing that two decades after the first Palestine War the Arab educational systems could not train enough mechanics who could service war planes and tanks, to say nothing of crew and pilots for these weapons of war?

There are, however, some redeeming features in the primary, preparatory and secondary education now provided in most Arab states. New schools are speedily being opened in rural, and some in beduin, areas; more pupils from these underprivileged areas climb up the educational ladder in higher schools in their locality; the number of girls attending school is increasing; at least all primary education is free; and within its limits, each national system affords equal opportunity for all children to reach the university.

University education will receive more treatment later on. Here it is briefly mentioned as the final step in the educational ladder, reflecting the perfections and imperfections of the lower steps. While it is possible to argue that education for citizenship and happiness requires that primary and secondary education should be made available for all children, it is equally possible to argue that university education should be for the education of an élite, the future leaders of the community and the professionals, unless the national resources, both financial and educational, justify it to be more comprehensive.

To generalize is to risk error. But it is safe to say that there is severe pressure on the older universities to admit more and more students, who cannot profit from higher academic education. On the other hand, some of the new universities find it difficult to muster enough students to make up sizeable faculties. There is in this contingency a danger to academic standards. If secondary schools in a given country are not well-established and their standards are not high enough or do not produce large numbers of pupils from whom the best could be chosen for higher education, then the wisdom of establishing a university on this basis may legitimately be questioned.

Content of the New Education

[3]

The content of modern Arab education is now, with one or two notable exceptions, European. It is true that none of the subjects taught in the modern schools is alien to the classical Arabic learning. Yet it is also true to say that traditional Islamic education did not concern itself with these subjects. In the scientific and technical field the subject matter is, to a great extent, European, and is mostly taught, particularly at universities, through the medium of one European language or another.

The only elements of the traditional Islamic curriculum that survived are the Arabic language and the Islamic religion. The one is taught as the national language in schools and is used, with few exceptions in north Iraq and North Africa, as the medium of instruction in primary and secondary schools. At university level the Arabic language and its literature are studied as academic disciplines as well as in conjunction with Islamic history and civilization.

The teaching of Islam as a religion in the primary and secondary schools goes sometimes under "religious education", so as to include as in Lebanon the instruction of Christian, as well as Muslim, children in the parental faith. But even where it is specifically put down as "Koran and Religion" as in Jordan, it is no more than a school subject with less time allotted to it than any of several other subjects. It has long lost its predominant place in the curriculum.

At a higher level several aspects of Islam are studied as academic disciplines in the universities. Veteran institutions like al-Azhar, which were entirely devoted to Islamic and Arabic studies, have been absorbed into the modern national systems. Thus az-Zaitunah is now a college of Islamic law at the state University of Tunisia. The much larger al-Azhar in Cairo became a state university and its scope widened by the institution of new colleges besides the traditional colleges of Islamic law and theology.

One balancing gain for the traditionalists is the prominence given in the curriculum of the modern schools to Arab history and Islamic civilization. This was of course a corollary to the stress the Arab states place on the cultivation of the sentiments of nationalism in the young. But if no national history can be taught completely dispassionately at school then it may be assumed that the Arab teacher is no exception. At a higher level in the universities Arab history and Islamic civilization are among the most popular subjects and are perhaps among the best taught.

No schools outside the modern national systems remained unaffected by the change in the content of education. As was pointed out in the second part of this book, the traditional Islamic schools, the original public system, have in the process of change become virtually private schools. They were subsequently either absorbed in the modern system or remained outside it. In either case their syllabus was changed to be closer to that followed in the state schools.

The communal private schools conducted by Christian Arab

authorities, ecclesiastical or lay, were not as radically affected. Belonging to different denominations their absorption into a state system would create educational difficulties and in any event would strain the communal balance which all national governments are keen on preserving.

No such considerations stood in the way of compelling foreign private schools to conform to the curriculum of the national system. Both the content of education and its spirit had to change in these schools. The missionary establishments in particular had to make substantial adjustment by abandoning their original aim of making converts. All foreign schools have to teach not simply a modicum of Arabic but an amount sufficient to pass state examinations, as well as Arab history and geography according to the official syllabus.

For different reasons, and in consequence of the growth of state control, the native Muslim schools and the foreign missionary schools are bound to decline at least in numbers, and may in the end disappear altogether as the state is more able to provide universal and free primary and secondary education. The same fate need not befall the native Christian denominational schools, given their continued resolve to maintain their identity and the constancy of state indulgence.

The position of the French schools in Tunisia, Algeria and Morocco is different because it is regulated by treaties which envisaged their ultimate absorption in the national systems. It is difficult to forecast accurately when this will be accomplished completely and successfully. The national educational systems in the three states still depend on French teachers, and the process of replacing French by Arabic as the language of instruction is so slow that it has not yet embraced the secondary still less the university stage.

To what extent the content of education is influenced by a foreign medium of instruction is perhaps a superfluous question. For language is not like a tool that can be used to do a job and then put aside; as a medium of instruction it leaves on the minds of the young almost uneffaceable marks which are inimical to the national language and culture. There is no telling how a child who reaches adolescence with such marks of a foreign influence, and who moreover proceeds to higher education through the foreign medium, will come out at the end.

Many argue that if this child is brought up as a Muslim there is no danger of his future cultural inalienation, and they point out the case of the Algerian Muslims whose Islamic faith conquered in the end both the French language and education. This is true up to a point. Many Algerians, Tunisians and Moroccans, sincere Muslims and patriotic Arabs, still find it easier to express themselves in French than in Arabic. These are the "philosophers" of the so-called bilingualism, which must be regarded as cultural capitulation if it means continued teaching through the medium of French in primary and secondary schools. French is indeed essential as a second language with Arabic, but there are dangers in allowing it to be its equal below the university and its superior in it.

Educational Planning

[4]

Some of the problems of the modern Arab educational systems, both regional and general, have been pointed out. They are all capable of solutions, but by the nature of things educational the solutions require time to be formulated and applied. Admittedly some haphazard measures are now in operation and may deceptively appear as solutions. At the same time there is a general recognition that such measures are temporary and are no substitute for systematic planning.

After the Second World War most Arab states devised plans of agricultural and industrial developments together with schemes for improved communications, health conditions and housing. These plans and other public services placed new demands on the educational systems, some sectors of which, notably science and technology, were unable to meet.

While on occasion foreign advice was sought, it was quickly realized that the national educational systems should produce the necessary personnel, from a skilled labour force to the engineers and administrators, for the operation of the development plans. But there is still little realization that effective educational development must go hand in hand with social, economic and other development, and that the advance must be coordinated on all fronts simultaneously, very much like the advance of all units of an army on the battlefield.

Needs differ widely and so also the national resources. In one or two states the structure of a modern system is still in the making, and the obvious need here is for more time, money and trained personnel. In other states with well-established systems the need is, apart from money, for more development with a view to overcoming the present imbalance noticeable in well-established as well as in newly established systems.

The imbalance is between the number of pupils in the primary stage and their numbers in the other stages of the educational ladder; between the number of boys and girls in all stages; between the quantity and quality of practical vocational education and abstract theoretical education throughout the system; and finally, and perhaps more seriously, between the quantity and quality of education in urban and rural areas.

Some of the imbalance is no doubt due to official action or inaction as we suggested under the head of voluntary or forced discontinued education. But a great deal of the imbalance is due to lingering social prejudices such as that attending female education. A similar prejudice is the respect paid to those who "wield the pen" and the contempt to those engaged in manual labour. Besides, the economic inequality, and the marked difference in living standards, between town and country is still reflected, to a lesser or greater degree, in an inequality of educational opportunity. These stark realities make the cries of "social justice" and "equality of opportunity" sound rather devoid of meaning.

It is true that to overcome these inequalities and to reduce and finally eliminate the imbalance between the different stages and types of education, immense resources are required which some Arab states simply do not possess. But there are other states with resources which are perhaps in excess of their own needs. This circumstance led Kuwait to establish an Arab development fund. This was before the Israeli attack on the neighbouring Arab states in 1967 led the oil-rich states to extend substantial financial aid to Egypt, Jordan and Syria.

These three states happened to have the most developed educational systems, and their expenditure on education among the most generous. But since 1967 a considerable amount of their resources had to be allocated for defence. Hence their need for aid both for defence and education. There is in the precedent set by Kuwait, and the defence aid from oil-rich states, a lesson which may be useful: the application of Arab capital where it is most needed irrespective of state boundaries. Might not this lead one day to the creation of a fund for educational development administered by the Arab League?

If such a fund is established it would help to mitigate some of the present inequalities. But with or without it, individual states cannot ignore the phenomenal increase in their population; they must plan for the minimum of universal full-time primary school of six years. If this first step in the ladder could be well-established, then it is the opinion of the writer that the development of vocational, technical and scientific education must be the second priority. No doubt teacher training is important; so also an evolving curriculum that allows frequent revision in the light of experience; and particularly for the newly-established systems, or systems newly-liberated from teaching through a foreign medium, suitable textbooks are indispensable.

Here it is important to point out at least one very serious impediment to efficient planning. Census of the population is seldom held in the Arab states. Lebanon for example is known to have held no census for more than thirty years. If such a census is held elsewhere within shorter periods, the census reports generally provide little that is of assistance to long-range planning, educational or other. Indeed some Arab countries possess only rudimentary apparatus for economic records.

Any attempt to study the social significance of the rise of new population centres as the new towns near oil fields, or the new villages in reclaimed agricultural lands, or the general drift from the villages to towns, will be impeded by lack of or insufficient official facts and figures. Even educational documentation and statistics are of comparatively recent date. What is worse is that the bureaucracy that disposes of whatever material is available does not respond easily to requests for information. This is even true when such information is known to be accessible in printed papers.

Aims of Education

[5]

There is a prevalent and very strong assumption, now almost amounting to a dogma, that through education the Arab nation can achieve the miracle of regaining its glorious past and catching up with the most advanced nations in the modern world. Politicians vie with educationists in calling for universal if not compulsory education in general as well as for the adoption of western science and technology in particular. The general aim of this modern education has been stated and restated within the last few decades without much precision. Article one of the Covenant of Arab Cultural Unity signed in 1964 defines it as follows:

"The creation of generations of Arabs, believing in God, loyal to the Arab homeland, confident in themselves and in their nation, aware of their responsibility to their nation and humanity . . . armed with science and morals, so as to share in the advancement of Arab society by maintaining the position of the glorious Arab nation, and safe-guarding its rights to freedom, security and dignified life . . ."

Beneath the rhetoric, somewhat mellowed in translation, the aim seems to be more ideal than practical, and of more national utility than of benefit to individual citizens. Compared with the traditional Islamic aim which has been succinctly put as "happiness in this world and in the next" the modern formulation is less concrete. However, the Covenant left it for member states of the Arab League to express in detail what is called "the philosophy of Arab education" and to define the aims of each stage of the process of education on the basis of the general principle embodied in article one.

No detailed and comprehensive philosophy has so far been formulated whether in general or in regard to a particular stage of education. There is still a great deal of generalization, but pertinent self-criticism is increasing, particularly in the publications of the cultural department of the Arab League. Of great significance are the reports on *ad hoc* and periodic conferences held under the department's auspices.

Among the aspects of the modern education frequently criticized is the disparity between technical and academic education. As may be deduced from our studies of individual state systems above there was, and still is, a social tradition that favoured academic at the expense of technical education. But colonial administration aggravated the situation by their policy of gearing the educational systems under their complete control to produce junior officials for government service. Despite their insignificance in numbers, the small officials, clerks and accountants thus educated, enjoyed the prestige of office, and an income, though itself very small, higher than any local artisan or labourer could hope to earn. In an underdeveloped society this circumstance intensified the traditional attitudes to manual labour which some form of vocational schools might have weakened.

Under national governments, and particularly where schemes of development in agriculture and industry are operated, the attitudes are steadily changing. With the increase in the number of skilled workers, technicians and engineers that the new schools are producing, and with the visible results of their higher earnings and better living standards, the balance has in places been redressed. But not yet adequately to divert enough students from academic to technical studies.

A report published in 1967 by the cultural department of the Arab League confirms the conclusions often reached above when discussing individual national systems. The great majority of pupils are still attracted to general academic courses in preference to the technical. To be precise technical education embraced no more than about 15 per cent of the aggregate Arab school population. The report recognizes the efforts made by some states to change an unhealthy situation, but it confesses to the neglect in the majority of other states.

Yet it is no good forcing the pace without ensuring that the product of technical schools and colleges will find employment. This is, of course, easier where there are plans of economic and industrial development in operation. That was the reason we insisted above that the two, development and technical education, should go hand in hand.

In all states, both those that operate development plans and those not yet doing so, there seems to be an urgent need to guard against two dangers that are inevitable results of academic education unleavened with the right proportion of vocational and technical education. The first danger, and the worst in a developing society, is the alienation of the educated youth from his environment. The second is the production of a class of unemployable intelligentsia.

To combat both dangers lessons may be learned from more advanced countries where the opportunities for employment are varied and adequate for practically all applicants. It is well-known that in such countries pupils are given, at certain stages of their advance up the educational ladder, advice as to what courses are suited to their aptitudes with a view to future careers. If similar, or even stronger, methods are employed in Arab schools they might create a system of "directing" talent, be it vocational or academic, in the right channels. For a system on these lines to succeed it must be coordinated with prospective employers whether they are government departments or development boards, or private enterprise in industry, commerce and agriculture. It must all be planned, and the state, in the absence of another authority must do it. In the centralized systems of education in the Arab world this is unavoidable.

Illiteracy

[6]

Any educational planning must take serious note of the curse of illiteracy. In the Arab world, and despite all efforts to reduce it, illiteracy still afflicts about two-thirds of the aggregate adult population. This grave malady is no doubt a major obstacle to social and economic advance. What is frightening is that it is being daily aggravated by an unprecedented increase in the birth-rate and consequently the number of children of school-age. In the absence of compulsory or universal primary education, the increase in the number of school-age children who do not find or do not seek places at school naturally augments in time the number of adult illiterates and reduces the chances of eliminating illiteracy.

Individual Arab states do conduct campaigns of varying degrees of efficiency to combat adult illiteracy. From 1964 the problem was regarded of inter-state interest and its solution essential for the development of Arab society as a whole. The Arab League itself declared that the elimination of illiteracy was an educational prerequisite for social, economic and political development, and that it must, for this reason, form part of any plan for national development.

A recommendation to this effect issued in 1965 envisaged uniform and parallel plans in the member states both for the elimination of adult illiteracy and for providing places in school for children of school-age. Fifteen years was the maximum allowed for the achievement of the two objects. Alas, this estimate proved too optimistic and the capacities of individual states were over-rated. Both problems are still as acute as ever, and there is moreover no sign of their final solution in the foreseeable future.

The difficulties are indeed great, but the inadequacy of funds may not be the greatest, at least for the wealthy states. The technical difficulties seem to be rather more intractable: the absence of detailed statistical material by age-group and sex of illiterates; the lack of agreed definition of an illiterate, or the minimum of the three Rs required for the attainment of literacy; the length of time and the cost of achieving this result; the books and teaching methods suitable for obtaining permanent results; and finally the supplementary training, both educational and vocational, required for ensuring permanent literacy.

Grandiose schemes often suffer from the defects of the virtue of ambition. Before they can be operated there must be at least some preparatory study together with careful selection of the "tools" and the personnel. To help adults attain and retain literacy is not simply an educational effort conducted in isolation. For its success it must be linked with social, economic or national needs for the employment of adults liberated from illiteracy.

This is not an easy task. It is so complicated and, in the Arab circumstances, so pervasive that it may be wise to establish some order of priorities, related primarily to family life and the need for intelligent manpower, local and national. The aim must be, in the first place, to make all mothers progressively literate and to give them at some time essential training in home management. In the second place, the aim must be to make all semi-skilled labourers in fields and factories effectively literate. Last but not least it must be to make every conscript in the armed forces, if he had missed school, permanently literate. Religious education as the moral basis of the life of the citizen is assumed to have been acquired through upbringing and practice. But its further cultivation is still necessary by precept.

In suggesting the above order of priorities it is assumed that the final solution of the problem of illiteracy requires longer time than Arab experts had hitherto allowed, and that in any event there is bound to remain a proportion of illiterates, adults or future adults, untouched. To meet this contingency private enterprise should be made to join forces with the state. Time, money and personnel must be found for on-the-job instruction in the three Rs of illiterate employees, if only with a view to increasing their productivity. But in the present state of Arab industry and agriculture this proposal is easier to apply to the former than to the latter.

On the basis of a survey report prepared by Unesco on the organization and financing of programmes for eliminating illiteracy in the Arab countries, published by the Sirs al-Layyan Centre in Egypt in 1965, the cultural department of the Arab League compiled an interesting comparative table showing the percentage of illiteracy in twelve of the fourteen Arab states. The two exceptions were Yemen for lack of information, and South Yemen which had not yet emerged as an independent state. The comparative table also shows the percentage of children of school-age who had no places in the existing schools.

The dates of estimating the percentage of illiteracy varied from 1950 (Saudi Arabia) to 1964 (Algeria). Also varied was the lowest age from which the rate of illiteracy was estimated, from five for Jordan and Iraq to fifteen for Morocco. The former calculation presumably took into account children of school-age who were not at school, while the latter did not.

In calculating the percentage of children of school-age who were not at school, generally between 1961 and 1964, the primary school was reckoned as from six to twelve in seven states, from five to thirteen in Algeria, from six to fourteen in Tunisia, from seven to ten in the Sudan and from seven to fourteen in Morocco. For Saudi Arabia no figures are quoted.

The imperfections of these calculations and the data on which they were based are obvious. They should reinforce the argument made above for remedying the deficiency. But even on the basis of incomplete scholastic and demographic data now available it is extremely doubtful whether the schools and the schemes for combating illiteracy have together greatly altered the situation. There is little evidence that the rate of illiteracy in the Arab countries as a whole is now much below 65 per cent. There is less evidence to contradict the assumption that there are no places in the schools for about 30 per cent of the children of school-age.

Teaching Methods

[7]

Are the present methods and apparatus of teaching suitable and adequate to achieve the expected results? So far as the campaigns for eliminating illiteracy are concerned there is reason to doubt their efficacy. There is also some doubt of their efficacy in the schools and some areas of higher education.

The problem is rooted in Arabic and Islamic practice in the age of decadence when reliance on memory and learning by rote, adherence to existing texts and respect for authoritative opinion became established at lower or higher levels of education. Once the original Arab oral tradition was superseded by fixed written material the teacher's function became more of a restrained transmitter and commentator and less of a resourceful adapter and innovator.

Under this system the pupil began his school life with learning portions of the Koran (or the Bible) by heart. In the modern schools he has to learn that as well as a prescribed amount of poetry. Teachers and taught tacitly understood that, *mutatis mutandis*, other material and not only the multiplication tables and rules of grammar, had to be committed to memory. Frequent competitive examinations confirmed the practice as embracing all school subjects. Knowledge of modern educational methods, psychology and the exhortations of progressive school inspectors availed little to change the practice. Thus in 1966 a conference of Arab teachers was held in Alexandria at which a paper contributed by the secretary general of the Egyptian ministry of education was read. In a restrained passage he wrote:

"It is noteworthy that despite the development of the subject matter of the syllabuses, their outstanding trends are still theoretical, and that despite the teachers' efforts to develop new teaching methods, the general mark of existing methods is still dictation and delivery. This is, of course, contrary to the call for giving prominence to the practical and applied aspects of the prescribed syllabus, and for stressing the functional sides in the syllabus and their relation to man's social environment. Indeed, it is contrary to the repeated recommendations by educationists that pupils should participate in the process of learning, use their hands and carry out experiments, and that teaching methods should accord with this technological age by the employment of visual and aural aids in teaching. But these calls and recommendations failed to evoke genuine response from the majority of teachers, and the scholastic work still goes on in its old ways."

There are, however, other reasons for lack of response from the teachers, and disrespect for authority cannot be among them. The reasons must be sought in the modern system itself, its own methods of administrative control and their application in the schools.

No teacher can teach what he does not know or what he was not taught. The frequent reference in the discussion of individual state systems above to shortage of teachers and the resort to the employment of insufficiently educated or untrained teachers must be recalled. Faced with a written syllabus, often very heavily loaded, such teachers are expected to do what is beyond their capacity to do.

A written syllabus, which is the order of the day in all the modern Arab systems, if taken as a target for teachers to aim at, and whose requirements they must meet may be useful. But to take it as a Koran, and there is evidence that even some well-educated school inspectors tend to take it as holy writ, is to ask for trouble and to create a strain between the guides and those who are to be guided. Perhaps the worst in a written syllabus rigidly applied is that it discourages initiative and frustrates efforts by enterprising teachers to adapt it to local conditions.

It is true that the syllabuses used in most systems do make allowances for rural as distinct from urban schools and that there are variations to suit girls' schools. But on the whole the content and range are too ambitious. To cover the whole ground must be taxing the ability of even the educated and trained teachers. It seems imperative to allow some latitude to the less educated and untrained or insufficiently experienced, particularly in a less developed environment where the living conditions are not very attractive. This seems to be more realistic and possibly more conducive to produce results.

Closely connected with teaching methods and the syllabus are textbooks. There are two noteworthy points on this subject: insufficient variety of texts in vital school subjects, and inadequate supply of books in Arabic for the school systems of three states formerly under French control. In the primary schools of most states it is still possible, for example, to find only one book prescribed for Arabic reading in each class, usually one part of a series by one author or a group of authors. Other than the prescribed book used by pupil and teacher alike there is sometimes no alternative, and for higher primary classes the amount available for supplementary or individual silent reading by the pupil is small particularly where it is needed most, in villages.

As to the supply of textbooks in Arabic for the schools of Algeria, Tunisia and Morocco, the matter is clearly connected with arabicization, the more classes in the schools use Arabic in place of French the more Arabic texts are required. When in 1964 the ministers of education of the Arab states held their second conference in Baghdad, their recommendations included one on the needs of Algeria, the last of the three states to be liberated from French control. Apart from the supply of teachers, there is specific mention of textbooks, visual and aural aids including Arabic maps and the donation to Algeria of five printing presses for the purpose of printing or re-printing Arabic textbooks.

Nor was this a mere symbolic gesture; it was in fact in accord with a policy laid down in 1961 by the fifth Arab cultural conference, and ratified by the council of the Arab League. Textbooks were to be written "within the framework of our national and educational aims", and all efforts were to be directed towards the arabicization of instruction in the national schools and the textbooks used in them.

One of the resolutions laid down that texts for the teaching of religious education, Arabic literature, Arab history and geography of the Arab world should be uniform in content and treatment. Another resolution insists that in general textbooks should bring out where relevant, "the part played by the Arabs in the development of civilization". Finally and perhaps inevitably the textbooks should expose where relevant "Imperialism and Zionism as the most dangerous enemies of the Arabs".

Technology and Education

[8]

Technology has now become a magic word in the Arab world; it is constantly on the lips of politicians and educationists alike. An Arab term has been found for "industrialization", but "technology" has either been adopted as it is or arabicized in a contracted form as *taqniyya*. Like most magic words, it means different things to different people, but all seem to be agreed that in technology, whatever the term itself may mean, lies the key to the economic and social development of Arab society and its success in peace and war.

To the educationist its meaning is more precise, even though there is as yet no common agreement on a graduated syllabus for its teaching in the schools, colleges and universities throughout the Arab world. Besides, technology may be the least developed subject of study, both in quantity and quality, as the above studies of individual educational systems bear out.

The educationist also knows the general aims: the training of the planners, technical managers, executive engineers, work foremen, skilled and semi-skilled workers, according to the needs of the developing industries and modernized farms, whether controlled by the state or private enterprise. But he is still trying to translate ideas and hopes into facts in the educational institutions. He is also faced with the harder task of coordinating vocational and technical education with state and private needs for personnel.

On the professional level the educational planner or administrator is faced with two related difficulties: a shortage of qualified teachers of science and technology and an inadequate teaching material in Arabic. Those qualified to teach these subjects through the medium of Arabic, particularly at higher level, are still relatively few. A good number of them had been trained, either locally or abroad, through a foreign medium. They need time and sustained effort to acquire facility in teaching through the medium of Arabic.

Such teachers are not the prospective writers of textbooks in their subjects. Nor are those qualified to write or translate into Arabic in a better position to do so since they lack the technical knowledge of the subject to be written or translated. This problem has been anticipated by the Arab academies of Damascus, Cairo and Baghdad which have been coining or translating scientific and other terms for the last fifty years.

However, because of the prevalence of two main currents of European thought in the Arab countries, the one French and the other Anglo-Saxon, there developed at least two sets of new terms, the one used largely in the countries formerly under French control and the other in those formerly under British control. This highly confusing development affected not only the sciences and humanities, but also legal, administrative and parliamentary usages. One of the functions of the Arabicization Institute in Rabat, established through the efforts of the cultural department of the Arab League, is to unify the usage in all these fields, particularly in the texts used in schools, colleges and universities.

In 1961 the fifth Arab cultural conference urged the educational authorities to double their efforts to achieve this object. Six years later the seventh conference re-affirmed the need for the "completion" of arabicization with reference to replacing French with Arabic as the language of instruction, but did not mention textbooks. It passed two resolutions, however, on the place of "technology" and science in the syllabus.

The wording of one of the resolutions reveals that the literary tradition lost none of its grip over the minds of Arab educationists. In the light of present conditions the possibility that science and technology could outweigh the literary subjects is remote. Yet the resolution implies that it is impending. "Continue" it recommends "the trend towards expanding scientific and technological education at all levels above the compulsory (i.e. primary) school, provided this does not weaken the theoretical and literary sides with their important role in educating the leaders in literature, art and law."

It seems that the proviso was to satisfy the fears of the *literati*. For elsewhere the same conference deplored the fact that small amounts were allocated in the budgets for technical education, and that only 15 per cent of the total pupils in secondary schools in all Arab systems received such education. The paragraph containing these pronouncements correctly ascribes the state of affairs to a response to the pressures of social expectations. "Our present society", it states, "does still attach more prestige to academic than to technical education".

Thus both society and the state are responsible for the slow pace of technological education. But it is also true that there is a steady increase in the number of students sent abroad to pursue scientific and technological studies and that they outnumber those sent for literary studies. The aim in sending such students to Europe and America is primarily to train not only managers and executives for industry, agriculture and commerce but also teachers for technical colleges and universities. Such teachers are, however, seldom able to teach their subjects through the medium of Arabic. Then it is obvious that it takes many years before their teaching notes can be translated into textbooks in that language.

To this problem we shall return in the next section when we deal exclusively with higher education. Now it is proposed to close this section with one or two remarks on the social and general cultural implications of technological advance. For in their eagerness to secure material advance for the people, Arab educationists sometimes forget the evils that attended such advance elsewhere. Consider some of the symptoms which are already there: the break-up of the tribal and clan relationship; the loosening of family ties; the drift of the rural population to the squalor of urban suburbs; the widening rather than narrowing the gap between rich and poor; the laxity of morals; the decrease in religious observance.

It cannot be denied that, in their way of thinking, cultural attitudes and moral values, a great many young Arabs educated in the modern sciences are now somewhat unsettled. They are all conscious of belonging, across regional boundaries, to a larger unity of the Arab nation and sharing in a common culture. But not all of them are aware that this heritage incorporated throughout its historical development important elements of western culture, and that this fact makes it the easier to adopt western technology. Fewer still are aware of the "values" of this technology and its background in western civilization. You cannot always divorce the technique from the ideas behind it.

On balance it seems that western technology alone is not enough. It may bring material prosperity to the few or the multitude as the case may be. But it will do so at a price. The Arab may become gradually more prosperous, but he may lose his soul in the process.

Higher Education

[9]

Writing in the May 1970 issue of *al-Arabi* monthly, Dr. Fakhir 'Aqil, Professor of Education at Damascus University, has hard words to say about the standards of Arab schools and universities. "The truth", he wrote, "is that the standard of the pupil who completes any Arab secondary school is below that of the pupil who completes a similar school in Britain, France, America and Russia". He then adds what must be a natural conclusion of this judgement, that the same applies to university graduates.

The great expansion in primary and secondary education after the Second World War, and particularly in the 1960s, was, as we have occasionally shown above, accompanied by a sacrifice of quality to quantity. There were political and social reasons for the haste, and the result is writ large in the structure of the education ladder, in the curriculum, in the recruitment and training of teachers and other aspects of modern Arab education.

In the universities the shortcomings of the lower steps of the educational ladder are intensified and reflected in the quality of students. Admissions vary considerably, from the open door in the newer universities to satisfying certain requirements of public examinations in the older universities. But even under the stricter system there seem to be more students than can profit from higher education. Egyptian universities, for example, produce more graduates per head of the population than do the British universities.

Overcrowding at the universities will certainly hinder attempts to raise the standards if it does not contribute to lowering them. Faced with great numbers, university teachers will continue to rely on lecturing. This pedagogic spoon-feeding assumes that the function of a university is to prepare students for examinations which lead to some paper qualification. One of the best features in Islamic education was the personal contact between teacher and pupil. As the tutorial system, it is now one of the characteristics of English education. The change to the impersonal lecture given to a multitude is not always one for stimulating thought. It affords the teachers very little opportunity for the discovery and development of talent to the maximum. In short the lecture is a poor method for educating the future leaders in creative thought and instilling in their minds inclination toward wisdom.

No doubt standards are not uniform, even when they are not high. They vary also between the literary and scientific faculties. But it may be assumed that the teaching standards in Arabic and Islamic subjects in the best Arab universities are at least as high as in any European or American university. A confirmation of this assumption may be seen in the confidence of Arab academic authorities who now scarcely send students to foreign universities in order to pursue the study of such subjects under teachers who are not much more qualified than their students.

Arabic and Islamic subjects are, of course, taught through the medium of Arabic. Science, technology and some of the social sciences are still taught largely or partly through a foreign medium, both by Arab and foreign teachers. Students who acquire in secondary schools insufficient command of the foreign language through which lectures are given at the university are bound, willy nilly, to influence the quality of the lecture. For if the lecturer is a realist he must go down to the level of his students, and this must adversely affect his own standards.

This brings us back to the problem of arabicizing the language of instruction at all levels of education, primary, secondary and university. Having rid themselves of political imperialism, wrote the secretary of the supreme council of universities in the United Arab Republic, it remains for the Arabs to get rid of "linguistic imperialism". How long this will take it is very hard to predict. Until this moment teaching through a foreign medium at Arab universities proved harder to change than the optimists expected.

In general progress towards achieving this object has not been uniform. Some states are still struggling to arabicize the primary schools while simultaneously making partial efforts at secondary and higher levels. Other states, with no problem at the primary level, are tackling it in secondary schools and universities. The results of their individual efforts are recorded in the second part of this book.

When in 1961 and again in 1964 delegates from the Arab states met under the auspices of the cultural department of the Arab League to discuss the problems of university education as a whole, arabicization naturally was one of these. While there was unanimity on its necessity both from the educational and national point of view, the recommendations were hedged with reservations. The process must be carried out "subject to local conditions". It must be gradual, and must not result in the neglect of the teaching of foreign languages. Both the writing of textbooks in Arabic and the translation of such texts into that language were to be encouraged and the authors or translators rewarded.

Except in the newer universities, however, professors and their assistants have to bear very heavy teaching loads which leave little opportunity for keeping abreast with new developments in their subjects, still less to write or translate books. Besides, university teachers educated through a foreign medium must first educate themselves out of the habit of thinking and lecturing in that medium. With very few exceptions the pre-university knowledge of Arabic possessed by such teachers is not, for the purpose of producing textbooks, as high as their technical knowledge of the subjects of their speciality. The exceptions are those who are at home with "the two cultures", whose command of Arabic is not less than their mastery of their speciality, be it scientific or literary. They are the pioneers and upon them must depend the success of arabicizing the language of instruction in the universities.

This is perhaps the place to question the notion that the function of the university is limited to instruction. As a matter of fact Arab universities are principally teaching institutions. They are the only centres for the training of men and women for leadership and the professions. But do they also inculcate in their students the capacity for independent thought and cultivate in them those moral habits which are the backbone of a civilized society? Do they encourage in their teachers the disposition, if not the duty, to contribute to learning through creative research?

As teaching institutions the universities like the schools rely a great deal on paper examination to test the attainments of their students. These tend to cram too much, and that leaves little room for independent thought and judgement. It has been said, and there is wisdom in the saying, that the best university education is that which teaches the least. This may be interpreted to mean traffic of ideas between teacher and pupil is more important than formal lecturing.

But the pressure of numbers and the force of old habits in administrators and professors tend to place students almost beyond the personal influence of their seniors. The tutorial system and the small seminar are still novelties. On the other hand lecture halls and laboratories are getting fuller, so full that at times amplifiers are used for the benefit of "listeners" in the corridors. How many lecturers, engrossed in this tedious routine, realize that knowledge is not "static", but constantly changing, even in the natural sciences? How many have the time, inclination or mental agility to revise their lecture at least every year? How many social scientists and men of letters do profit from and adopt the scientific method? How many realize the loss to themselves and their speciality which results from the lack of close contact and exchange of views with the young?

Arab educationists are alive to such questions and recognize that all is not well with all the universities in the Arab world. One of them pointed out in conversation with the writer that the lecture is the standard French method of instruction, and that the English tutorial system, though admirable, is very expensive for adoption on a large scale in Arab universities. Another said that bursary students who experience the benefits of the tutorials, the seminars and live research in Europe do on return find it difficult to adopt them for administrative, financial or even personal reasons.

No doubt these remarks are cogent. Bursary students do, however, cross-fertilize the atmosphere even if they cannot radically change it. They are usually among the most inspired teachers and the most productive in the lecture hall as well as ultimately in books and articles in learned journals. It is salutary that the general policy is now to send for training abroad graduate students, relatively mature and more acquainted with their culture and thus more prepared to absorb the shock of a foreign environment. Students below graduate level are not sent abroad unless they cannot be trained locally.

But the sending of students for study abroad has its risks. One of them is the "brain drain". It happens so often that when they complete their training, students from developing countries, Arabs as well as others, prefer the better living conditions and higher pay in the host country to returning home where their service, and sacrifices, are expected and needed. Lebanon, for example, is the loser of roughly half the students who go to the United States for study but never return. The United States also attract a large number of Egyptian students. An authoritative study of the files of 148 such students who never returned revealed that 107 of them settled in America even though only 85 of these received their training at American institutions.

A few years ago a similar "brain drain" from Britain to the United States, involving mainly scientists and doctors, raised a storm of protest. The deserters pleaded that apart from attractive material reward the American facilities for research were more generous. The Arab deserters may be impelled by similar considerations, but surely they must know that their desertion is a symptom of diminished regard for the aspirations of their homelands. In the present circumstances of these homelands the desertion of a scientist must be regarded as the desertion of a soldier from the battlefield.

Idealism and radicalism go well with youth. Disregarding the disturbing symptom of the "brain drain", and the tendency to seek education for livelihood and not for life, Arab youth at the universities, at home or abroad, are imbued with a large measure of both. Most if not all of them are eager to offer themselves for the service of their country and society and a great many of them are burning with enthusiasm to transform the social order more by revolution than by evolution. Their ideology and radicalism, have various shades and are derived from sources easily identified in national or foreign ideology. But speaking from limited knowledge and experience, it must be admitted that the idealists and radicals are not always well-informed or capable of clear expression devoid of rhetoric and slogans.

Although Arab students are very responsive to political developments around them and do initiate or take part in political demonstration, the present unrest among them has two other manifestations, both radical if not revolutionary. The one is directed at the university administration and teaching and the other at the social order and the political leadership. The first is, of course, part of a world-wide movement which seeks participation in university administration and changing the approach, method and content of teaching. The second is peculiar to the Arab scene: students are impatient of the politicans of all kinds not simply for political reasons but also for comparative failure to civilize the masses by education and other means. If the students of today are the leaders of tomorrow, it is possible that the challenge of today will surely be flung back in their faces tomorrow.

On the professional level the students have good reason for complaining. The most frequent complaint is of the impersonal manner in which instruction is generally conducted. Brilliant students are often frustrated by the remoteness and inaccessibility of their teachers. But as stated above university teachers are overworked. The student-teacher ratio is sometimes that of secondary schools. Thus in the universities of the United Arab Republic this ratio is on the average 36 students to one teacher.

Furthermore, the pay is rather low, except perhaps in the new universities of the oil-rich states and in one or two foreign universities. It is so low that sometimes professors need some part-time jobs in order to supplement their income. Nevertheless the post of a university professor carries with it social prestige. The state does often "borrow" the services of professors in advisory, executive or sometimes ministerial capacities.

Those who go that way, mostly economists and lawyers, cannot avoid dabbling in politics. The universities themselves are autonomous corporations, and despite their total financial dependence on the state they are free to conduct their internal affairs and to devise the curricula as they please. But without being actually dictated to they are not insensitive to the changes in the political climate. Professors are free within the curriculum to teach according to their own lights. It is true, however, that even without specific prohibition there are areas, say in contemporary history, which the prudent teacher will have to traverse with great care. Once students at a state university rebelled against an Arab nationalist rector for some alleged indiscretion. On another occasion a foreign professor at a foreign university in Beirut had to leave his post for prescribing a textbook containing derogatory remarks on Islam and Muhammad.

There are now three foreign universities in the Arab world: the American University of Beirut, the Université St Joseph also in Beirut, and the American University at Cairo. The small Jesuit establishment in Baghdad, al-Hikmah University, has since the writing of the section on Iraq been absorbed into the University of Baghdad. Because these foreign universities are subject to the laws of the Arab states where they are located, and because their students are Arab, they are striving to supplement but in no way compete with the national universities.

The American University of Beirut in particular has greatly changed its image, first from missionary to secular and then from predominantly American to largely Arab personnel. The pay of teachers and the student-teacher ratio are better than at most state universities. The institution began as a college with funds contributed in Britain and the United States. A board of trustees based in New York collected and controlled the necessary funds. But with the growth of the college into a university more and more funds were required. After the Second World War American oil companies and American foundations supplied much of the money. But even they could not meet all the needs for development and current expenditure. Recently the United States government began to pay generous contributions. For a private independent institution to accept money from an unpopular government in the Arab world must be embarrassing, to say the least.

Under the present set up the AUB is a collection of faculties, arts and sciences, each going its own way with little coordination. Unlike the college and university in their early days, the present institution seems somewhat devoid of a unifying philosophy. The teachers are of heterogeneous backgrounds and philosophies of life, and with the exception of the departments of Arab history and Arabic literature there is little unity of purpose to bind them together.

Foreign universities are in general similar to the national universities in that they do not seem to communicate to their students the scientific method and spirit, or they do not communicate them in sufficient measure, despite the great advance in their teaching of all the sciences. The result is that the amount of "scientific" thinking that some well-educated Arabs bring to bear on general problems is not always very profound. Many will readily blame the literary tradition which makes men more adept to rhetoric than close analysis. But there is a simpler explanation; it is no doubt the teacher. If as the poet Shauqi said, the teacher is inspired, he can do wonders and rank almost as a messenger of God:

Rise and give honour to the teacher
Verily, the teacher is almost a prophet!

The General Cultural Aspect

[10]

As may be deduced from declared aims, modern Arab education is sought for the social, national and personal benefit it is supposed to confer on society, the nation or the individual. This is a philosophy that leaves important elements out. It does not for example stress sufficiently, or it does not mention at all, the necessity for intellectual, moral and aesthetic development. If "spiritual values" are mentioned they are often concealed beneath generalities or obscured by rhetoric.

The Egyptian revolution came nearest to a frank admission of these limits. In formulating the guide lines for constitutional and other development there is specific mention of education and the importance of science and the scientific approach to social and national questions, but with a significant reservation:

"Science or learning for its own sake would place on the state responsibilities that are beyond its present capacity. We must therefore seek science for the benefit of society . . . leaving our participation in the universal quest for learning for its own sake to a later stage. But "science for society" must not be interpreted narrowly to mean simply "the loaf of bread" . . . Let us always remember that the spiritual energies which nations derive from the ideals of their divine faiths, or from their cultural heritages, are capable of performing miracles".

Every educational system is caught between conflicting pressures, such as respect for tradition and the necessity for change. Partly on this account and partly because of the complexity of the process of education, every system is liable to fall short of its objectives. The above quotation indicates a desire to link the present with the Islamic past or at least to assert the Islamic values. Yet it does not mention Islam. The circumlocution signifies the climax of the gradual secularization of the state and education. In the Arab world the process was dictated largely by the necessity of enlisting the active participation of the Christian Arab minorities first in the struggle together with the Muslim Arab majority against foreign control and then in the national life after independence.

Those who still accuse the Islamic system of rigidity might reflect on this silent revolution that took place in an orderly manner. The transformation of the Arabic-speaking peoples from separate religious communities to one Arab nation, cutting through geographical boundaries and religious affiliations, is a miracle in which education played a major if not the major part. The Arabic language and Arab history are the two unifying common elements in the education of young Arabs, Muslims and Christians.

The greatest publicist of the ideas of this unity was himself the most prolific writer on education. Sati al-Husri was sometime minister of education and retired from the important post of director of the cultural department of the Arab League. He wrote, mostly *ex post facto*, rationalizing accomplished facts. But he is the only Muslim writer to exclude Islam by not naming it as an essential element in Arab nationalism:

"The most important element in the formation of a nation and the building up of nationalism is the unity of language and history. . . . But neither religion, nor state, nor economic interests, nor geographical unity is basic among the fundamental props of the nation. . . ."

Islam or Arab nationalism in education has now become a sterile question. More relevant is the practical question of whether the modern system produces better leaders. It would be hard to determine whether the traditional *madrasah* was more or less adequate to the needs of its day than the modern Arab university to the needs of a more complex society. But it is a demonstrable fact that, despite the great increase in educational facilities, there appears to be no great surfeit of enlightened, imaginative and wise leaders.

Can this be due to a lack of binding convictions, or to obscure sense of direction or moral malaise? To attempt even short answers to these questions would give the impression of preaching. But one side of this perplexing problem must not escape notice—the apparently limited scope for the rise of inspired teachers with prophetic vision and missionary zeal.

Every educational system, primitive or advanced, does in the course of its history produce this rare species. A great teacher always succeeds in overcoming material and technical handicaps. In the closing decades of the nineteenth century al-Azhar produced a few prominent teachers, so also did in its early days the modern Egyptian

University. But there is nowadays little news of great teachers in Egypt or elsewhere in Arab universities. One wishes the reason to be that there are too many outstanding teachers for the few to shine.

Teachers, especially university teachers, can make or break an educational system. They train the élite who will lead the nation to its declared aim of catching up with advanced nations—an aim which alas seems more elusive than ever. For the gap between Arab and Western educational progress, at least in science and technology, is widening not narrowing, and the consequences are not simply educational or even social and economical. They have also direct bearing on the position of an educationally, scientifically and technologically advanced power now in occupation of Palestine.

It is fashionable in the West to scoff at the Arab leadership. To some observers the Arabs have a propensity to regard a few slogans as ideology and worse still as substitute for sustained effort. This is a harsh judgement, even if it contains an element of truth. The Arab countries are, of course, at widely different stages of social, economic and political development. Arab education is apparently expected by foreign observers to achieve miracles quickly—levelling up these differences in the various countries and raising the standards in each country. Because the former is still an aspiration, an outsider tends to see some appearance of divorce between the ideal and the actual. The truth is that the tree of education takes time to bear fruit and more so in a developing area.

While even educated Arabs often take offence at such criticism, Arab educationists are one with the politicians in recognizing the inadequacies as well as the need for the best that Western education, science and technology can offer. It has been shown in the second part of this book that despite Western journalistic exaggerations the great majority of Arab students seeking higher education abroad go to Western Europe and America, not to the Soviet Union and Eastern Europe. This is a clear indication that the Arab world has not abandoned its modern cultural orientation developed during the last century and a half.

But political developments after the Second World War, particularly the fate of the Arabs of Palestine, created a new situation which is bound to affect future cultural orientation. The alternatives are three in number. First, there are good reasons for a continued, if diminished, Western orientation. Secondly, there are signs of a possible halt or even reaction. Thirdly, there are other signs of a possible new venture towards Marxism.

Ideally learning and science must be regarded as neutral, transcending geographical and national boundaries, as they were in the golden age of Islamic civilization and in medieval Christendom. Education was then the servant of religion as it is now that of the state. With religion reigning supreme, the aims of education were to teach a faith, to uphold a universal social order, to transmit a universal culture, to train the leaders clerical or lay, and to enlighten the masses. After the dethronement of religion in Christendom and the weakening of its position in Muslim and Arab lands, not all of these aims are still operative.

Nationalism occupied the spiritual vacuum, and this gave rise to agnosticism and even atheism. At present "humanism" is a respectable disguise for these and other idols. Religion, in the accepted sense, has retreated to places of worship and the hearts of believers. The consequences are still in the making and the future is unpredictable. But in history the weakening of ideals, or their invasion by alien forces, contributed to the breakdown of civilization.

Even its most ardent prophets cannot deny that narrow nationalism can be a dehumanizing influence on the conduct of states and individuals. Arab nationalists in particular have a continuous object lesson in the horrors perpetrated by other nationalists against the indigenous Arab population of Palestine. Education—Arab or other—must rise above these tendencies, and without betraying national loyalties, cultivate the brotherhood of man and the universal unity of the mind across geographical and ideological frontiers. The modern Arab educationist has a great Islamic tradition in education to look up to for inspiration.

Once the noted Cambridge historian, Professor Sir Herbert Butterfield, wrote that he and some of his friends in early youth dreamt of "the light that might come from the Orient". I confess that I often please myself with a similar thought when I imagine moral civilization retreating eastward towards its original cradle, in the heart of the Arab world.

APPENDICES

APPENDICES

EDUCATION OF THE CHILDREN OF THE PALESTINE ARAB REFUGEES
(up to June 1967)

Since the Palestine tragedy in 1948, the United Nations Relief and Works Agency assumed jointly with Unesco responsibility for the education of the children of the Palestine Arab refugees in Jordan, Lebanon, Syria and the Gaza area (under Egyptian control.) From the beginning the Agency followed the same organization and curriculum and used the same textbooks in its schools as in those of the host country.

With this as a general policy the Agency offered either in its own schools, or through grants on behalf of refugee pupils to private or state schools, six years primary and three years preparatory education in Jordan, Syria and Gaza, but four years preparatory in Lebanon.

The Agency itself did not operate secondary schools but it subsidized refugee pupils at private or state schools. It operated, however, its own training colleges and centres for vocational and technical training, for both males and females. In addition the Agency subsidized some refugee students at other training centres in the area and sent others overseas for further training. For higher education it awarded a number of scholarships to outstanding students at universities in the area. In 1966–67 the Agency's educational budget was just under $13 million.

UNWRA Schools only (1966–67)

	Boys	Girls	Total
Jordan			
(Refugee population 732,400)			
primary	34,699	32,100	66,799
preparatory	8,212	4,845	13,057
Gaza			
(Refugee population 321,100)			
primary	21,936	19,676	41,612
preparatory	8,784	8,027	16,811

UNWRA Schools only (1966-67 (*continued*)

	Boys	Girls	Total
Lebanon			
(Refugee population 165,800)			
primary	11,517	9,570	21,087
preparatory	2,366	1,139	3,505
Syria			
(Refugee population 146,900)			
primary	11,068	8,728	19,796
preparatory	4,211	2,413	6,624

UNWRA Schools, Training Colleges, Vocational Centres and subsidized students at all levels (1966–67)

Level or Type	Jordan	Gaza	Lebanon	Syria	Total
Elementary	84,345	41,612	26,776	25,763	178,496
Preparatory	20,382	16,811	5,396	8,159	50,748
Secondary	6,489	8,264	1,221	2,201	18,175
Pre-Service Teacher Training*	649	279	168	—	1,096
In-Service Teacher Training	560	450	256	273	1,539
Vocational and Technical Education	974	511	514	399	2,398
University Scholarships	261	142	93	94	590
Total	113,660	68,069	34,424	36,889	253,042

*Distributed by Country of Origin

(Source: UNWRA-UNESCO Department of Education—Statistical Summary for the School Year 1966–1967)

THE EMIRATES OF THE PERSIAN GULF

Bahrain

The Arab rulers of Bahrain Island in the Persian Gulf entered into treaty relations with Britain in 1820. The relationship produced little or no change in the social conditions till about a century later when the discovery of oil in the 1930s enriched a small country that could afford modernization of state services including education.

Education is now free. The ladder is formed of six years primary and four years secondary. In a population now estimated at two hundred-thousand the number of pupils in 1950–51 was 5,092 (including 2,086 girls). There was then one secondary school (131 pupils) and one school for arts and crafts (90 pupils). A great many of the teachers came from Egypt, Palestine, Syria and Lebanon. From 1947 a handful of selected students were sent for further education in the neighbouring Arab countries.

According to the latest available figures, in 1967–68 there were 35,222 pupils (including 14,379 girls) in primary schools, 5,262 pupils (including 2,066 girls) in intermediate schools and 4,334 pupils (including 1,483 girls) in secondary schools. Post-secondary education was received by 107 pupils (including 40 girls).

Qatar

Britain established treaty relations with the Shaikh of the Peninsula of Qatar on the Arabian side of the Persian Gulf in 1868. From 1950 oil made a poor country with a population now estimated at eighty thousand inhabitants fabulously rich. As in other oil-rich principalities in this area, Qatar provides free education with free meals at school, clothing and transport as well as an allowance per pupil for attendance.

The first primary school for boys was opened in 1951–52 with 240 pupils, and the first primary school for girls in 1955–56 with forty pupils. Since then a complete system of six years primary, three years intermediate and three years secondary was constructed. In 1956–57 an industrial school was opened with 13 pupils and three instructors.

The latest available figures for 1967–68 show 11,871 pupils (including 5,068 girls) in primary schools, 1,501 pupils (including 453 girls) in intermediate schools and 477 pupils (including 113 girls) in secondary schools. There was one teacher-training school with 103 students (including 17 girls), one commercial school (55 pupils), one industrial school (201 pupils) and one religious "institute" (128 pupils), all males.

Abu Dhabi

In 1892 Britain established treaty relations with this country on the Arabian side of the Persian Gulf. Its present population is estimated at fifty-thousand and the revenue from oil, first discovered in 1962, at sixty-five million pounds sterling per annum. The sudden accession to wealth was utilized to establish an apparatus of a modern state. In a five-years' plan launched in 1968 education figures prominently with an over £12 million allocation.

The first modern primary school was established in 1960 with teachers from Jordan. Three years later the first primary school for girls was opened. For the supply of teachers Abu Dhabi depended on Jordanians and Palestinians. Small wonder that it was convenient to adopt the Jordanian school syllabus. Education in Abu Dhabi is free, so are school meals, clothing and transport. Pupils moreover are given allowances for attendance.

In 1967–68 the intermediate state was started, together with an Islamic "institute". In that year there were altogether nine schools with 1,499 pupils (including 724 girls).

Sultanate of Muscat and Oman

As a reaction to Napoleon's invasion of Egypt in 1798 Britain entered into treaty relations with the sultan, since revised or replaced. With a population estimated at over half a million the sultanate was and largely remains isolated. In 1959 a development board was created with British advice. Education, as well as agriculture, health and communications figure on its programme, but little was heard of tangible educational results. Oil has been discovered in commercial quantities and its export began in 1968. It may lead here, as in Kuwait, Qatar and Abu Dhabi, to educational and other social development in the near future.

THE COVENANT OF ARAB CULTURAL UNITY*

Responding to the feeling of natural unity between the sons of the Arab nation, and believing that the unity of thought and culture is the main foundation of Arab unity, and that the preservation of the Arab cultural heritage and its continuous transmission to the successive generations guarantees the solidarity of the Arab nation and the performance of its pioneering and inventive role in the sphere of human culture and world peace, . . .

And in view of the effectiveness of cooperation in education, culture and science . . . in guaranteeing the right of the individual Arab to education, freedom dignity and comfort . . ., and in the evolution and progress of Arab society on firm bases of its original spiritual values and of modern science and its application,

And in view of the belief that this cooperation is conducive to projecting a [favourable] image of the Arabs in the world, enabling them to resist the world evil forces as represented by Imperialism and Zionism, to participate in the maintenance of world peace, and to perform their part in the development of human civilization,

The Arab states approve the following covenant of Arab Cultural Unity:

Article 1: The aim of education shall be to bring up generations of Arabs, enlightened, believing in God, devoted to the Arab fatherland, confident in themselves and their nation, aware of their national and human calling, . . . armed with science and morals. . . . Member states shall draw up and apply the [?individual] Arab philosophy of education that will attain these objectives.

Article 2: Member states shall cooperate fully in the spheres of education, culture and science . . . and in particular coordinate their educational organizations, exchange experts, teachers and the results of scientific and technological research.

Article 3: Deals with the establishment, under the Arab League, of the Arab Organization for Education, Culture and Science.

Article 4: Member states shall equalize educational standards, adopt the same educational ladder and unify the substance of the syllabus.

*Abridged translation of the text approved by the second conference of Arab ministries of education held in Baghdad, February 1964.

Article 5: Member states agree to coordinate higher and university education . . . and encourage scientific research.

Article 6: Member states shall cooperate towards making at least the primary stage of education compulsory, eliminating illiteracy, diversifying secondary education, promoting the higher education of the talented, and cultivating technical education.

Article 7: Deals with the encouragement of the establishment of scientific, educational and cultural institutions by one state in the territory of another.

Article 8: Member states shall endeavour to bring up the rising generations in the devotion to the principles of religion.

Article 9: Member states agree to promote female education in accordance with religious principles, Arab [moral] values and modern scientific progress.

Article 10: Member states agree that the Arabic language shall be the language of instruction, study and research at all educational levels, or at least in the primary and secondary stages.

Article 11: Deals with the need for each state acquainting its citizens with the social, economic, cultural and political conditions in the other states.

Article 12: Deals with the need for a "source book" for the writing of textbooks for schools on Arab history, geography, language, literature, etc.

Article 13: Emphasizes the importance of training the teacher.

Article 14: Recommends the formation of national unions of teachers in each state.

Article 15: Recommends cooperation for the revival and diffusion of the Arabic heritage, the translation of its prominent books into foreign languages, the spread of Arabic-Islamic culture and the Arabic language in Islamic and foreign countries.

Article 16: Recommends the encouragement of translating important works from foreign languages into Arabic.

Article 17: Member states agree to make efforts towards the unification "of scientific and cultural terms" in cooperation with the permanent centre for arabicization in Rabat.

Article 18: Recommends the formation of a union of Arabic academies with a view to promoting the object of the previous article.

Article 19: Deals with cooperation between libraries and museums.

Article 20: Deals with cooperation and exchange of experts in music, theatre, cinema, press and the like.

Article 21: Recommends state legislation for copyright.

Article 22: Recommends legislation for deposition of printed books in national libraries.

Article 23: Deals with the exchange of professors, teachers, experts, etc.

Article 24: Deals with the exchange of pupils and students, and equation of certificates subject to the fulfilment of conditions under article 4.

Article 25: Member states shall cooperate in rendering cultural assistance to the Arab countries that need it.

Article 26: Recommends the encouragement of inter-state cultural, scout and sport tours.

Article 27: Member states shall take the necessary measures to make their legislative trends in education and culture as near as possible to one another and to unify what is possible to unify, and shall introduce comparative studies of Arab legal systems.

Article 28: Recommends the coordination of Arab cooperation with international bodies especially with Unesco, and the establishment of Arab cultural centres in friendly countries.

Article 29: Deals with the ratification of the covenant.

Article 30: Arab countries not yet member states of the League may adhere to the covenant.

Article 31: Deals with the date of the covenant coming into force.

Article 32: Deals with possible withdrawal of a member state.

Baghdad   16 Shawwal 1383
                29 February 1964

APPENDIX 4

AREA AND POPULATION

Country (in the order of mention in this book)	Land Area (in sq. km)	Population
1. Iraq	438,446	8,600,000
2. Jordan	96,610	2,100,000
3. Egypt (U.A.R.)	1,002,000	38,800,000
4. Sudan	2,506,800	14,800,000
5. Lebanon	10,400	2,600,000
6. Syria	185,180	5,740,000
7. Libya	1,759,540	1,800,000
8. Tunisia	164,150	4,700,000
9. Algeria	2,381,743	12,100,000
10. Morocco	444,000	14,600,000
11. Saudi Arabia	2,150,000	7,000,000
12. Kuwait	15,000	540,000
13. Yemen	192,000	5,000,000
14. South Yemen	287,683	1,500,000

(Source: *The Times*, a special report on The Arab League, 3 April 1970)

CIRCULAR SENT TO ALL ARAB MINISTRIES OF EDUCATION AND ARAB EMBASSIES AND LEGATIONS IN LONDON

University of London Institute of Education

22 March 1968

Your Excellency,

This Institute has a large number of students from Arab and Islamic countries following various courses from the Postgraduate Certificate in Education to Master of Arts and Doctor of Philosophy. The undersigned teach and supervise the work of many of these Arab and Muslim students. One of us is at present writing a book on Islamic education and its development in the national educational systems of the Arab states from Kuwait to Morocco.

Your assistance is sought to provide the kind of information which Sati al-Husri's surveys contained. These surveys have been discontinued, with the result that up-to-date information is now lacking. We would welcome copies of all official reports, new laws and regulations, long-range development plans, university calendars, school curricula, statistics, etc. on any and all aspects of education from kindergarten to university, including private schools, native and foreign.

The information will be welcome whether in Arabic, English or French, and it would be gratefully acknowledged by the Secretary, Arab Education Project, 25 Woburn Square, London W.C.1, to whom please cause correspondence and material to be sent.

Yours faithfully,

J. A. Lauwerys
L. J. Lewis
A. L. Tibawi

BIBLIOGRAPHY

This is not an exhaustive list of the sources, still less of numerous secondary works, miscellaneous reports and articles in learned journals, used for the writing of this book. I doubt the utility of the very lengthy lists so fashionable these days; they provide little or no guidance to the specialist and may baffle the uninitiated by including works with no direct bearing on the subject. The following lists, longer than originally intended, are strictly selective but fairly inclusive; they were prepared largely with the needs of students in mind.

An asterisk against a title denotes its special importance.

General Background

Arnold, W. T. and Guillaume, A.	*The Legacy of Islam*, Oxford, 1931
Gibb, H. A. R.	*Mohammedanism*, London, 1953
Hitti, P. K.	*History of the Arabs*, London, 1958
Europa Publications	*The Middle East and North Africa: A Survey and Directory*, London, 1968
Royal Institute of International Affairs	*The Middle East: A Political and Economic Survey*, London, 1958

Part One

The substance of this part of the book is largely derived from the following works by the author:

Muhadarat fi Tarikh al-Arab wa al-Islam (Lectures on the History of the Arabs and Islam), Vol. I, Beirut, 1963

Muslim Education in the Golden Age of the Caliphate
   (*Islamic Culture*, XXVIII/3 (1954) pp. 418–38)

The Origin and Character of al-Madrasah
   (*Bulletin of the School of Oriental and African Studies*, XXV/2 (1962) pp. 225–38)

Philosophy of Muslim Education
   (*Islamic Quarterly*, IV/1–2 (1957), pp. 78–89)

The following books, different in approach and ranges, are useful to the students:

Dodge, Bayard	*Muslim Education in Medieval Times*, Washington, 1962
Salama, Ibrahim	*L'Enseignement Islamique*, Cairo, 1939
Shalaby, Ahmad	*History of Muslim Education*, Beirut, 1954
Totah, Khalil	*Contributions of the Arabs to Education*, New York, 1926

Part Two

For factual surveys of educational developments in the Arab world from 1948 to 1962 the six volumes of *Hauliyyat* (annuals) issued by the cultural department of the Arab League and edited by Sati 'al-Husri are indispensable. Before 1948 a survey of the educational systems in six Arab countries was conducted and the result published by Roderick Mathews and Matta Akrawi under the title of *Education in Arab Countries of the Near East* (Washington, 1949). This book is now out of date, but it is still useful as a record of the conditions in the mid 1940's.

To supplement Husri the student will find occasional articles by specialists in *The Year Book of Education* issued by the University of London Institute of Education. A different annual publication is *The International Yearbook of Education* issued by Unesco from the International Bureau of Education in Geneva, reproducing official national reports. It fills in the gap, though not adequately, left by the discontinuance of Husri's annuals. These national reports, thus printed in a collective annual volume, are not listed separately under the countries concerned.

A new series started in 1962 by French scholars based on Aix-en-Provence under the title of *Annuaire d'Afrique du Nord: Algérie, Maroc, Tunisie* is particularly useful. It is clearly concerned with the three Arab countries formerly under French control, but the affairs of Libya are also covered. For Arab countries, formerly under British or French mandates (Palestine, Trans-Jordan, Iraq, Lebanon and Syria), the annual reports of the mandatory powers submitted to the League of Nations up to 1939, contain sections on education. More important than the reports themselves is the record of their examination by the Permanent Mandates Commission whose minutes are of particular interest.

In the two decades following the end of the Second World War, several missions from the International Bank of Reconstruction and Development were sent to study the possibilities of economic development in a number of Arab countries. Their reports contain important sections on education relating it to economic and social plans. Here again the reports are not cited under the countries concerned.

Two books were published in 1966 on higher education, both in the nature of surveys. The first is by Fahim Qubain, *Education and Science in the Arab World* (Baltimore, Johns Hopkins Press), and deals rather unevenly with seven out of the fourteen Arab states. The second is by Jean-Jacques Waardenburg, *Les Universités dans le Monde Arabe Actuel* (The Hague), and deals also unevenly with institutions in more countries including those omitted by the first author.

General history and travel books are cited only if they give special attention to education. For consideration of space, syllabuses, university calendars and national statistical reports are not cited. Of the publications of the cultural department of the Arab League the following are of particular utility:

I'dād al-Mu'allim al-'Arabi (Training of the Arab Teacher), 1958
Mushkilāt at-Takhṭīṭ at-Tarbawi (Problems of Educational Planning), 1967
Mushkilāt at-Ta'līm al-Jāmi'i (Problems of University Education), 1964
Nashrat al-Iḥsāāt at-Tarbawiyyah lil-Bilād al-'Arabiyyah, 1966–67 (Educational Statistics for the Arab Countries 1966–67)

A few references are now given for each country in the order of mention in the text:

Iraq

| Bowman, H. E. | *Middle East Window*, London, 1942 |
| Clark, V. | *Compulsory Education in Iraq*, Unesco, 1951 |

*Dujaili, Hasan — *Taqaddum at-Ta'līm al-Āli Fil-'Iraq* (Development of Higher Education in Iraq) Baghdad, 1963

*Hilāli, 'Abdur-Razzāq — *Tārikh at-Ta'līm fil-'Iraq fil-'Ahd al-'Uthmāni* (History of Education in Iraq in the Ottoman Period) Baghdad, 1959

Ministry of Education Baghdad — *Taqrīr 'an 'An-Nastāt ath-Thaqāfi wat-Tarbawi wat-Ta'līmi, 1968* (Report on Cultural and Educational Development)

Jordan/Palestine

*Bowman, H. E. — *Middle East Window*, London, 1942

Luke, H. and Keith-Roach, E. — *The Handbook of Palestine and Trans-Jordan* London, 1930

*Tibawi, A. L. — *Arab Education in Mandatory Palestine*, London, 1956

Tibawi, A. L. — *A Modern History of Syria including Lebanon and Palestine*, London, 1969

Egypt (U.A.R.)

*'Abdul-Karīm, Ahmad Izzat — *Tārikh at-Ta'līm fi Miṣr 1848– 1882* (History of Education in Egypt 1848–1882) Vol. II, Cairo, 1945

Boktor, Amir — *The Development and Expansion of Education in the U.A.R.—* Cairo, 1963

Cromer, the Earl of — *Modern Egypt*, Vol. I, London, 1908

*Dunne, J. H. — *An Introduction to the History of Education in Modern Egypt*, London, 1938

*Husain, Ṭāhā	*Mustaqbal ath-Thaqāfa fi Miṣr* (Future of Culture in Egypt) 2 Vols., Cairo, 1938
Sami Pasha Amin	*At-Taʿlīm fi Miṣr* (Education in Egypt), Cairo, 1917

The Sudan

Beshir, Mohamed Omar	*Educational Development in the Sudan 1885–1956.* Oxford, 1969
*Mahgoub, El-Fatih	*Secondary Education in the Sudan 1905–1955.* Unpublished London M.Phil. Thesis, 1967
*Sanderson, Lilian M.	*History of Education in the Sudan with Special Reference to the Development of Girls' Education.* Unpublished London M.A. thesis, 1962
Sudan Government	*Directory of the Republic of the Sudan,* London, 1959
Sudan Government	*Ten Years Plan of Economic and Social Development,* Khartoum, 1962

Lebanon

*Dodge, B.	*The American University of Beirut,* Beirut, 1958
Chapman, E. L.	*A Study of the Educational System of Lebanon,* Washington, 1966
Fayen, Abdul Hamid	*Dirāsah ʿan at-Taʿlīm wa Taṭawwur al-Manāhij fil Marḥalah al-Ibtidaiya al-ʿĀliya fi Lubnan.* (A study of Education and Curricula in the Higher Primary Cycle in Lebanon.) Beirut, 1970.
*Tibawi, A. L.	*A Modern History of Syria including Lebanon and Palestine,* London, 1969

Tibawi, A. L.

"The Genesis and Early History of the Syrian Protestant College" in *The Festival Book*, American University of Beirut, 1966

Syria

Ministry of Education

At-Tarbiya wat-Taʿlīm fil-Jumhūriyyah al-ʿArabiyyah as-Sūriyyah, 1962 (Education in the Syrian Arab Republic)

Taqrīr ʿan An-Nashāṭ at-Tarbawi Wath-Thaqāfi 1967–68 (Report on Educational and Cultural Development)

Ministry of Higher Education

Jamiʿat Dimashq, Jamiʿat Halab, etc. (The Universities of Damascus, Aleppo, etc.) Damascus, 1968.

*Ministry of Planning

Report on the First Five Years Plan. Damascus, 1965.

Tibawi, A. L.

A Modern History of Syria including Lebanon and Palestine, London, 1969

*Tibawi, A. L.

American Interests in Syria—A Study of Educational, Literary and Religious Work. Oxford, 1966

Libya

*Mansury, Shoeib

Education and Socio-Economic Development in Libya. Unpublished London M.A. thesis, 1966

Ministry of Education

Nuẓum at-Taʿlīm fi Libya (Educational Systems in Libya) Tripoli, 1968

*Steele-Greig, A. J.

History of Education in Tripolitania from the Ottoman Occupation. Tripoli, 1948

Tunisia

Basset, A. et al.	*Initiation à la Tunisie.* Paris, 1950
*Debbasch, C.	*La République Tunisienne.* Paris, 1962
Micaud, C. *et al*	*Tunisia, the Politics of Modernization.* London, 1964
Secretariat of State for Planning	*Report on the Implementation of the First Year of the Three Years Plan, 1962–64.* Tunis, 1962

Algeria

*Alazard, J. *et al*	*Initiation à l'Algérie.* Paris, 1957
*Gordon, D.	*The Passing of French Algeria.* London, 1966
Mazouni, Abdallah	*Culture et enseignement en Algérie et au Maghreb.* Paris, 1969

Morocco

*Fāsi, 'Allāl	*Al-Harakāt al-Istiqlāliyyah fil Maghrib al-'Arabi.* (Independence Movements in Arab North Africa). Marrakesh, 1948
Ministère de l'Education Nationale	*L'enseignement au Maroc.* Rabat, 1963
Royal Cabinet	*The Three Years Plan.* Rabat, 1965
*Tourmeau, R. le	*Evolution politique de l'Afrique du Nord musulmane.* Paris, 1962

Saudi Arabia

*Hibshi, Muhammad	*The Development of Higher Education in Saudi Arabia, 1945–65.* Unpublished London M.Phil. thesis, 1967
Philby, H. St. J. B.	*Saudi Arabia.* London, 1955
*Ministry of Information	*Education for Girls* (n.d.)

Wahbah, Hafiz   *Jazīrat al-ʿArab fil-Qarn al-ʿIshrīn* (The Arab Peninsula in the Twentieth Century). Cairo, 1935

Kuwait

*Department of Education   *A Brief Account of the Educationa, Department.* Kuwait, 1958

Government of Kuwait   *Kuwait Today.* Nairobi, 1963

Government of Kuwait   *Education and Development*, 1958

*Ministry of Education   *Taṭawwur at-Taʿlīm fil-Kuwait* (Development of Education in Kuwait). Kuwait, 1967

Yemen

ʿAṭṭār, Muḥammad Saʿīd   *Le sous-développement Economique et Social du Yemen.* Algiers, 1966

*ʿAẓm, Nazīh al-Muayyid   *Riḥlah fi Bilād al-ʿArabiyyah as-Saʿīda* (A Journey in Arabia Felix). Cairo, 1938

Dunne, J. H.   *Al-Yaman: Social, Economic and Political Survey.* Cairo, 1952

*Great Britain, Colonial Office   *Aden and the Yemen.* (London HMSO, 1960)

Part Three

It is difficult to give even a selective list here. While most of the sources listed above, and many others, contributed to the content of this part, the ideas and their development are the author's own. In "The Cultural Aspect", a lengthy contribution he made to volume II of *Religion in the Middle East* edited by A. J. Arberry (Cambridge, 1969), the author dealt with the origins and evolution of modernism in the Arab world, including education.

For a long time the author has been interested in problems of primary education in an illiterate environment. He tried to draw some lessons from the history of education in Palestine under British administration, in an article entitled "Primary Education and Social Change in Underdeveloped Areas", published in *The International Review of Education*, IV/4 (1958).

Unesco publications on literacy, fundamental and compulsory education, and teacher training provided ready material on which to base judgement. On higher education the literature is too voluminous to be encompassed. I have, however, re-read while writing this part of the book, two works by well-known British scholars. The first is *The Universities and Education today* by Professor Sir Herbert Butterfield (London, 1962). The second is *The Universities in the Modern World* by Professor Lord Robbins (London, 1966).

Journals and Newspapers utilized:

Al-'Arabi (Kuwait)
The Egyptian Gazette (Cairo)
Al-Kulliyyah (Beirut)
Al-Manār (Cairo)
Al-Muqtaṭaf (Cairo)
The Times
The Times Educational Supplement

INDEX

The entries below are concerned with purely educational matters, not political history. They are classified principally under institutions, ideas and activities rather than countries or cities. In the text personal and place names (and also dates) were deliberately reduced to a minimum. Even fewer personal and place names appear in this index. The test of inclusion or exclusion has been the direct relationship of the material to the educational thought or activity as discussed in this book. Thus Aristotle is excluded but Averroes is included, because it was through the Arabic works of the latter that the former was introduced to Europe.

The Arabic definite article *al*, when it occurs at the beginning of a name or a word, has been disregarded in listing entries. The Western custom of listing Arabic personal names has been varied. For example, Muhammad Abduh appears under M not A.